The Light of Knowledge

EXPERTISE

CULTURES AND TECHNOLOGIES OF KNOWLEDGE

EDITED BY DOMINIC BOYER

A list of titles in this series is available at www.cornellpress.cornell.edu.

The Light of Knowledge

Literacy Activism and the Politics of Writing in South India

Francis Cody

Cornell University Press
Ithaca and London

First published 2013 by Cornell University Press
First printing, Cornell Paperbacks, 2013
Printed in the United States of America

Library of Congress Cataloging-in-Publication Data

Cody, Francis, 1976– author.
The light of knowledge : literacy activism and the politics of writing in South India / Francis Cody.
pages cm
Includes bibliographical references and index.
ISBN 978-0-8014-5202-4 (cloth : alk. paper)
ISBN 978-0-8014-7918-2 (pbk : alk. paper)
1. Arivoli (Organization : Tamil Nadu, India) 2. Literacy programs—India—Tamil Nadu. 3. Literacy—Political aspects—India—Tamil Nadu. 4. Tamil Nadu (India)—Rural conditions. I. Title.
LC157.I52C63 2013
379.2'4095482—dc23 2013009771

Cornell University Press strives to use environmentally responsible suppliers and materials to the fullest extent possible in the publishing of its books. Such materials include vegetable-based, low-VOC inks and acid-free papers that are recycled, totally chlorine-free, or partly composed of nonwood fibers. For further information visit our website at www.cornellpress.cornell.edu.

Cloth printing 10 9 8 7 6 5 4 3 2 1
Paperback printing 10 9 8 7 6 5 4 3 2 1

Contents

Foreword

It is with the greatest pleasure that I introduce you to Frank Cody's *The Light of Knowledge*. In it, Cody brilliantly analyzes the work of the Arivoli Iyakkam, one of the largest literacy movements in the world, which mobilized millions across Tamil Nadu between 1990 and 2009. The Arivoli Iyakkam sought to increase the political participation and leverage of rural women and aspired to help them attain new, enlightened autonomy through literate access to science and knowledge. A range of socialist literacy movements inspired the movement, especially Paulo Freire's "pedagogy of the oppressed." Beginning as a volunteer-driven, nongovernmental project, such was the complicated and transitional situation of Indian statecraft during the period—as Nehruvian national developmentalism increasingly gave ground to visions of liberalization and globalization—that the Arivoli Iyakkam quickly found itself drawn into the interstices of nongovernmental and governmental authority. Cody shows how the work of the movement was strained by competing conceptions of development and citizenship in the 1990s and early 2000s. Yet literacy was a locus of aspiration and a zone of social imagination claimed by all, whether to deepen the basis of national citizenship and collective purpose or to open a gateway to a new regime of individuated liberal freedom and autonomy.

As fascinating as the backdrop of "socialist politics in a decidedly neoliberal age" is, competing regimes of governmentality are not the real story here. Drawing on the analytic techniques of both linguistic and cultural anthropology, Cody delves deeply into the epistemic practices of the Arivoli Iyakkam movement itself. Here, Cody pinpoints a crucial tension between, on the one hand, faith in the promise of literacy to emancipate the self from social restraint and, on the other, recognition that literacy is a power-laden social practice in its own right. Cody does not argue that there is some fundamental incommensurability between the lifeworld of Tamil peasants and enlightenment accounts of the interconnection between literacy, science, and freedom. Instead, he gestures to the deeper paradox "at the heart of . . . pedagogical practice" within "charismatic Enlightenment" activism that people must, in essence, be charmed and trained to be free. In this respect, Cody finds that the pedagogical practices of the Arivoli Iyakkam often chafed against its principles, leading him to consider the generative intellectual labor of village activists to produce a coherent, and coherently "Tamil," practice of enlightenment. He argues that it was the critical and reflexive practices of activists themselves that aligned, so far as this was possible, the senses of freedom incorporated in traditional Tamil culture with socialist models of emancipatory enlightenment. The Arivoli Iyakkam thus mutated Freirean pedagogy into a distinctively Tamil form, creating a new "rural humanism," as Cody terms it. It is the epistemic and linguistic virtuosity of the activists, as well as their considerable social and cultural impact in rural Tamil Nadu, that is the beating heart of Cody's account.

When the Expertise series began three years ago, *The Light of Knowledge* was exactly the kind of transversal, horizon-opening project I had hoped to be able to recruit. Knowledge has long been a crucial zone of inquiry in anthropology and the human sciences. Indeed, anthropology's long rumination on knowledge—whether, in the beginning, on "reason" and "belief," later on "culture" and "identity," or more recently on "expertise" and "epistemology"—has contributed generously to the conceptual apparatus of the discipline. The Expertise series has sought to recognize and extend this generosity. By centering the series in the anthropology of knowledge, my colleagues at Cornell and I have hoped to solicit rich and compelling ethnographies that demonstrate that epistemic practices and forms remain crucial objects of inquiry for anthropology and the human sciences. This is a question, on the one hand, of finding effective ways and research objects through which to narrate and analyze the broader complexities of human experience. But it is also a question of the search, after the (timely or untimely) diminishment of culture theory, to nurture anthropological theory that speaks effectively across many fields and subfields of the human sciences.

Our goal is not to develop a new unifying signature concept (for example, to replace theory of "culture" with that of "knowledge"). Rather the idea is to use the foundational importance of epistemic factors across many domains of life to encourage, for example, studies of politics to connect conceptually with those emerging from media studies or to help research on medicine to form new links to studies of religion. We human scientists seem increasingly suspicious, and reasonably so, of unifying signature concepts in the era of the lateral connectivities of digital media. Still, the premise of Expertise is that more can and should be done to augment the capacity of the plurality of ethnographic field knowledges to communicate more effectively with one another. This seems to me an appropriate horizon for anthropological theory in the digital era. Thus one might think of the Expertise series as a constellation of experiments to highlight different research nodes or meshes through which the anthropology of knowledge can help provide new connectivities between and among other fields. Daromir Rudnyckyj's book, the first in the series, elicited unexpected connections between anthropological research on development, modernity, and religion through a study of New-Age managerial ideology in Indonesia. In Iver Neumann's ethnography of a diplomatic corps, the first of its kind, we found a reimagination of states and their relations with each other through the eyes and hands of those who perform the intimate expertise of managing status, honor, and reputation between governments.

In the case of Cody's book, the operational node is "activism." The trajectory of the Arivoli Iyyakam's literacy activism transects and connects anthropological research on power and governance, movements and ideologies, media and knowledge. His project helps define and extend the analytic potential of an emergent area of ethnographic research that highlights activism as a key mediating expert practice in the transformation of social and political subjectivities. Comparable work in recent years includes David Graeber's and Jeffrey Juris's research on antiglobalization and direct action movements, Angelique Haugerud's research on satirical activism in the United States, Cymene Howe's research on sexual rights activism in Nicaragua, Sally Engle Merry's work on human rights activism, and Maple Razsa's research and films on Croatian anarchism. In each case, we find studies of what goes on behind-the-scenes in social movements and public political discourse, of the work of activists to leverage the legitimacy of universalizing principles (like human rights or freedom) for what are nevertheless always very local purposes. And, just as in Cody's book, we find that activists often solicit unique mediations between translocal and local knowledges. This entire field of research, but Cody's book particularly, makes us rethink how transnational political discourses operate, how ideologies like Freirean pedagogy are translated and transformed by grassroots political actors and intellectuals, forcing seemingly universalist principles to acquire a plurality of distinct cultural inflections (inflections that, at the same time, are also able to reshape the local knowledges on which they draw). Cody and his colleagues thus reveal activism as a crucial and generative juncture of modern power and knowledge, perhaps especially as neoliberal governance has sought to rely more and more on civil society and social movements to take on vital projects of social and political subject formation.

With these preliminaries in mind, I invite you to enjoy what is also simply a remarkable story of one of the most impactful social movements of the past century.

Dominic Boyer

October 2012
Oaxaca de Juárez, Mexico

Acknowledgments

This book is the product of many conversations and exchanges with family, friends, activists, and colleagues. I thank the friends and families who have made me feel at home in Pudukkottai. S. A. Karuppiah, an activist whom readers will come to know well through the course of this book invited me to come live with his family in Kovilpatti. Karuppiah remains a lifelong friend and his interpretations of the Arivoli Iyakkam and life in Tamil Nadu more broadly have played a very large role in shaping my own. I thank him and everyone in Kovilpatti, especially S. Arangulavan, S. A. Tangavelu, K. Rajalakshmi, N. Nadiyammai, and D. Minakshi for their care, companionship, and affection. K. Amutha and her sisters, D. Nadiyammai and T. Sridevi, helped me with survey work. In Katrampatti Colony, N. Velan and V. Rajalakshmi taught me about the pasts of a village. Many thanks to A. Chithra, A. Govindammal, K. Kuttaiyamman, V. Marakatham, K. Nadimuttu, S. Nalayini, K. Palaniyayi, N. Parimala, N. Racamani, A. Santhi, S. Santhi, K. Sudha, K. Sumathi, T. Vinitha, and all those who opened their hearts to me in

Katrampatti. Poets R. Neela, Subi, and family in Mangalapuram provided not only generous doses of affection and sustenance but these friends and fellow writers also provided a space, along with the room in Alangudi, to discuss literature, philosophy, and politics. Nothing I can write could possibly convey the gratitude I feel for those who have welcomed me as part of their *ūr*.

Conversations with Senthil Babu first convinced me that this was a story worth telling. His own work inside and outside the academy continues to inspire, as does his desire to interrogate the gap between the production of scholarly knowledge and politically effective activist praxis. I thank him and the TNSF and PSF leadership, especially Dr. V. B. Athreya, who took the time to help in developing a historical and regional perspective on the events I saw happening before me in Pudukkottai. Poet Muttu Nilavan and other members of the Progressive Writers and Artists Association in Pudukkottai and Alangudi consistently engaged with my work at a number of meetings, formal and informal. I continue to reflect on these discussions over the years and I look forward to many more. I also thank Usha Nandini and the Vidiyal Kalai Kulu of the Alangudi region and R. Rajkumar, the former district coordinator of the Arivoli Iyakkam in Pudukkottai, as well as Arokiyarani, Arumugam, Chitra, and Nagarattinam, at the literacy office, and especially the block coordinators, Abu Bakar, Chinnalagan, Ilango, Megala, Paramasivam, Ramalingam, Sivakumar, Sheik Muhammad, Sundari, and Vallal. Their ceaseless reflection upon their own work contributed greatly to the shape of my research in Pudukkottai.

In Chennai, I benefited greatly from frequent meetings with my guide at the Madras Institute of Development Studies, A. R. Venkatachalapathy, during my fieldwork. The friendship continues, now across continents. V. Geetha has been a model of intellectual courage and generosity. Aruna Rathnam's insights and friendship have been critical to this project. François Gros and M. Kannan of the French Institute in Pondicherry also provided stimulating discussion of this work and of a related research project on village history.

In the United States, I thank Webb Keane, Judith T. Irvine, Gloria Goodwin Raheja, and Sumathi Ramaswamy for their contributions and generous support in helping me formulate and execute the research for this book. Others at the University of Michigan who deserve special mention include Fernando Coronil, Alaina Lemon, Bruce Mannheim, Barbara Metcalf, Thomas Trautmann, and Katherine Verdery for their parts in building the atmosphere of engagement that contributed to this work. Fernando is dearly missed by so many who had the good fortune to study with him. Sharad Chari deserves perhaps the most immediate credit for helping me to think about the relationship between political activism and the materialities of language. Lee Schlesinger has been a mentor since I first arrived at Michigan. I am indebted to Professor K. Karunakaran for introducing me to Tamil and to South Asian sociolinguistics. Friends Laura Brown, Naisargi Dave, Karen Hébert, Olivera Jokić, Emil Kerenji, Jonathan Larson, Edward Murphy, and John Thiels provided an amazing community in Ann Arbor. William Nelson and Eliot Tretter have been my brothers and intellectual companions since childhood, and Aparna Balachandran and Chandan Gowda have been dear friends and fellow researchers both in India and in the United States.

Friends and colleagues who have generously engaged with this work, sharing encouragement and insights over the years, include Shahid Amin, Barney Bate, Ruchi Chaturvedi, Val Daniel, Ujala Dhaka, Susan Gal, Matthew Hull, John Kelly, William Mazzarella, Lisa Mitchell, Anand Pandian, Nate Roberts, Ravi Sriramachandran, Ajantha Subramanian, and Anand Vaidya. Michael Silverstein has been a longtime interlocutor who saw big things in small signatures early on in my research. Cornell University's Society for the Humanities and Department of Anthropology provided the perfect environment in which think about how to develop the manuscript for this book. Thanks to everyone at the society's seminar for feedback on an early formulation, and I especially express my gratitude to Paul Nadasdy and Marina Welker for their friendship and gracious hospitality in Ithaca. Toronto has proven to be an inspirational place to work because of the people I have come to know there. Darshan Ambalavanar, Ponni Arasu, R. Cheran, Sudharshan Duraiyappah, Chelva Kanaganayakam, Srilata Raman, and Aparna Sundar have become friends and fellow travelers in the field of Tamil studies. Friends and colleagues in Toronto who have helped me refine the story I tell include Joshua Barker, Ritu Birla, Girish Daswani, Naisargi Dave, Christoph Emmrich, Andrew Gilbert, Jennifer Jackson, Kajri Jain, Michael Lambek, Tania Li, Paul Manning, Bonnie McElhinny, Andrea Muehlebach, Natalie Rothman,

Jack Sidnell, and especially Alejandro Paz, who read through the entire manuscript. I have been very fortunate to teach a remarkable set of graduate and undergraduate students whose questions and comments have helped define the writing of this book.

I learned much from comments and critiques made by workshop, seminar, and colloquium participants in a wide range of venues, including the Stockholm University Department of Anthropology, Princeton University South Asia Colloquium, Harvard University South Asia across Disciplines Colloquium, Cornell University Anthropology Colloquium, University of Chicago Anthropology Seminar, Yale University Vernacular Public Spheres in South Asia Workshop, Madras Institute of Development Studies Seminar Series, and Johns Hopkins University conference on Signatures. I have also benefited from presenting my work at meetings held by the American Anthropological Association, American Ethnological Society, Association for Asian Studies, American Comparative Literature Association, Canadian Anthropology Society, Annual Conference on South Asia in Madison, Wisconsin, Annual Tamil Studies Conference in Toronto, and Michicagoan Linguistic Anthropology Conference. Portions of chapter 5 were previously published in 2009 as "Inscribing Subjects to Citizenship: Petitions, Literacy Activism, and the Performativity of Signature in Rural Tamil India," *Cultural Anthropology* 24(3): 347–80, and parts of chapter 1 in 2011 as "Arivoli's Humanism: Literacy Activism and the Senses of Enlightenment," in *World without Walls: Being Human, Being Tamil*, edited by C. Kanaganayakam, R. Cheran, S. Duraiyappah, and D. Singh (Toronto: TSAR). I thank the reviewers of these pieces and the editors, especially Kim and Mike Fortun, for their suggestions.

The research for this book was funded by the Connaught Foundation at the University of Toronto, the Mellon Foundation and Society for the Humanities at Cornell University, a Fulbright-Hays Dissertation Research Grant, the Wenner-Gren Foundation for Anthropological Research, and a Rackham Fellowship from the University of Michigan. In India, institutional affiliation was kindly extended by K. Nagaraj and A. R. Venkatachalapathy of the The Madras Institute of Development Studies.

Dominic Boyer and Peter Potter at the Cornell University Press have been exemplary editors. I thank them for their expert guidance, and I thank Susan Specter, who saw the manuscript through production, and Lisa DeBoer, who created the index. I also extend my gratitude to Barney Bate for an extremely useful set of comments on the manuscript and to the second reviewer at Cornell for providing important contributions as well.

My mother and stepfather, Ariane and Ron Thompson, raised me in a house full of books, helped me first go to India, and have supported me every step of the way. They and my sister, Melinda Cody, my father, Edward Cody, and my nieces, Lola and Chloe, have put up with a lot while I conducted research and wrote this book. My grandparents, Andrée and Gaston Espinasse, who passed away during my research, were perhaps my most important role models. No expression of gratitude could begin to repay the debt I owe them. The Ramans and the Ramachandrans have given me yet another home in Chennai. Uma and Mohan Raman have followed my work in Pudukkottai with curiosity and encouragement. They gave me a place to rest and reflect, and they have become family. I would like to acknowledge Mr. M. Ramachandran, whose great heart and love of Tamil touched everyone who met him. And finally, Bhavani Raman has acted as my eyes through this entire process. This book could not have been written without her care and critique. Her love and intellectual companionship have made this work what it is, and me who I am.

Abbreviations

AIADMK	All-India Anna Dravida Munnetra Kazhagam
BGVS	Bharat Gyan Vigyan Samiti
BPL	below poverty line
CEC	continuing education center
CEP	continuing education program
CPI(M)	Communist Party of India (Marxist)
DK	Dravida Kazhagam
DMK	Dravida Munnetra Kazhagam
DRO	district revenue officer
DSMS	District Supply and Marketing Society
DWCRA	Development of Women and Children in Rural Areas
GAD	gender and development
GONGO	government organized nongovernmental organization
IAS	Indian Administrative Service
ICS	Indian Civil Service
IPTA	Indian People's Theatre Association

IRDP	Integrated Rural Development Program
KSSP	Kerala Sastra Sahitya Parishad
NGO	nongovernmental organization
NLM	National Literacy Mission
PDS	Public Distribution System
PSF	Pondicherry Science Forum
SGSY	Swarnjayanti Gram Swarozgar Yojana
TNSF	Tamil Nadu Science Forum
UNESCO	United Nations Educational, Scientific, and Cultural Organization
VAO	village administration officer
WID	women in development

Note on Transliteration

Tamil terms have been transliterated in the text and in transcripts using the University of Madras Tamil Lexicon scheme. For the sake of readability, names of people, deities, political parties, castes, and places appear in their more recognizable Anglicized forms, for example, "Pudukkottai" or "Rajalakshmi." When appearing as discrete words, Tamil terms are pluralized in the English manner, by adding an "s." Most non-Tamil Indian terms are employed without diacritics, using commonly recognized Anglicized spellings. All translations from Tamil speech and from written texts in Tamil are mine unless otherwise noted. In a number of passages and transcripts I have represented spoken forms according to local spoken convention rather than literary spelling conventions, in the same manner as Tamil fiction authors but in transliteration.

THE LIGHT OF KNOWLEDGE

Introduction

Of Light, Literacy, and Knowledge in the Tamil Countryside

People in Katrampatti had nowhere to cremate their dead. Or, as the residents of this small, southern Indian hamlet would put it more bluntly, "We've got no place to croak" (*maṇṭaippōṭṟatu iṭam illai*). The Dalit community of Katrampatti had been allotted a small plot of land some years back to use as a cremation ground, since they were barred from sharing a cremation ground with the caste-Hindus who lived in nearby villages. This land was surrounded by fields owned by the dominant Kallar caste. While the fields were left fallow, no one bothered about the cremation ground's location. But when farmers began planting on these fields with the advent of bore-well irrigation, they started objecting to the passage of dead bodies through their fields, already polluting and thought by some to be dangerous to crops. There is a long history of caste violence in this region.

The problem of the cremation ground had been troubling the whole village for a number of years. Justice was not forthcoming in the village council and all appeals to local political party cadre had failed. It was only when a young man from a neighboring village began teaching literacy lessons that the possibility of a different kind of solution arose. Karuppiah, an activist working for the political Left, had organized a study group composed of women from the village who toiled together transplanting rice for meager daily wages. He was determined to make literacy relevant to their lives and to prove that these Dalit women could make a difference in the dispute over land. It was therefore with a great deal of encouragement from their activist neighbor that the women of Katrampatti finally decided to write a petition requesting that provisions be made for a cremation ground. Their petition would be addressed to the collector, the administrative officer who heads district governance. The Katrampatti literacy group had been convinced through Karuppiah's pedagogical efforts to exercise their rights as citizens by participating in the weekly "Grievance Day," when peasants and rural workers have an opportunity to bring their problems directly to the attention of the powerful officer and the district-wide bureaucratic order he represents. Most important for Karuppiah, they would bring their grievance to the state through the medium of writing. Their trip to submit a petition at the collector's office in the town of Pudukkottai represented not only the culmination of over one year's worth of work learning basic reading and writing skills; it also represented a new form of social action. Most of the petitioners would be signing their names in an official context for the first time in their lives.

When people asked where we were going as we left the village on that cloudy monsoon morning, the women all answered with a degree of newfound confidence, "We're going to see the collector. We need to give him a petition!" Before going to the office, the women first had to feed their families breakfast and take time to tie on their best saris. They had stopped at the bus station after the one-hour ride to town to put flowers in their hair. Karuppiah had been talking with the literacy group about this petition for months. But it was only that morning that he could finally persuade these women to skip a much-needed day of work during the transplanting season to go to town. We arrived at the office a little later than hoped for. Karuppiah knew that the collector would leave at exactly one o'clock and that it was necessary to file one's name early to get a chance to see him. Because we were so late, he ended up quickly writing a petition by hand himself. The literacy group would then not be able to show off their literacy skills to the collector, other than to leave their newly acquired signatures. Karuppiah thought that at least they would have the satisfaction of handing their petition over to the collector as a group and telling him about their problem in person.

An unhappy intersection of the rural laborers' schedule and bureaucratic time conspired against even that form of participation. We stood in line with hundreds of villagers, from all over the district, waiting for their number to be called, until one o'clock, at which point the collector promptly got up and left for his next appointment. The Katrampatti literacy group simply filed their signed petition at an office downstairs, rather than being able to hand the petition in person to the collector. The signatures they had been learning and practicing for the past year would have to take on the full burden of representing an absent subject. Everything rested on a written piece of paper. On the bus ride home, the women seemed disappointed at not being able to see the collector, but everyone agreed it had been a very important day.

The act of petitioning the state was in no way an ordinary or obvious course to take for these women, who had never stepped foot in a school. It was the result of massive amounts of work. The people described above were all participants in the *Arivoli Iyakkam*, the "Light of Knowledge," or "Enlightenment," movement.[1] The villagers from Katrampatti, their activist neighbor, Karuppiah, and even the collector were taking part in this social movement, which sought to make political agents of rural women and to disseminate scientific knowledge through the spread of written language. Over the course of nearly twenty years, from 1990 until the movement ended in 2009, the Arivoli Iyakkam managed to mobilize huge numbers of people from across the Tamil countryside. In the small, rural district of Pudukkottai over three hundred thousand villagers participated in literacy lessons, science demonstrations, and other Arivoli events. Across southern India the number reached the millions. By the time of my fieldwork in the early 2000s, it was no longer unusual for groups of women like those from Katrampatti to write petitions or to pursue other forms of interaction with local state offices. This was, by all accounts, a very new phenomenon.

Literacy activists worked for the Arivoli Iyakkam in the name of enlightenment, citizenship, and development. They claimed acts of written self-representation, such as composing and signing petitions, for a politics of emancipation from the traditional power structures of caste, class, and gender. Teaching everyone to read and write would lead to India's "true independence," as many workers in the literacy movement and sympathetic allies would put it. To activists, the petition submitted by the women of Katrampatti represented a form of self-determination and stood as a sign of their participation as agents in the political process. But the forms of knowledge and social life that the Arivoli Iyakkam had, in fact, enabled cannot be grasped adequately within these terms of enlightened citizenship.

In rural India, as elsewhere, the enlightenment ideals of citizenship and self-determination couple easily with new forms of subjection to state power and bureaucratic rationality. The Dalit petitioners from Katrampatti were ambivalent about their encounter with the logic of official writing. Petitioning was a means by which people like them, otherwise excluded from government offices and politics, could meet the collector in person. The petitioners had expected that their intense efforts to learn to write over the course of the year would culminate in a face-to-face encounter to make their case for social justice. Their palpable disappointment on the bus ride home illustrated how their desire to engage directly with political processes remained unfulfilled. The written signs left by these women in the petition "efface as they disclose," to borrow a phrase from Gayatri Chakravorty Spivak (2010, 21). There is no simple correlation between literate interaction with state offices and empowerment (Gupta 2012, 191–233). We can see that what activists had promoted as a medium of transparency and agency was experienced by the women of Katrampatti as an erasure of sorts. Disappointments like this about the impossibility of pure self-representation routinely challenged activists' understandings of literacy's promise of emancipation.

This book is about contradictions in the project of Enlightenment that emerged over the course of two decades in rural Tamil Nadu. In their endeavors to remake the Tamil countryside through literacy activism, workers in the movement found that their own understanding of the politics of writing and enlightenment was often transformed in the encounter with deeply rooted practices surrounding entirely different notions of language and imaginations of social order. Arguing that the Arivoli Iyakkam faced contradictions and reformulations in its quest to enlighten the countryside through the spread of literacy and scientific rationality, however, is not to claim that Indian villages are somehow ill suited for, or even resistant to, such a project. The Tamil region has a long history of philosophical literature beginning before the Common Era, missionary efforts and colonization have substantially altered orientations to language and society since the eighteenth century across southern India, and Tamil Nadu has seen a wide range of modernist political movements over the course of the twentieth century. My study of the Arivoli Iyakkam instead seeks to foreground irreconcilable elements and paradoxes of agency within an Enlightenment pedagogy that would claim to remold the very people it aimed to emancipate through the written word.

In postcolonial studies it has become common to criticize discourses of modern progress for the way Enlightenment reason encompasses alterity through a narrative of historical incompletion (Chakrabarty 2000). Talk about national development, for example, tends to assume movement along a universal scale of time, such that people may express anxieties about being "left behind" or "not yet modern" because of the particularities of their culture. Anticolonial politics had already developed a counterargument to this logic. For many anticolonial thinkers, cultural resistance to the instrumental rationality of Enlightenment stood as the realm of national autonomy (Chatterjee 1993; Cheah 2003). Liberal thought, on the other hand, continues to divide the world into those who enjoy the freedom of rational self-determination and those who are constrained by their culture (Mahmood 2005; Povinelli 2011). To the degree that these positions require one to be *for* or *against* Enlightenment reason, they recapitulate what Michel Foucault (1987, 167) once called the "blackmail" of the Enlightenment. But is it possible to construe a contemporary activist movement carried out in the very name of enlightenment in terms other than the binary of cultural resistance and instrumental rationality? What if something else was also at stake in the practice of literacy activism, which neither those championing the cause of Enlightenment nor their critics fully recognize? How might a critical analysis of the Arivoli Iyakkam offer an escape from the blackmail of Enlightenment?

These are certainly difficult questions in light of the ongoing legitimation crisis of both liberal and left political thought in recent Indian history. I raise these concerns, however, after some years of reflection on ethnographic materials suggesting that the Arivoli Iyakkam's mass mobilization gave rise to forms of social relation, immanent to the field of activism, that are reducible neither to the utopian world envisaged by literacy activists nor to the putatively traditional society that was supposed to be transformed through literacy activism. In fact, activists of the movement successfully mobilized large numbers of rural women through logics that often pushed against the very Enlightenment rationality they hoped to foster, and the results of their efforts were often unanticipated. It is in moments where activism hit the limits of its own ideology that we can catch glimpses of forms of sociality overlooked not just by the activists but also by the conceptual vocabulary of social science.

This story must account for the perspectives of a wide set of social actors, from Dalit literacy students, to activists from a range of backgrounds, and on to government administrators from across India, all of whom were brought together in novel ways through the Arivoli Iyakkam. Among these protagonists, I focus in particular on the women and men who worked as rural activists, because it is they who wrestled most squarely with the contradictions of bringing Enlightenment to the Tamil countryside through literacy. Arivoli's workers were caught between a vision of literacy as radical freedom from social constraints and the realization that writing is an embodied technique as well as a technology of governance. They continually reflected on this as well as other tensions in their quest to produce newly empowered villagers through the spread of literacy. Compelled to address these problems, activists undertook numerous experiments with pedagogy. Their efforts to respond to the contradictions of Enlightenment allowed the Arivoli Iyakkam to become a mass movement extending deeply into the wider social world of the Tamil countryside. Within this particular story lies a more general narrative about knowledge, representation, and Enlightenment in the postcolony. It is the workers of the Arivoli Iyakkam who will serve as our guides in this journey of leaps back and forth, between specific moments of activism in Pudukkottai's villages and intellectual problems that have universal significance for those of us interested in questions of self-determination and mediation in politics.

Pedagogies of Enlightenment and the State

The Arivoli Iyakkam was indebted to visions of emancipation upheld by the political Left that stood in constant tension with the neoliberal conditions of possibility allowing for the movement to grow so quickly. The ideology of the Tamil literacy movement resembles certain earlier mass literacy programs that could also lay claims to inheriting and elaborating a modernity based on the principles of Enlightenment. Early Bolshevik experiments, for example, were carried out by the "liquidators of illiteracy" of the youth and women's wings of the Communist Party in the name of the People's Commissariat of Enlightenment (*Narkompros*). Later in the twentieth century, Mao Tse-tung initiated campaigns to persuade villagers to "believe in science" through the spread of literacy, and we can find numerous examples of similar efforts among the socialist revolutions of Latin America, many of which were inspired by the Brazilian philosopher Paulo Freire's *Pedagogy of the Oppressed* (1970), as was the Arivoli Iyakkam.[2] Naming the literacy movement the "Arivoli Iyakkam" was therefore not an arbitrary choice. The Tamil literacy movement drew on a long tradition connecting the written word to the project of producing a rational and self-determining human subject. But in some important respects the Arivoli Iyakkam also differs from these earlier state-led experiments in modernization at the level of political organization. It began as a nongovernmental initiative that was then absorbed by a rapidly changing capitalist state.

The Arivoli Iyakkam was originally conceived as a social movement to spread Enlightenment rationality through literacy by an activist organization. The volunteer movement that became the Arivoli Iyakkam was first initiated by the largely urban, middle-class members of the Tamil Nadu and Pondicherry Science Forums in the late 1980s as a means of teaching basic science and literacy to villagers and the urban poor in the cities of Chennai (then called Madras) and Pondicherry. In addition to teaching people how to read and write in Tamil, these scientists and academics

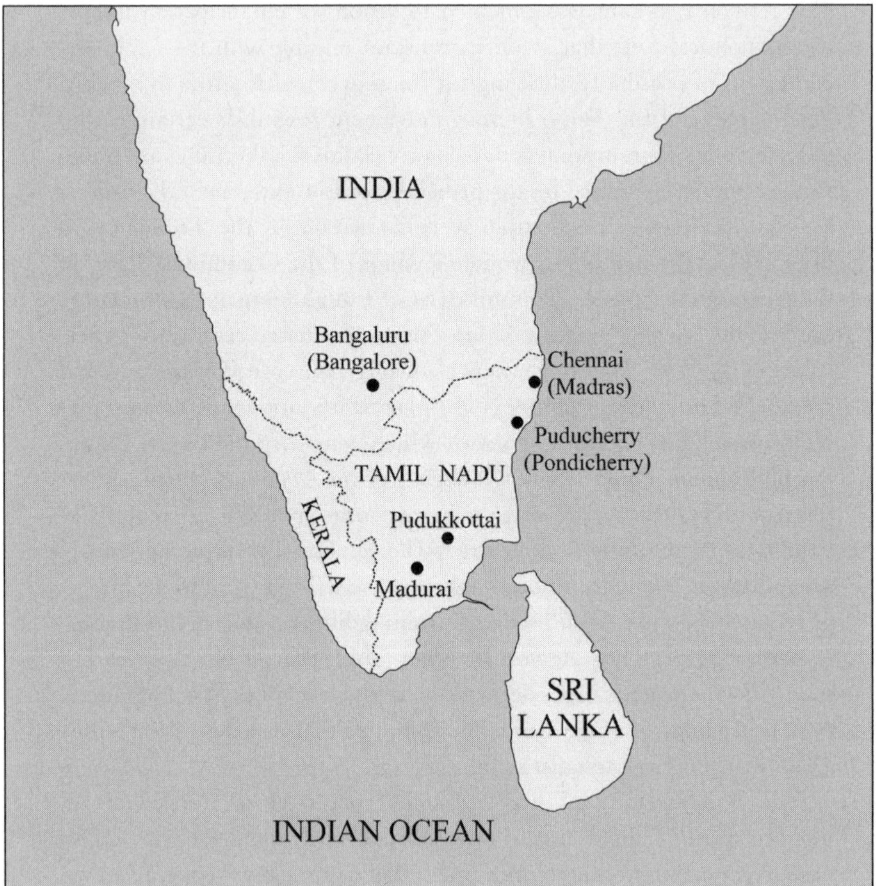

INDIA
Bangaluru
(Bangalore)
Chennai
(Madras)
Puducherry
(Pondicherry)
TAMIL NADU
KERALA
Pudukkottai
Madurai
SRI
LANKA
INDIAN OCEAN

also held public demonstrations to explain basic science using microscopes, telescopes, and globes. These were efforts to awaken a general curiosity about the world among the poor, and more specifically to argue that the subaltern classes had political stakes in government science policy. It was only through their literacy classes, however, that the Science Forums were able to recruit large numbers of volunteers among the urban and rural poor. Their success captured the attention of the central government of India.

In 1990, a joint NGO-state initiative advanced the Arivoli Iyakkam model of mass literacy through volunteerism under the newly established National Literacy Mission. Activists across the Tamil region sought to replicate the successful experiments in Chennai, Pondicherry, and the neighboring state of Kerala on a much larger scale. From a small volunteer initiative run by academics and scientists to recruit activists for a "people's science," Arivoli had become a development program. This move allowed activists to make use of central government funds to print primers and gave them access to material resources such as jeeps from the Collector's Office. The Arivoli movement also garnered a new form of legitimacy in the eyes of other government workers whose cooperation was necessary if the movement was to grow. Local administrators become involved and university professors were offered a year of paid leave if they decided to work for the literacy movement. The move to inhabit the state's development infrastructure allowed the movement to recruit many more volunteers than it would have otherwise.[3] But unlike the state-led efforts of the Bolsheviks and Cuban revolutionaries, the convergence of state interests and activism came at a very different time in Tamil Nadu.

The literacy movement was launched at a time of political upheaval and economic restructuring that signaled what many consider to be the demise of the Nehruvian state in India. The once-unquestioned national dominance of the Congress Party had eroded. With the rise of Hindu nationalist politics new anxieties emerged about the future of secularism across much of the country. But perhaps most important, the Arivoli Iayakkam's initial mass-mobilization in the early 1990s coincided with policies of economic liberalization.[4] As a number of scholars have noted, many of the functions of governance and rural development were formally shifted into the nongovernmental sphere as a result of neoliberal socioeconomic reorganization (Ferguson and Gupta 2002; Gupta and Sivaramakrishnan 2010; John 1996; Kamat 2002; Menon and Nigam 2007; Sharma 2008). The Nehruvian state had claimed a paternalist legitimacy through its monopoly on modernity through development.[5] Under this older regime, nongovernmental organizations worked in a clearly separated sphere, and they affiliated themselves with social movements that were often critics of state-led development. Under the new development regime, these divisions were increasingly blurred as the state took the initiative to administer its welfare projects precisely through these nongovernmental organization forms.[6] In the process, issues surrounding social redistribution, once discussed in terms of political struggle, were often reframed as technical problems with the old, inflexible, state-led development regime.

Research on the neoliberal reorganization of welfare projects frequently draws on Foucault's (2007) concept of governmentality. Scholars working in this tradition have noted that the demise of high-modernist development planning strategies does not necessarily mark a retreat of state power as much as it facilitates the dissemination of governmental rationalities across the domains of state, society, and family. The Arivoli Iyakkam certainly fits this global pattern of neoliberal governmentality. Governmental communicative logics, epistemologies of enumeration, and moral narratives of self-development were strengthened through volunteerism and entrenched by institutions that blurred the divide between the state and nongovernmental organizational forms. Arivoli activists remained volunteers rather than paid government workers. They worked for the betterment of their society without the security of government employment that their predecessors in the Nehruvian development apparatus would have enjoyed. This form of development work was facilitated at the national level by organizations, like the Bharat Gyan Vigyan Samiti (BGVS), which were established in the late 1980s to connect movements like the Arivoli Iyakkam both to the central government and to social movements in other regions.[7] Much like other organizations, such as the Mahila Samakhya women's development initiative studied by Aradhana Sharma (2008), the BGVS and its affiliated social movements were led by activists whose political upbringing was in the parties of the leftist movement in the 1960s and '70s. Arivoli Iyakkam activism was therefore the curious product of a state-sponsored volunteerism under conditions of neoliberal governance that was nevertheless shaped by radical traditions of the organized Left.

The concept of governmentality focuses our analytical attention to the political structure of the Arivoli Iyakkam as well as to the forms of instrumental reason propagated by this form of activism. But as Aradhana Sharma's work makes clear, the world inaugurated by neoliberal governmentality does not only consist of the "antipolitics" described by earlier critiques of development in anthropology (e.g., Escobar 1995; Ferguson 1994). Drawing on the work of Akhil Gupta (2001, 2012) and Partha Chatterjee (2004), she notes that the strategy to install a hierarchical technocracy in the name of "empowerment" may also "spawn political activism centered on redistribution and justice" (Sharma 2008, xxi), sometimes drawing on older roots in the Nehruvian welfare state. Sharma represents the second generation of critical development studies in anthropology when she argues that development is, in fact, generative of struggle and politically ambivalent. My own concern is that too strict an adherence to the analytic of governmentality and the instrumental rationality undergirding this strategy of power might easily obscure a politics that is neither about the demand for state welfare nor about the rhetoric of "self-help" and entrepreneurship that has been propagated as a technically superior form of development in the age of neoliberalism.

The questions guiding this book are not only about the enabling or disabling of agentive life under neoliberalism, but also about how the Arivoli Iyakkam arose through modes of mobilization that cannot be captured through received narratives of agency in the first place. As we will see, the Arivoli Iyakkam advocated the empowerment of women through a language of individual rights, but its successes came from a practice that upheld obligations to others. It was a movement to foster autonomy that worked instead through duty. It was a movement designed to craft a disembodied public sphere through writing that gained traction through embodied forms of orality and traditions of recitation. These are just some of the paradoxes that have convinced me that the pedagogical practices of Arivoli activism often worked against its own Enlightenment ideals, and that the political logics fueling the movement produced a field of social action exceeding that which the lens of governmentality can bring into focus. An account of Arivoli activism demands that we listen carefully to the echoes of socialist politics in a decidedly neoliberal age, but also that we attend more carefully to the contradictions of Enlightenment at the heart of pedagogical practice.

A Linguistic Infrastructure for Citizenship

Contemporary pedagogies of citizenship have been shaped by a history of colonial domination and postcolonial statecraft. Much of what postcolonial theory has taught us revolves around the question of this historical inheritance that continues to animate a wide range of political interventions in contemporary India (Chakrabarty 2000; Chatterjee 1993; Dirks 2001; Gupta 1998; Kaviraj 2010; Scott 1999). Postcolonial statecraft, for instance, rests on the persistent premise that the subaltern classes do not *yet* have the full capacity to represent themselves as rights-bearing citizens.[8] Literacy rates and the ability to sign one's name, in particular, have long stood as indexes of the capacity for self-representation and even as signs of fitness for democratic self-rule in both colonial and postcolonial India (Cody 2009). But it was only just as women were becoming the primary targets of development policy, in the 1990s, that mass literacy came to the fore as the solution to this problem of incorporation within the nation-state. It was therefore according to the tenets of this particular form of statecraft that villagers were taught to embody literacy as an infrastructure, enabling erstwhile subjects to become citizens through pedagogical projects like the Arivoli Iyakkam.[9]

Mass literacy held out a promise that formerly excluded women among the rural poor might one day join the homogeneous space and time of the Indian nation. Written language would work as a medium allowing for the imagination of a modern subject that has been abstracted from an immediate context, enabling the production of large-scale identities commonly understood to transcend the worlds of kin and caste. National citizenship has, in fact, been the paradigmatic case through which academics as well as activists have understood the unifying effects of mass literacy and print publication.[10] The theoretical perspective on language taken in this book, however, argues that it is not the technology of writing itself that causes such radical changes, whether positively valued in terms of the evolution of rationality, as Jack Goody (1977, 1986) would have it, or negatively construed as the violent intrusion of modernity, as in Claude Lévi-Strauss's (1973) famous lament in his best-selling *Tristes tropiques*. India's acquaintance with the written word dates back to the Bronze Age, and Tamil has an unbroken literary tradition that spans over two millennia. If Lévi-Strauss (1973, 300) was perhaps correct to argue that "the fight against illiteracy is connected with an increase in governmental authority over citizens," he was certainly wrong to assume that the appropriation of written language initiates an irreversible fall into the iron cage of instrumental rationality and the end of a transparent, face-to-face community. This view attributes an unmediated nature to nonliterate people by ignoring the textual dimensions of language use more broadly, in addition to assuming a monolithic effect of writing technology.[11] Writing, like other media technologies, has unpredictable uses, effects, and value.

Philosophies that claim literacy as a medium of political emancipation, such as Freire's *Pedagogy of the Oppressed* (1970), often share more with Goody and with Lévi-Strauss's theories of the modern subject than they appear to on the surface. There is a common assumption in social thought on literacy, often shared by activists, that writing breaks the bonds of orality by objectifying the world through processes of mediation and abstraction. Variegated logics of textuality and language already operating in the Tamil country, such as the modern devotional orientations to the power of language studied by Sumathi Ramaswamy (1997) and Bernard Bate (2009), inevitably pose problems for a pedagogy that would conflate literacy with humanist emancipation or Enlightenment. The variety of textual genres at play in Tamil literature, many of which are circulated orally, cannot be captured through any general theory that would seek to account for the effects of literacy. Traditions of cultivating virtue through the embodiment of ancient poetry at the core of Tamil pedagogies, for example, may well be seen as incommensurable with the approaches to language that the literacy movement had adopted from Freire's philosophy. The cultural relativism of what has been called the "new literacy studies" (e.g., Gee 1996; Street 1984, 1993; cf. Collins and Blot 2003) that has dominated in the discipline of anthropology, however, does not suffice to engage with the universalizing claims being made on behalf of writing in the Arivoli Iyakkam's Enlightenment project.

Where writing works both as an ideational and a material infrastructure of citizenship, as it does in India and elsewhere, to argue that there are alternative literacies is not enough. Critical social theory must instead focus on the historical intersection of technologies of mass mediation with ideologies of self-abstraction and stranger sociability that have come to determine our understanding of political modernity. The task, as I see it, is to understand how citizenship acts as a link between democracy and the nation-state through technopolitical assemblages that limit or enable the agency of the modern subject qua citizen. This is not to claim that literacy is a requirement for electoral participation, nor is it to assume citizenship is the only form of political agency.[12] Rather, it is to develop a broader understanding of political participation from which much of the population is excluded owing to the uneven distribution of literacy and formal education (Drèze 2004). More specifically, the persistent structural violence of poverty, caste, and gender requires detailed attention to the bureaucratic logics and practices of inscription that determine the everyday course of postcolonial state formation (Gupta 2012; Hull 2012; Rao 2009). It has become clear in recent years that the narrative of modern citizenship, understood broadly as a capacity to make demands on the state, remains compelling for large numbers of rural women where the very infrastructural means of entry into the sphere of citizenship is not something that people can expect of the state itself. A great proportion of the education system in rural Tamil Nadu is now privatized, for example. It is as a result of such large-scale political and economic reorganization in the direction of unfettered capitalism that so much social responsibility had fallen onto the shoulders of literacy activists.

Methods in Activism and Ethnography

People living in districts where the Arivoli Iyakkam was strong commonly liken the movement to India's epic struggle for freedom from

British rule, calling it the "*second* independence struggle."[13] There are number of reasons for people, even those who were not affiliated with the movement, to make such a weighty claim. It is partly the sheer scale of social mobilization that seems to invite this comparison. But there are other respects in which the similarities between these movements, which are separated by half a century, resonate with more depth. Both moments in history have been experienced as tangible breaks with the past, as ruptures that were animated by new forms of collective action. Just as important, both the independence and Arivoli movements produced a set of remarkable people who acted as catalysts in focusing social energies among the marginalized in rural India. In the otherwise dreary world of development expertise, it was the activists who made the Arivoli Iyakkam a social movement of political importance.

Activists are intellectuals, not only in the general sense of being people who self-consciously produce new modes of thought and conceptions of the world, but also in a more limited, sociological meaning of the term. If everyone can be said to be an intellectual in the former sense, what distinguishes some people is what Antonio Gramsci would call their intellectual "function" within a "general complex of social relations" (1971, 8–9). It is in this particular sense of playing a mediating role in the production of social relations that I would like to place literacy activists as intellectuals. Although ostensibly working as volunteers under the auspices of India's Delhi-based National Literacy Mission, activists often viewed their job as that of standing between what they would often call a "machine-like" state bureaucracy, on one hand, and the aspirations of rural Tamils in a struggle for forms of social justice that had been denied them because they could not read and write, on the other hand. Like the schoolteachers of West Bengal described by Chatterjee to illustrate his conception of political society, activists "mediate between domains that are differentiated by deep and historically entrenched inequalities of power . . . between those who govern and those who are governed" (2004, 66). The expertise of activism drew from professional development discourse; from transnational feminist politics; from communist and rationalist social thought; from idioms of Enlightenment and social service that are widespread in the Tamil countryside; and from a range of other intellectual traditions that I describe in greater detail in the following chapter. The field of knowledge entailed in mobilization and pedagogy in the Arivoli movement therefore sat at the intersection of a number of otherwise disparate domains.

Many workers with relatively little schooling from farming families had entered the movement through personal or political-party connections, fully inhabiting the intellectual function through their engagement with activism. It was also through activist practice that many rural workers developed the "attention to the formal properties and values of semiosis" that characterizes intellectual life (Boyer 2005b, 43). These were the activists who tended to devote their whole life to the cause, like Karuppiah, the young man who had organized the petitioning expedition described above.[14] Some were university professors, teachers in small towns, or some other type of knowledge professional before entering into a social movement that would forever change their relationship to rural life. Professionals who worked for the movement nevertheless ended up returning to their jobs after some time, or they took up other causes. Both women and men were drawn to the movement from the range of caste and religious backgrounds representative of the region where they worked, although the state-level leadership was certainly dominated by upper-caste Hindus. What the workers of the movement generally had in common was an orientation to intellectual life that could make no claims to being autonomous or independent of the social relations of knowledge production. This awareness of the socially and materially grounded nature of knowledge was due in part to the importance of Marxism in the movement, and perhaps also because activists came from such a wide range of social backgrounds. Like the nationalist struggle, the Arivoli Iyakkam specialized in attracting and eventually producing people who learned to inhabit multiple lifeworlds that others would find to be irreconcilable.

Activism is, in many respects, a search for pedagogies that would provide the right fit, adhering to historical inheritance as experienced in the present, while also pulling toward an imagined future. Karuppiah's best friend and colleague in the Arivoli Iyakkam, R. Neela, for example, is one the activists I came to know who had developed a keen sense that the movement must ground its methods of mobilization in contemporary forms of social life among the rural poor. An avid reader and local intellectual who had never finished the tenth standard of primary schooling because her labor was needed at home when she was being raised by a single mother, Neela had risen through the ranks to become the Arivoli coordinator for the whole development block of Tiruvarangulam. It was in her capacity as a coordinator also involved in more formal political organizing that Neela made frequent trips to the state capital in Chennai, and that she once went to the National Literacy Mission offices in New Delhi, for training. She also worked closely with the Dalit literacy group from Katrampatti that Karuppiah had organized. But when she visited this group, they would never go through the normal lessons plans of learning the script and practicing signatures. They would simply talk about work in the fields and compare the songs that the women of Katrampatti sang while transplanting rice paddy with those sung in other parts of the same district.

Once, early in my fieldwork, Neela saw that I was somewhat surprised that an Arivoli lesson need not be about literacy at all. She explained to me: "We get all these instructions about how to run classes, but we really need to run this movement according to the qualities of the mud of this place [*inta maṇ tavunta mātiri inta iyakkam naṭakkaṇum*]." Using this potent agricultural metaphor to invoke the substantial powers of locality, Neela was explaining to me the importance of working with that which learners themselves bring to Arivoli lesson. She told me that it was more important that the group keep coming and finding in the Arivoli literacy circle some relief from their difficulties than it was for them to go through the lesson plans that had been devised for them by activists and academics in Chennai. Knowing very well that she was participating in a national literacy program that held lessons across India, Neela was often driven by her work to reflect on what is particular to the places where she conducted lessons. For Neela too, then, I came to understand that visiting the literacy group in Katrampatti was part of a larger *research project*. Neela's village is not far from Katrampatti, where material living conditions are quite similar. It was therefore not some generality about rural life that interested her, as it might some anthropologist. Rather, it was the details of an unorthodox ritual that intrigued her, or the imaginative lines that some field laborer had inserted into a work song she already knew. How might a story or song collected in one village be used to pedagogical ends in another? These were the questions motivating her research.

Neela's orientation to pedagogy tells us much about the Arivoli Iyakkam's broader methodology, and can furthermore help serve as a guide to my own approach insofar as the questions activists ask have deeply influenced the shape that this research has taken. Neela's research project was centered on those idiosyncratic aspects of everyday life that could be turned into grounds for building something new. It is important to explain here that Neela is a widely published poet and short-story writer, in addition to being a literacy activist. Also a very active member of the Tamil Nadu Progressive Writers Association, Neela collects stories both for their aesthetic qualities and for the value they have as pedagogical tools, and she does not necessarily distinguish between the two. She has shared some of her work with Tamil readers in the form of a collection of short essays based on her activism, called *Pāmara Taricanam* (Darshan of the Common Folk [2002]), and she is a frequent contributor to a range of literary weekly magazines in Tamil. Within Pudukkottai District, Neela discovered a whole world of cultural differences tied to religion, caste, and location that she feels compelled to share with a wider world. She taught me that the fishermen of the Palk Strait coastline, for example, sing in a particular rhythm that is timed to the motion of their rowing, and she further explained how her colleague in the movement wrote Arivoli Iyakkam songs about women's emancipation and composed them in this meter to be sung among the literacy groups in fishing villages. Activists like Neela would often echo a claim that Mao is said to have made, that they were simply "giving back to the people with more clarity what they have already given us." Activist methodology was based on a self-conscious reciprocity, wherein workers in the literacy movement objectified aspects of rural life that could then be represented to build a progressive politics, mobilizing experience to shape visions of the future. Active programs of research and reflexivity on the part of activists like Neela and Karuppiah were an integral part of this process.

Most of my research time was spent following these activists to literacy lessons and events around the district, learning from their research. After living for one year on my own in the town of Pudukkottai, where I worked closely with the district leadership, I ended up living with Karuppiah in his village for another year, focusing on activism in the village of Katrampatti and in the surrounding area. We would meet with Neela and other activist friends and colleagues nearly every day in the room Karuppiah rents in the small town of Alangudi. I have hence focused my ethnography on this particular class of people to understand the styles of reflexivity that had come to define the creative process of activism. There were certainly many working for the Arivoli Iyakkam at the grassroots level who did not share in Karuppiah's or Neela's intellectual endeavors, and some of the movement's leadership had developed such a close relationship with state institutions that they did not share in the sense of mediating between cold bureaucratic machinery and the aspirations of villagers. Some activists had become full-fledged development professionals and consultants over the course of the movement. It was a particular variety of activist, then, who had developed a sense of their work as that of yoking the particulars of village life to some grander narrative of Enlightenment, and rethinking key elements of this narrative in the process. This form of activism shares some ground with ethnographic research, and I became friends with Neela and Karuppiah precisely because we were interested in similar questions about language, culture, and power, even if we have cultivated our methods for pursuing these questions in relation to somewhat different ends.

Anthropology has often used stories like the one I have just presented about Neela to engage concretely with the abstractions of social theory. Victor Turner's (1967) memorable portrait of Muchona, "the Hornet," is an example of how the ethnography of a rural intellectual can be used to question epistemological hierarchies. Much late twentieth- and early twenty-first-century ethnography has furthermore responded to earlier critiques of the discipline's compulsion to exoticize by developing a fieldwork program specifically among subjects who appear to share certain styles of thinking with anthropology (Boyer 2005b, 2007; Brenneis 1994; Holmes and Marcus 2005, 2008; Maurer 2005; Riles 2000). For instance, Bill Maurer (2002) draws attention to striking parallels between the rhetorical structure of Islamic accounting and that of anthropological accounts, as each attempt to reconcile theory and data tends to be encompassed by a higher level of abstraction in both of these knowledge systems. Many ethnographers who have studied experts and intellectuals have emphasized the sociological reflexivity developed by their interlocutors, as I do in this book, raising the question of methodological traction in a world where the knower and the known appear to operate with the same theoretical tools.

Anthropologies of activism have been particularly concerned both with the place of anthropological knowledge in activist discourse (e.g., Merry 2006; Warren 1998) and with the potentials of activism to reshape anthropological knowledge (e.g., Hale 2006; Tsing 2004). Sally Engle Merry (2005), for example, has emphasized the "porous borders" between activism and anthropology when studying the globally circulating discourse on human rights and gender violence. Although greatly inspired by the new anthropological attention to intellectual production among activists, the investigations presented in the following chapters take a somewhat different tack from that pursued by those who have focused primarily on the similarities between ethnographers and their subjects. There are indeed similarities between some of the conclusions reached by activists and those arrived at through academic research. Activists and ethnographers often share an engagement with problems of legal normalization and ethical closure in political mobilization (Dave 2012) and a deep antipathy toward centralized state power (Graeber 2009). Sometimes our forms of knowledge even share a common source, as when I went to interview the Arivoli activist and author S. Tamilcelvan in his home in rural Tirunelveli and found him reading a photocopied version of Clifford Geertz's *The Interpretation of Cultures* (1973). But there is often a substantial difference between activist and anthropological perspectives. This difference has more to do with our differential relationship to the social world at hand than with some cultural gulf that lies between us. Activist knowledge is shaped by epistemologies and deeply embodied affects tuned to lifeworlds that I have only traveled through as a part-time resident. The very fact of my being in the position of an outside observer in the world of agrarian labor renders my understanding of the events unfolding around me as reflections of a different order than those produced by activists, for whom such research constituted an immediate social necessity.[15] Work on activism has wrestled anxiously with questions of representation raised by this differential relationship to the social world that activists work to change, especially when scholarship itself also aims to produce activist knowledge (Chari and Donner 2010; Hale 2008; Sanford and Angel-Ajani 2006;

Scheper-Hughes 1995). This book can make no such claims to identification, but it is nevertheless resolutely partial and concerned with the question of how to represent activist experience and activist research.

It is in their retrospective accounting of what happened in the Arivoli Iyakkam that activists have engaged in the sort of work that more closely resembles the perspective of social science, and I draw liberally from the Tamil writings of activists such as S. Tamilcelvan (2003, 2004b), N. Karunanidhi (2003), and R. Neela (2002, 2004) and publications of the Tamil Nadu Progressive Writers Association (1993, 2002, 2006), in addition to the English-language reports of administrators and academics who played a part in the movement.[16] Tamilcelvan's *Iruḷum Oḷiyum: Aṟivoḷi Iyakka Aṉupavaṅkaḷ* (Darkness and Lightness: Experiences in the Light of Knowledge Movement), published first as a series of essays in the Tamil cultural studies journal titled *Tīmtarikiṭā* (Drumroll) while I was conducting fieldwork (2002–4), and later as a book in which the questions of enlightenment and political responsibility are turned back onto his readers has been my most important guide in this respect. His post hoc analyses of the pedagogical experiments he undertook as an Arivoli leader in Tirunelveli exhibit a depth of insight and a degree of reflexivity that allowed me to conduct fieldwork in a much more effective manner. His work has also helped me develop the understandings of ethnographic data that I present in this book. Breaking with an anthropology that would assume a perspective of objective distance with regard to "local" knowledge production, whatever that may be in this age, my investigation therefore places itself in conversation with literature written by activists with a full understanding that we often write with different ends and for different publics.

Outline of the Chapters

The structure of this book makes an argument concerning the Arivoli Iyakkam's struggle to mediate the everyday lived reality of villagers and the movement's vision of literacy as transcendent Enlightenment. Having begun with the story of women submitting a signed petition at the district administrative headquarters, we must now go back to learn about how these unlikely agents of social change had come to the center of rural governance by means of activism around written language. The first half of the book is about mobilization in the literacy movement, and the second half focuses on pedagogy. In each chapter we will see how attempts to spread light and knowledge through the written word hit certain limits, forcing those involved to rethink their strategy and orientations toward literacy.

The first two chapters of this book introduce Arivoli Iyakkam activism by focusing on how the movement sought to unify experiences of space and time and to produce new forms of agency through literacy. Combining ethnography of the movement in the early 2000s and historical reflections on the movement's origins in science activism and the broader Left, in chapter 1 I seek to understand how and why the literacy movement built its self-image through the trope of enlightenment. In trying to account for how the Arivoli Iyakkam came to attract many more women than men, in chapter 2 I then develop this exposition of the movement's vision of progress with a sharper focus on the different models of agency and gender used in activist pedagogy. The Arivoli Iyakkam worked through a range of idioms in developing their version of grassroots feminism. I argue that the movement was, in fact, successful to the degree that it developed a style of "reciprocal agency" through which women paradoxically participate in a movement designed to foster a sense of autonomy out of a sense of obligation or duty to activists themselves.

Moving closer to the ground of language as an embodied knowledge, in chapters 3 and 4 I concentrate on the teaching of literacy in village lessons organized by the Arivoli Iyakkam. I first explain the development of Paulo Freire's liberation pedagogy, in which subjects understand themselves to be agents through processes of verbal objectification. In an attempt to develop a radical pedagogy suited to awakening adults' sense of their own agency, the Arivoli Iyakkam used models of personhood and language that map only partially onto those that obtain among the movement's villager learners. Learners themselves provided a critique of this pedagogy through questions they asked about the poetics of Tamil learning traditions and about how written language becomes memorable and meaningful, forcing activists to reconsider their methods.

Tracking a shift of emphasis in the Arivoli Iyakkam's critical pedagogy toward reading aloud, in chapter 4 I argue that experiments with literary approaches had forced a new awareness of the social and embodied qualities of language among activists. As a result of the struggle to devise a new mode of literary production fit for activism, the Arivoli Iyakkam turned away from vanguardist pedagogy toward folklore in their attempts to shape a literature appropriate for neoliterates to read aloud. Experiments in education constituted the search for a linguistic practice that would be both enlightening and true to forms of expression characteristic of village life. Once again, activism was confronted with the question of which cultural forms can be recontextualized so as to suit the vision of progress fueling the movement.

In the final ethnographic chapter in the book I return to the scene of petitioning first described in the introduction. Providing ethnography of petition writing, scribal mediation, and signature in the practice of governance, in this chapter I follow the social life of discourse as village-level complaints are performed orally for scribes and volunteers outside administrative offices, and then rendered in writing so as to be presentable to state power. Attempts to reorder the political economy of language through literacy activism, such that people can be said to represent themselves in writing, nevertheless inscribe neoliterate petitioners as "underdeveloped." It is the Arivoli Iyakkam's pedagogy that held out the promise of a future alignment of communicative frameworks allowing for the transparent self-representation of an already-constituted citizen.

Arivoli activism made an argument for why mass literacy would enable new forms of agency among the most disenfranchised, all the while reflecting on the paradox that the movement must remake the very people that it aimed to empower and recognizing that the movement worked through forms of social life that cannot be fully captured through the lens of Enlightenment. What insights this book might offer are often critical elaborations of problems activists themselves report to have faced in their work. I draw on ethnographic examples from across the district of Pudukkottai, as well as interviews with activists from other districts and cities to make sense of the larger contradictions within the project of Enlightenment through literacy. But it is my experience with Neela, Karuppiah, and the literacy group from Katrampatti, accumulated through two years of fieldwork and through yearly visits to this hamlet ever since, that serves as a grounding reference point throughout. These people will serve as our companions for the remainder of this book.

1

On Being a "Thumbprint"

Time and Space in Arivoli Activism

I first started to understand the extent to which literacy activism is really a form of cultural work, not simply a matter of teaching people how to read and write, one evening in a seaside village. It turns out that many villagers were taught to desire literacy and they learned a number of other things about themselves and their place in the world along the way. The occasion of my awareness was a street-theater performance by the Dawn Arts Group, a drama troupe that had been organized by Karuppiah and Neela to encourage people to join Arivoli classes and to recruit more volunteers for the movement. The central street of the fishing village where this performance took place was loud and lit brightly, lined with blaring loudspeakers interspersed with neon tube-lights fastened to bamboo poles. The saturated atmosphere would have reminded everyone of the yearly temple celebrations of local gods that also take place in the dry season. Young actors of the Dawn group started their performance by singing a song in the folk style of the Pudukkottai region. Their voices were distorted by the mic and speakers, which broadcasted their song powerfully into the air. The lyrics announced that this evening's event was indeed a festival, but one devoted to the dissemination of a specific kind of knowledge:

> Street by street, we come in festive procession;
> We rise up and come to spread literacy.
> (Vītiyilē vītiyilē ūrvalam varukiṉṟōm
> Eḻuttaṟivai pōtikka eḻuntē varukiṉṟōm.)
>
> Because the Light of Knowledge movement comes to teach
>   the darkness of ignorance
> Because we are waging yet another independence struggle.
> (Kallāmai iruḷakaṟṟa aṟivoḷi iyakkam varuvataṉāl
> Iṉumoru cutantirap pōr nāṅkaḷ naṭatta iruppataṉāl.)

Like the procession (*ūrvalam*) of a deity in a temple festival, the Arivoli Iyakkam had come to dispel the forces of darkness.

Following this song, the dramatic performance began by depicting a man, played by Karuppiah, sitting in his doorway attending to some sort of work with his hands. He wore a wrapped towel on his head signifying his status as a rural worker. A woman, presumably his wife, was sitting next to him preparing food. Two of the younger actors in the group held straight sticks at a right angle over their heads, giving the visual impression of a house. Another man walked up to the house carrying a clipboard and some papers in his hand. As he was approaching, the peasant told his wife to go inside the house. The stranger introduced himself as someone who was taking a survey for the government and asked the character played by Karuppiah how many people were living in the house. The peasant responded with some suspicion in his voice, and when asked to sign his name on the survey form as head of household, he refused. Wondering why he would refuse to sign his name, the survey taker went on to the neighbor's house asking the same information, this time successfully collecting a signature. He then asked the neighbor why his first respondent had refused to sign. The neighbor explained that the peasant's son was wanted by the police, and that he was probably afraid to talk to anyone from the government. The survey taker, still a little perplexed, went back to the first house calling Karuppiah's character, explaining that this was only a government census and had nothing to do with the police.

Still he would not come out and sign his name. The neighbor finally said, "He's just a thumbprint [*kaināṭṭu*]," trying to explain his unwillingness to sign his name and also indicating that he should be counted as an illiterate in the census. All the actors froze in place. Leaving a few seconds of silence after the play ended, giving the audience time to absorb the lesson, the whole Dawn Arts Group stood in a straight line facing the audience, pointed at them, and sang:

> This is the time of footprints on the moon.
> Shame on you for using your thumbprint!
> (Itu cantiraṉ mēle kāl vacca kālam
> nī kaināṭṭu vaikkiṟatu alaṅkōlam!)

Some in the audience seemed stunned by the accusation coming from the mouths of these young actors. After this short play ended, there were a few moments of silence before the Dawn Arts Group launched into their next play, which was similarly about the difficulties nonliterates face in the modern world, but this time peppered with a healthy dose of comic relief. Following the performance that evening, our hosts in the village fed the actors a late meal, thanking them for the efforts they had made to come to this relatively remote part of the district. Songs from a cassette player continued to blast from the loudspeakers as the drama troupe packed their microphones and instruments back into the van. Before leaving, Karuppiah had managed to secure a promise from the local Arivoli Iyakkam volunteer that she would make renewed efforts to start a literacy group among the women of the village. The drama troupe's van then drove into the night, stopping to drop off the actors in their respective villages.

Chronotopes of Enlightenment in the Tamil Country

It is now quite well known that the social imaginary of the development state is premised on a sense of a temporal difference attributed to those who are considered not yet modern. To claim that this is the "time of footprints on the moon" as the drama troupe did, for example, is to invoke a sense that those who do not read and write are living in the past. Akhil Gupta (1998) has provided a detailed ethnography of such temporal difference in agricultural development discourse among villagers in northern India. He explains how farmers feel behind in the race to become fully developed even if many had also become critical of what they see as an urban bias in government policy. Writing about Egypt, Lila Abu-Lughod (2005) shows how state and development agency–funded television serials worked in conjunction with adult literacy programs to fulfill a national pedagogical project by teaching the rural poor from Upper Egypt their marginal place in a broader story of modernity centered in the city of Cairo. It seems that in Egypt, as in India and elsewhere in the postcolonial world, political modernity "generates a tension between two aspects of the subaltern or peasant as citizen. One is the peasant who has to be educated into the citizen, . . . the other is the peasant who, despite his or her lack of formal education, is already a citizen" (Chakrabarty 2000,10). But there is still much to understand about the contradictions that arise in attempts to cultivate and manage the sense of dual temporality splitting these two aspects of the subaltern as citizen. The tension between these two aspects of the subaltern as citizen is, in fact, contradictory, profoundly unstable, and given to constant reformulations. Where the two aspects of the subaltern as citizen jostle each other is the very space of politics.

In this chapter I explore how activism works to produce senses of time and place among activists and villagers in the Arivoli Iyakkam. I focus in particular on ideological conflicts ensuing from a pedagogical desire to bring villagers within the narrative of the Indian development state, on one hand, and countervailing recognitions that Tamil villagers are already citizens with their own histories and senses of self that are not easily folded into the national narrative of progress, on the other. After examining the intellectual foundations of the literacy movement in the projects of state building, Left politics, and modern science, I then move on to examine how the discourse of Enlightenment itself has undergone significant transformations in the process of the Arivoli Iyakkam becoming a mass movement in villages across the Tamil countryside. In their attempt to build a mass movement among villagers, the leaders of the Arivoli Iyakkam found that they had to ground their narrative of national awakening in forms of experience and knowledge that would make sense to those they would seek to compel.

It is for these reasons that I find it useful to think of the cultural work of the Arivoli Iyakkam in terms of what the linguist and literary theorist M. M. Bakhtin (1981) has called "chronotopes," the frameworks of time and space that serve to ground the movement of events and characters in a narrative structure. A national vision of progressive time sat at the core of this Enlightenment activism. Activists sought to teach villagers to think in terms of an affiliation to this large-scale chronotope, connecting villagers to their fellow citizens. The accusation that was often made of those who refused to participate in the Arivoli Iyakkam was that they were caught up in the narrow, hierarchical, and anachronistic socialities of kin, village, and caste, unaware of the role they have to play in the larger national drama. But this chronotope of national progress would constantly have to contend with other senses of time and place that could appear to activists either as resistance to the universalizing narrative of Arivoli or as narrative resources that could be used in the service of propelling the movement, and thus encompassed within the narrative of Enlightenment.

The festival-like drama performance, described above, is only one example of the techniques used by the Arivoli Iyakkam to teach, not only that everyone must read and write, but also the particular senses of time and place that characterize the developmental imagination. The peasant played by Karuppiah, who continued to live in the "darkness of illiteracy," could not be counted as a full member of the national community. He could not legitimately represent himself to the state through a written signature and he would be counted in the census as an "illiterate." To "teach the darkness of ignorance" to such people, such that they might mend their ways, is therefore to inaugurate what activists commonly call a "second independence struggle," the true arrival of the nation in its tryst with destiny. In fact, among the signs of illiteracy that have been stigmatized as anachronistic departures from the narrative of progress perhaps most prominent has been the use of a thumbprint (*ḳaināṭṭu*, or, *ḳairēḳai* "hand line") in lieu of a signature on official documents. The thumbprint that many among the rural poor still use to identify themselves on government documents has, for a long time, carried connotations of ignorance and even criminality.[1] A "thumbprint" is not something someone would call themselves. It is an epithet that is likely to be hurled at someone who cannot sign their name, indicating not only they do not write, but also that they are not smart and can easily be fooled.[2] But to be "just a thumbprint" is no longer only a sign of being an uncultivated person; it is increasingly seen as a sign of a person who is living in the past. Many activists who ended up devoting much of their youth to the movement point to plays like the one described above depicting the lowly condition of a "thumbprint" as the reason they joined. Such plays invoked a collective sense of shame, serving as a call to action.

Figure 1. An Arivoli Iyakkam image produced by S. P. Raju for a World Literacy Day poster depicting a woman being saved by a pen from drowning in her own thumbprint. Reproduced with permission from the Tamil Nadu State Resource Centre.

Work on the cultural politics of citizenship and statecraft has underscored the extent to which the modern state is not only defined by what Max Weber famously identified as a "monopoly over legitimate violence," but also by what Pierre Bourdieu would call "a monopoly over the legitimate use of physical and *symbolic* violence over a definite territory and over the totality of the corresponding population" (1999, 56). This second form of state power, or "metacapital" can be defined simply as a capacity to determine the legitimacy and political efficacy of signs within state space. Distributions of social power are calibrated in relation this field of value to the degree that the state can set the basic parameters of what counts as a successful performance of citizenship and what does not. The task for an anthropology of state power must then be to account for how a semiotic monopoly is produced and maintained.

How do people come to think that they are lacking certain qualifications for entry into the sphere of full citizenship? It is in plays and images like those above that we can begin to appreciate how the politics of time and space is integral to the project of producing a monopoly over legitimate sign usage in the context of postcolonial state formation. It was the capacity to be counted in the census as a literate person and, by extension, as a full-fledged citizen, and not simply as a body, that was at stake in the drama. The desire for full literacy, I argue, was premised on the unification of a field of social and political power that would determine the value of semiotic acts such as the thumbprint and the personal signature. This is a politics of time and space insofar as entry into the sphere of legitimate intercourse with the state through signature correlates with entry into the very chronotope of "footprints on the moon" depicted in the song above. To the degree that activists working in the Arivoli Iyakkam were devoted to such a unification of time and space in the homogenizing narrative of progress, they participated in reproducing a form of state power premised on the destruction of older structures of semiotic legitimacy. But these claims remain rather abstract at the moment. Let us return to the modes of cultural work employed by the movement to produce the "allochronic" (Fabian 1983) effect that would render these structures and modes of social behavior as archaic or out of time, and specifically to the question of how this effect is related to the very technology of writing.

Divisions of Linguistic Labor

Arivoli Iyakkam activists' understanding of the difference between progress and retrograde social habits was built in part on their experience of change over the course of their lives. Rural Tamil Nadu has seen massive transformations in the social division of linguistic labor, for instance, such that there is now a more generalized stigmatization of "illiteracy" and of dependence on others to mediate interactions with the worlds of writing and state officialdom. Norms had been shifting away from the assumption that literacy and education are the domain of a privileged few, and activists saw themselves as agents in establishing a new consciousness (*viḻippu ṇarvu*) of the need for everyone to read and write. This new understanding of one's place in the world also turned on the premise that the lowliness or humiliation (*ḳēvalam*) of illiteracy must be identified as such, and as subject to change through pedagogy. But this was a process of raising consciousness that remained grievously incomplete in the eyes of many, requiring the ongoing "second independence movement" announced in the song reproduced above.

While chatting one afternoon on the front veranda of her small home in the village of Mangalapuram, Neela once explained to me the positive changes she had seen as a result of the Arivoli Iyakkam in particular:

> Now common folk [*pāmara maḳḳaḷ*] know about the necessity of literacy and education. Before they would have just relied on others and avoided going to government offices or the banks themselves. But now they go, and if everyone else is signing their name and they have to put a thumbprint, they'll be shy [*veṭḳappaṭuvāṅḳa*], they'll face difficulty [*ḳaśṭappaṭuvāṅḳa*]. People will say, "Oh, she's just a thumbprint [*ḳaināṭṭu*]." They will see the necessity of literacy [*eḻuttaṟiviṉ avaciyam*].

The empirical claim that Neela was making, that everyone now understands the need and uses of literacy, remains open to question, as we will see in a moment. Even if villagers were perhaps more ashamed to leave a thumbprint now than in the past, and they were more likely to find themselves in situations in which literacy is required, it was not necessarily the case that they were conscious of a need for total literacy. But Neela was also making several other claims worth our attention. First, she identified illiteracy as an undesirable social identity, as something that should and can be overcome. Second, Neela was also making a normative claim, providing important clues about the strategies of Arivoli activism. She was in a sense arguing that people *should* be made to feel ashamed, that "shyness" and facing difficulty are in fact signs of progress spurring "common folk" and "thumbprints" to pursue literacy. As Neela's fellow activist, the famous essayist and short-story writer S. Tamilcelvan, wrote of the Arivoli Iyakkam's efforts, "Our strategy to get the uneducated to come, sit and learn at Arivoli lessons, was to make them feel guilty and to use that feeling" (2004b, 18). He recounts how he would go out to villages and give speeches quoting from classical Tamil texts, saying that lack of literacy is like wearing two sores on your face instead of eyes, trying to shame people into joining a literacy group. But, he continues, in the reflexive mode, the Arivoli mission was also "to make educated people understand that it is shameful for us [*nammai*] to be surrounded by so many uneducated people" (19). In the second quote, Tamilcelvan uses the inclusive first-person plural pronoun to include his readers. Activists consistently argued that nonliterates would be partaking in a general national shame, which must be felt by all Indian citizens.

Many unlettered villagers I talked to during the course of my fieldwork, however, remained unsure whether learning to read and write as adults would lead to any significant positive change in their lives. They might well have felt ashamed of their lack of literacy skills, but many villagers who were targets of literacy mobilization lived in a world in which lack of literacy was just one problem among many problems of more immediate consequence. Such people had long lived in a world in which it is perfectly normal for some people to read and write on behalf of others. Literacy appeared to many to have a marginal place in a more encompassing division of labor and political power, making it difficult for activists to organize literacy groups based on a shared assumption that literacy was the most pressing need for everyone. For activists, the question of literacy must be objectified as a solvable problem and as a means to greater freedom. I would like to now discuss, through two episodes, how this shared understanding of the power and meaning of literacy was cultivated. Both cases are about people who took their inability to read and write as self-evident, but in different ways and from different perspectives. These cases also illustrate how literacy activists engage with the division of linguistic labor and seek to reframe it as out of date.

Quarry Workers' Perspective on Literacy in the Wider Political Economy

I once accompanied Neela's fellow activist, Sheik Mohammad, as he was visiting a hamlet near his own village in the evening to persuade the mainly nonliterate quarry workers there that they should form Arivoli Iyakkam literacy circles. Although not a quarry worker himself, Sheik was from a very modest background, and he worked in his father's small corner shop when he was not working for the literacy movement. The village we visited that evening, like many that the Arivoli Iyakkam targets for mobilization, was a Dalit "*cēri*"—a hamlet that is spatially separate from the main caste-Hindu village settlement.[3] Sheik had already told me that this was a particularly impoverished area, as most of the residents worked in the nearby granite quarries as bonded laborers for a daily wage of less than twenty-five rupees, about fifty cents. The soil is too rocky for agriculture in this area. As we pulled up on our motorcycle at about eight thirty in the evening, the hamlet was completely dark. Thinking that this was a temporary power outage, a common problem even in well-off villages, Sheik went around from house to house asking people to come out for a meeting. While initially reluctant to leave their duties at home, many came outside to sit in the central square in the dark.

Sheik started by introducing me as a researcher from the United States who had come to study the important work that the literacy movement was doing in helping the rural poor. He then told them how they too could take part in this important movement to improve their own lives, when one young woman stood up and said, "Sir, get us electricity and streetlights first! Then we can talk about holding literacy classes. How can we study when there's no light?" Our eyes followed her hand as she pointed up to the lamppost and we saw that there was a very faint flickering, but that there was insufficient power to illuminate the fluorescent bulb. It seems that the darkness that evening was not from a simple power outage, usually the result of a blown fuse or a scheduled "load shedding," but that this village had not been supplied with enough electricity even to light a street lamp. The lack of electricity resulted from the villagers' lack of political power to influence a village council controlled by upper castes, those who owned the very quarries where these Dalits worked. A transformer had broken down months ago and no one had been called to fix it. Several others from the crowd also complained of lack of water for drinking and washing.

Sheik was dismayed that I should see such a difficult state of affairs in his own area. He responded to the young woman and other villagers, saying that he would try to press the local panchayat to fix these problems. But Sheik also told the villagers that evening that if they learned to read and write, they could themselves write a petition addressed to the district collector, who would order the block-development officer to take action. When faced with such opposition, Arivoli workers tried to turn such situations into pedagogical opportunities, telling villagers that if they could read and write, then they too could be more effective in demanding basic services from the government. Activists would often tell literacy groups that the district authorities would take special interest in a petition written by an Arivoli literacy groups, because it would show their commitment to development and to national progress (Cody 2009). Petitions from literacy groups were understood as signs of entry into legitimate interaction with the state bureaucracy.

Lack of literacy was only one sign among many distinguishing Dalits, women, and wage laborers more broadly in terms of lack or lowness—what villagers might call "*ḳēvalam.*" This lack is measured in many ways: not only are lower-caste settlements spatially separated and sometimes poorly connected to government services, I have been told by people from a range of different communities that the very work of transplanting rice, the domain of labor associated with Dalit women, is a "lowly work" (*ḳēvalamāṉa vēlai*).[4] Construction and quarry work fit into a similar category. The task of literacy mobilization, as Sheik himself demonstrated, was to therefore objectify literacy as a separate and solvable problem that can help solve other problems, like the manifold ways in which the rural poor face social domination and exploitation. Here we begin to see the layered difficulties facing literacy activism and the type of cultural work required to persuade people of literacy's importance.

A Neighbor's Perspective on the Political Economy of Literacy

A second illustration of these issues presented itself when my neighbor from across the road in the village of Kovilpatti wanted to apply for a ration card. While not in the same marginal social position as the Dalits, because he belonged to the dominant Kallar community and because he owned some land, Arumugam was nevertheless another person for whom learning to read and write was not a priority. When I asked about his education and whether he wanted to learn to read and write, like many villagers he responded, "I'm too old to learn to read and write, what's the use of it now?" Arumugam was in his early thirties when I moved to Kovilpatti. He was the married father of two children and he worked both on his own half a hectare of land as a farmer and on a crew that went across the state drilling bore-wells for irrigation. This second job took him away from home for days, sometimes weeks, at a time. Although Arumugam had gone through two years of schooling as a child, he could do little more with written language than sign his name and recognize a few words. He was unable to read the newspaper. While not quite a "thumbprint," he was considered by most in the village to be a "*paṭikkātavaṉ,*" someone who is uneducated, or unable to read.

Arumugam had separated from his older brother's household soon after his wedding. The two families lived on two sides of the same structure, but they maintained separate cooking areas and finances. They had divided the land between them and were considered by all to be separate households. Although Arumugam had split the joint family household some years back, he was still relying on his elder brother's ration card to buy government-subsidized supplies at the ration shop in nearby Kilattur village.[5] Ration cards are issued to the head of every family and may be used by anyone in that household to buy supplies. The card lists members of the household by name and can also serve as an official form of identification for other interactions with the government, such as requesting an electricity connection. Arumugam bought mainly sugar and kerosene there, and unlike those who had no land, did not need to buy rice at the shop. For Arumugam, getting his own ration card would increase his spending power because there are limits to how much can be bought on one card over the course of the month. More important, getting a card for his family in his name would mark the final step toward independence from his older brother.

Obtaining a ration card is not easy. One must first obtain a proof of address from the local village administrative officer (VAO).[6] Arumugam also needed the VAO to certify that his family was indeed living below the poverty line, allowing him to buy supplies at a lower cost.[7] While in principle this should not be difficult, the problem was that in Kovilpatti, the VAO lived in the town of Alangudi. He rarely showed up at his office in neighboring Kilattur village. One had to go by bicycle to check every day in order to catch him in his office at the right time to make the request. The VAO would then take his time, sometimes weeks, to verify the address and notarize an official document attesting to financial status and residence. The VAO was also known to demand some money in the form of a bribe in exchange for this document. Once Arumugam had obtained his verification, he would have to have it photocopied and take it, along with two passport-sized photographs, to the Taluk Supply Office in Alangudi Town to fill out the application. This is where the process became even more difficult.

Rather than fill out and submit a form on his own, Arumugam explained to me how he had to find an application vendor outside of the Taluk Supply Office and pay fifty rupees, about one day's wages for him, to have the vendor fill out the form. Along with the address, financial status, and personal information for everyone included on the card, applications for a new card require a written memo explaining why the applicant had not filed for a card earlier. Although he had been told by others to expect this, and he assumed that this was how an application must be made, Arumugam complained to me later about the price. "First he asked for a hundred rupees in addition to the twenty-five I gave him for the sheet [application]. But we talked and I paid him fifty. Already, I had to skip a day's work on the bore-well in Mattur to go there." The vendor had also promised to submit the application to someone he knew in the office to make sure it was properly filed. Every vendor claims to have a special connection to a bureaucrat on the inside. Having no choice but to trust the document vendor, Arumugam paid him and then went home. He was then to wait a few weeks for the inspector from the supply office to come to Kovilpatti village and verify the claim before actually filing the application.

Arumugam waited at home, but no one ever came. Again, he had to decline a bore-well drilling job to wait for the inspector. He went back several times to look for the scribe who had sold him the written application in Alangudi, only to be told by the other vendors that Arumugam's document seller had not been around for some days. So, after much frustration, Arumugam ended up buying a new form from another vendor, and this time asked Tangavelu, Karuppiah's younger brother and a schoolteacher, to fill it out for him. Tangavelu filled out the form after giving Arumugam some trouble for not asking him sooner and for not being able to do it on his own. Arumugam was used to such comments and appeared unfazed. Karuppiah's uncle, who was also in the process of establishing a separate household, saw that Tangavelu was helping Arumugam fill out the application and decided to get his own form and ask his nephew to do the same for him. Tangavelu did so without complaint.

This account of Arumugam's trials provides an illustration of how many in rural Tamil Nadu manage the world of written documents. Arumugam, when asked about literacy, saw no reason to learn to read and write. The actual writing of the application and explanation for why he had not applied earlier appeared to him as just one task in a whole series of tasks involved in the application process. He found it perfectly normal to ask and even pay others to do this work for him, just as it was natural for him to go to the tea stall and simply listen to people read the newspaper headlines aloud and discuss them to get his news. Getting the ration card was a matter of asking the right person and being a little patient. Like many other villagers who had had limited or no schooling, he took such difficulties for granted. Arumugam and Karuppiah's uncle had always relied on a well-established social division of linguistic labor. Just as it was normal for only women of lower castes to transplant rice, or for men of the Pandaram caste to act as priests at the village temple, it was quite normal for some people to do the work of reading and writing on behalf of others.

Karuppiah, while seeing Arumugam's search for a ration card unfold from across the street, however, shook his head in disappointment. This whole process appeared to him as symptomatic of what is wrong with how government works and with village life. "The government should respond to people's needs," he would often complain. But Karuppiah was critical not only of the labyrinthine application process. While more forgiving of his older uncle being unable to manage these things on his own, Karuppiah was especially critical of his age-mate, Arumugam. Watching his brother come home after work at the school, only to fill out the application for Arumugam, Karuppiah remarked to me, "Look at that guy. . . . What a lowly situation [*evvaḷavu kēvalamāṉa viśayam*]. Whatever you say he won't listen," explaining that he had tried long ago to persuade Arumugam to join a literacy class and learn. But the problem was that his neighbor had "head weight" (*talai kaṇam*), like many men, and would not listen to reason. The word "*kēvalam*" (lowliness) was here again used by Karuppiah to characterize the condition of illiteracy. Although he had a good deal of affection for Arumugam as a neighbor and as his "*maccāṉ*" (fictive cross-cousin), Karuppiah attributed the stubborn refusal to learn as a sign of what he called "*piṟpōkku karuttukaḷ*," retrograde, or backward looking ideas. This is lowness that was understood by Karuppiah through a distinctively temporal lens. It was in fact because they had grown up together that he would get so frustrated with Arumugam and other young men of the village who refused to go to school. It was probably to avoid Karuppiah's moral condemnation in the first place that Arumugam had gone to Tangavelu instead of his older brother for help.

Karuppiah was working to reframe this social division of linguistic labor as deviant and out of date through his dramatic performances with the Dawn Arts Group and other forms of activism in the Arivoli Iyakkam. Seeing a great deal of exploitation in unequal control of writing, activists like Karuppiah and his colleagues were convinced that people must learn to manage these sorts of affairs on their own and assert a certain independence before government offices and other bureaucratic authorities that require literacy. In fact, the first among the measures of functional literacy according to the National Literacy Mission is "achieving *self-reliance* in literacy and numeracy," followed by "being aware of the causes of deprivation and moving towards amelioration of oppressive conditions through organization and participation in the process of development," and "imbibing the values of national integration." In order to be true, fully belonging citizens of India, villagers should be able to petition the government on their own, and Arumugam, for example, should be able to apply for a ration card on his own. For the Arivoli Iyakkam, it was crucial that they have not only the literacy skills to do so but also the consciousness and self-confidence to do so. Arivoli activists wanted someone like Arumugam to go beyond seeing the application for a ration card as a personal or local act of completing the separation from his brother's household. Activism was premised on tying such local acts to a chronotope of enlightened citizenship and to the ongoing emergence of the nation from a backward state.

Science Activism, the Left, and the Development State

The reason that Karuppiah's criticism of the division of linguistic labor should correspond so closely to India's national policy was not only because of the many official training programs he had attended as an Arivoli Iyakkam volunteer. The sense that literacy is a technology enabling emancipation, progress, and even secular-rational thought is of course widely shared. This is a position that has been articulated perhaps most systematically by the Nobel Prize–winning economist and philosopher Amartya Sen (1999), who has demonstrated correlations among literacy rates, health, effective governance, and gender equality across India in his influential arguments for a social capabilities approach to the question of freedom. Sen has gone so far as to cite low adult literacy rates in the "Hindi belt" of central and northern India as indexes of the "gullibility" and "militant obscurantism" that fuel Hindu chauvinist threats to secular democracy in these regions (1993, 17–20).[8] In the case of Arivoli Iyakkam activism in Pudukkottai and India's National Literacy Mission, however, the shared vision of literacy as a project of encouraging self-reliance, becoming aware of the causes of one's deprivation, and integrating the rural poor into the nation-state points back to a common pedagogical source that is more firmly rooted in the political Left.

The Arivoli Iyakkam was first imagined and organized as such by urban, middle-class intellectuals from Chennai and other cities in their capacity as members of the Tamil Nadu Science Forum (TNSF) and of the Pondicherry Science Forum (PSF). In the early 1980s, nearly a decade prior to their entry into the field of large-scale activism, the Science Forums first started as discussion groups among graduate students and professors from the prestigious Indian Institute of Technology and

Indian Institute of Science. These groups initially formed with the aim of organizing a public critique of the government of India's science policies from within the scientific community itself. Decades of centrally planned development efforts focused on big science, dams, and, by the 1970s, nuclear technology had done very little to improve the lives of the majority of Indians, many of whom continued to live in poverty. The environmental costs of the Nehruvian mode of development were also becoming more and more apparent, with the poor, once again, suffering more than anyone. "We were all training to join the government as scientists, and so we began asking questions," explained one of the founding members, a mathematician who now works for an NGO in Delhi, where I interviewed him in his office. He continued, "Why does nuclear research get more attention than solar energy? Who decides that the science of weapons needs more money than the science of agriculture? Why should the government subsidize research that benefits only the rich? Why must we pour our money into big dams instead of local rainwater harvesting? These are questions of social choice and they decide what science is done." Such were the concerns that drove early meetings, leading these socially conscious researchers and teachers to register their organizations as the TNSF and the PSF in 1986.

It was also around this time that the Science Forums began to find that if they wanted to democratize the way in which decisions are made about how science would operate in India, they would have to reach out precisely to those communities that are most affected. As part of the effort to bring villagers and the urban poor into a discussion on the political significance of science, then, the Science Forums began organizing extra training in science outside the classroom. Science activists would often hold their tutorials in the government school building itself, after school hours. The project to engage in criticism of government science policy had, by the late 1980s expanded into efforts to educate people about science more generally, eventually leading to science classes designed for those who had never gone to school.

"The science movement has tended to view the propagation of science as a virtue in itself," explained Dr. T. Sundararaman, in an interview I held in his Pondicherry apartment. "In some sense it would be materialist, it would combat superstition, it would lead to more rational thinking and the soil would be more fertile for radical thought."

Dr. Sundararaman was an important figure in the Left movement, the president of the Pondicherry Science Forum, and one of the early leaders of the shift to concentrate on science education among the poor and eventually on the more basic issue of literacy. As I asked him about other movements that had influenced him and his generation of science activists, he continued, "The science movement draws consciously from the Marxist ideology. And that also is atheistic. That also sees science as intrinsically materialist, and science as an ideology, which is not necessarily the Marxist paradigm, but commonly interpreted by our friends in that framework, somewhat filling the gap that religion would do for a believer."

The Science Forums drew on what Sundararaman would repeatedly mention as the "Bernalian science and society framework," referring to J. D. Bernal, the Irish Marxist scientist and sociologist of science whose book *The Social Function of Science* (1961 [1936]) provided twentieth-century modernizers with a theory of scientific enlightenment as much concerned with the social as it is with the natural and material. This book is required reading for all in leadership positions in the Science Forums. According to Bernal, "science implies a unified and co-ordinated and, above all, conscious control of the whole of social life; it abolishes, or provides the possibility of abolishing, the dependence of man on the material world. Henceforth society is subject only to the limitations it imposes on itself" (1961 [1936], 409). Heavily influenced by the Soviet model, he therefore comes to the conclusion that "the full development of science in the service of humanity is incompatible with the continuance of capitalism" (410), because capitalism leaves too much agency to economic forces beyond direct human control. Sundararaman continued his description of the science movement: "It is not a political movement in the narrow sense, and not an agitational movement, though in specific circumstances this may become essential. It is a political movement in the broader sense, defining what issues elections should be fought on."

The friends Sundararaman had alluded to when explaining the rise of the Science Forums include the All India People's Science network, a nationwide alliance of groups modeled on earlier efforts of the Kerala Sastra Sahitya Parishad (KSSP). This latter organization of what is sometimes called the "Indian new left" was founded in the early 1960s, and has played a very important role in shaping the course of decentralized planning policy under Communist Party of India (Marxist) rule in Kerala (Heller, Harilal, and Chaudhury 2007; Isaac and Franke 2002; Menon and Nigam 2007; Zachariah and Sooryamoorthy 1994). Many of the founding members of the Science Forums, the KSSP, and other science activist groups had studied elsewhere in India or abroad. M. P. Parameswaran, one of the leaders of science activism in India and an important planner of the Arivoli Iyakkam campaigns in Tamil Nadu, for example, had studied physics at the University of Moscow in the late 1950s before returning to India to eventually become president of the KSSP and a leader of the adult literacy movement. It is, in fact, through the stories of science activist leaders like Parameswaran that we can gain a deeper understanding of the relationship between village-level activism and globally circulating theories of Marxism, science, and the question of freedom.

When I visited him at home in Trissur, on a Kerala monsoon-soaked afternoon, the spritely white-haired man who had inspired generations of activists told me how he had first been exposed to Marxian approaches to the liberating role of science in society while in the Soviet Union.[9] During this time, Parameswaran was a science journalist for the Malayalam newspapers in Kerala, reporting on his experience as a student. "I was incredibly impressed with the social progress I saw, how they were able to take care of children and the way they were catching up to America, but I also found the party structure very hierarchical and undemocratic." On his return to India, he started a science activist group in Bombay (now Mumbai) and eventually moved back to Kerala, where he joined the CPI(M) in 1970, and ultimately played a leading part in shaping Kerala politics for the next thirty-five years, both within the party structure and without. Parameswaran was central in shaping the KSSP, redirecting its aims from providing simple science education to pursuing the cause of "Science for Social Revolution," and bridging a range of social gaps between academics, grassroots activism, and party bureaucracy (Zachariah and Sooryamoorthy 1994, 64–65). It was under his leadership in the 1970s that Marxism was promoted across Kerala and southern India as a "science of society" through village activist efforts supported by the party. He went on to organize science and literacy activism at a national level through the

Total Literacy Campaigns of the 1990s. Parameswaran was eventually expelled from the CPI(M) while I was still doing fieldwork in 2004 for his persistent demand that the party democratize its decision-making process at the state and local levels.[10]

Unlike the KSSP, which had already grown into a mass movement by the 1980s, prior to their work in the field of literacy activism the Tamil and Pondicherry Science Forums had very small memberships, limited primarily to urban academics. J. Krishnamurthy, a teacher from Pondicherry and a longtime science and literacy activist, explained, "People were keeping their distance from the science movement and from our ideas. There was a gap [*iṭai veḷi*] between us. We saw the literacy movement as an instrument [*ḳaruvi*] to reach the people and get closer to them." Kerala already had high literacy rates and a robust Communist tradition, and Tamil thinkers such as M. Singaravelar had already tried to fuse scientific rationalism and working class politics in the early twentieth century (Babu 2004). But since the mid-twentieth century, Tamil politics had been dominated by parties that, while receptive to secular rationalism, worked through forms of ethnolinguistic populism and critiques of caste dominance that left little room for the type of internationalist claims made by the largely upper-caste Science Forums. Many activist leaders I interviewed over the course of my fieldwork attested to the fact that the slide shows and science experiments they conducted in villages in the late 1980s, prior to the literacy movement, failed to attract many people's interest and enthusiasm. Activists would sometimes travel to villages with posters explaining scientific principles that few people could read.

Members of the Science Forums found their opportunity to broaden activities and engage villagers in 1989 by entering into partnerships with the central government of India for large-scale science education and mass-literacy campaigns in what would come to be known as the Arivoli Iyakkam. Experiments with district-wide literacy movements that year in Kerala, where the KSSP had partnered with the newly established National Literacy Mission, provided inspiration. In order to mediate this new partnership, Parameswaran had worked with members of the Congress government at the Center and established a national nongovernmental organization, called Bharat Gyan Vigyan Samiti (BGVS), specifically designed to coordinate science and literacy activist efforts from the political Left with a government policy that had become increasingly invested in promoting "grassroots" and "participatory" development initiatives. The BGVS therefore acted as the institution through which the government of India would provide a limited set of funds and allow movement organizers to make use of the district development apparatus, while activists and volunteers would do the work of mobilizing villagers and holding science and literacy classes. Over the course of only one year, in 1991, some twenty thousand volunteer teachers had been recruited for the movement in Pudukkottai District alone, and a good number went on to become members of the Science Forums. It was at this time, for example, that villagers like Karuppiah and Neela became involved with science activism and Left politics more broadly. This model of activism worked so well in part because government workers, like schoolteachers and university professors, were given paid leave from their jobs for one year to devote themselves to the movement. But as much as the Arivoli Iyakkam campaigns required state support, they soon found that such partnerships could come at a very high cost.

In 1992, only two years into their Arivoli Iyakkam mass-literacy campaign, the Pondicherry Science Forum found themselves under attack from local politicians in a legislative assembly that eventually shut the movement down in the Union Territory of Pondicherry, on the Tamil coast. It appears as if the Arivoli Iyakkam and the Science Forums were posing a threat to the monopoly on political action that parties had established, because villagers were going to local literacy volunteers for help with their problems instead of going to representatives of the political parties. "We had over twenty-thousand people attend one of our rallies, much more than either party could manage. They got scared," Sundararaman explained. According to Nitya Rao, a journalist who was covering the movements at the time, "One lesson in the literacy primer raised issues of poverty and unemployment in India and of the inequitable distribution of resources, and called people to struggle for a just society. Citing this chapter as 'evidence' the speaker of Pondicherry's legislature actually called the Total Literacy Campaign 'anti-national' " (1993, 915). Both the ruling Congress Party and the opposition DMK eventually teamed up and terminated government support for the Arivoli Iyakkam in the middle of the Postliteracy phase in the state legislature, claiming that it was "subversive."

While perhaps strengthening the state's general monopoly on legitimate representation, in this case the literacy movement had shown that its might and charisma could rival that of the established political parties and their capacity to mediate access to state power.

Even after officially severing relations with the government of India in the mid-1990s because of such friction, Science Forum activists continued to occupy almost every position in the Arivoli Iyakkam, and the literacy movement continued to act as the means by which people joined other Left activist groups and political parties. Science Forum activities that Arivoli Iyakkam activists carried out in Pudukkottai's villages during my fieldwork, for example, included performing simple physics experiments for the public and bringing telescopes into villages to teach people the basics of astronomy or microscopes for biology lectures.[11] Science Forum visits to villages also consisted of demonstrations of the ways in which god-men and magicians perform what appear, in the eyes of some, to be "miracles," such as producing sacred ash from the palm of one's hand. Such scientific demonstrations in villages predate the mass-literacy movements but have continued in Pudukkottai and elsewhere under the name "*Mantiramā Tantiramā*" (Magic? or Trickery?). Science Forums hold public functions to commemorate the abuses of science in the service of violence and political expedience, not answerable to more generalized human material needs, through annual public presentations on the anniversaries of the Hiroshima and Nagasaki bombings. In the words of the TNSF's own policy document, the aim has been to "create a scientific culture, building on the heritage of the freedom struggle and of democratic, socialist, and women's movements."

The convergence of orientations between science activism and a wing of the state represented by an Indian Administrative Service cadre in district administration had rested on a broad set of shared assumptions about modernization, rationality, and the unification of spheres of social action. For science activists, literacy was initially seen as the means to a much larger project of building a "rational society" through knowledge of a wider world. J. Krishnamurthy, a teacher, Science Forum leader, and organizer of literacy campaigns across Tamil Nadu, explained in an interview I held with him at his house in Pondicherry,

> Look at all the things happening around you. There is a need for some kind of platform to get them to understand these things. That is, many things don't reach them. Things reach through oral language, through their ears, whatever they see on TV, or they will say what they read in the newspaper. Someone will read and tell them. But if they hear it, see it on TV, or in a newspaper, this needs to be discussed in a group. To decide what is wrong or right, what is needed or not, they need to be in a group, right? One needs to build a structure, right? We thought that's it, that's all we need to bring. So we could use writing as a vehicle to develop a structure for all these things.

There was a lack of integration of sorts, from Krishnamurthy's perspective, requiring a structure or platform for critical debate and understanding of the world outside villages. It is not only that "many things don't reach them"; the Arivoli Iyakkam would provide a forum through which people could exercise their reason in a group.[12] Both the government and science activists were concerned with villages being left behind in the race for development, and it was this shared concern that led to their partnership in conducting the Total Literacy Campaigns of the 1990s. Even in Pondicherry, where serious opposition came not from district administrative offices but from political parties, Krishnamurthy explained to me with a chuckle, "The government shut it down, and then gladly accepted the UNESCO King Sejong award for achievement in the field of adult literacy!"

The general model of partnership between local science and literacy NGOs and district administration offices proved tremendously effective in mobilizing large numbers of people in support of the mass-literacy movements. The Science Forums quickly changed from relatively marginal groups of politicized academics to leaders of one of India's largest social movements. The Science Forums' effectiveness in gaining a public legitimacy that would extend well beyond political party affiliation lies in using a reformist language already well rehearsed in the anticolonial and Dravidian nationalist struggles of the early twentieth century. The TNSF was able to enter into a sometimes uneasy relationship with the central government of India for the purposes of organizing mass-literacy movements precisely because it is devoted to the popularization of science. This has been a powerful nationalist theme since the Nehruvian era and was given renewed salience with Rajiv Gandhi's tenure as prime minister (1984–89) shortly before the Arivoli Iyakkam began, and more recently with Abdul Kalam's presidency (2002–7). The All-India People's Science Network that grew around the literacy movements is now one of the largest voluntary organizations in the world with nearly 2 million members.[13]

Although the Science Forums' desire to build a structure for public debate through literacy and science activism might have brushed against entrenched party interests in monopolizing access to state power, they were nevertheless able to appeal to an urban audience by drawing on the theme of national modernization along secular lines. This is a familiar way of narrating the progress of the nation's movement forward through the homogeneous time of history, as Benedict Anderson (1991) has famously argued. But how did the Science Forums come to appeal to Tamil villagers, and how was their message absorbed on a mass scale through the literacy campaigns? How were these goals of Enlightenment interpreted by activists and other Arivoli Iyakkam participants in Pudukkottai's villages? And what happened to the "gap" between Science Forum activists and the villagers they sought to reach? Science Forum discourse on Enlightenment and literacy was grafted onto already existing ideas about education and progress through a number of interdiscursive resonances, introducing alternative histories and temporalities into the narrative. It is to this process that I now turn.

Resonances: The Senses of Enlightenment

We have so far focused on one aspect of the chronotopic politics underpinning the Arivoli Iyakkam's claims to bring light to the Tamil countryside through literacy and science, namely the narrative of modernization that would construe other orientations to agency as out of date. Yet even radically modernist attempts to remake the world require histories and memories that would resonate with those who must be mobilized for such purposes. The need to build a past in the service of a revolutionary present is a point that was articulated forcefully, if somewhat pessimistically, by Marx (1963 [1852], 15) himself when he wrote that efforts to create "something that has never yet existed . . . conjure up the spirits of the past to their service in order to represent the new scene of world history in this time-honored disguise and this borrowed language." We saw in the opening to this chapter, for example, how Arivoli Iyakkam mobilization drew both on the dramatic techniques of temple festivals, with their bright lights and songs carried over loudspeakers, and on forms of realist theater to produce a moral narrative of national progress that would resonate with a village audience. Activists attempted to suture otherwise heterogeneous orientations to time and space through such dramatic performances.

Another mode of emplotting the Arivoli Iyakkam with reference to a prior text was to depict Arivoli as the "*iraṇṭāvatu cutantirap pōrāṭṭam*" (second independence struggle). This strategy of invoking the independence movement was used by activists of all sorts, even by bureaucrats affiliated with the movement and by many other villagers in Pudukkottai. In this example, the national struggle for independence is targeted as an event that is available to all as a template for interpretation through which Arivoli's struggle for emancipation through full literacy can be grasped as one of world historical significance. Indian independence acts as an intertext, mediating interpretations of the present by framing a chronotope of progress toward freedom and by situating the nation as the correct locus of agency. Participants in the Arivoli Iyakkam would thus be responding to a call for collective self-determination that was first made a century before.

Whereas the text of national liberation is one that was likely to be shared by everyone, other narrative pasts are more likely to be used by some participants in the Arivoli movement than others. Some activists draw heavily on more specifically Tamil traditions of thought on education as the fusion of light and knowledge in order to frame or ground their own activism, while some draw on traditions that they take to be more global in reach. As we will see shortly, the choice of which past and which cultural forms to invoke in the service of narrative propulsion is conditioned in large part by the activist's place in a social structure, and this fact of a less-than-unified narrative framework across social classes has led to some contradictions in the project of making autonomous subjects—a point I will return to later in this chapter.

The simpler point I would like to make here is that invocations of existing discourses or intertexts are means of fashioning the present, and not simply restrictions on agentive action as in Marx's complaint with the pull of the past. Such texts mediate self-understanding. For Marx, the narrative forms of the past sit like a weight, indeed, "like nightmare on the brain of the living" who would seek to revolutionize themselves (1963, 15). However, Arivoli activism reveals that the past need not only appear as weight, a source of pure drag, but the appropriate past can also appear as an ethical source in the project of remaking the social world. Jürgen Habermas, writing on the problematic developed by Marx, expresses it quite nicely: "A modernity that has been evaporated into what is actual at any given time, as soon as it attains the authenticity of a now-time, must constantly take its normativity from mirror images of pasts whose services are enlisted for this purpose. . . . Inasmuch as we appropriate past experiences with an orientation to the future, the authentic present is preserved as the locus of continuing tradition and innovation at once" (1987, 11–13). It is this production of tradition that is "enlisted" to shape horizons of future projection that I would like to focus on. Bernard Bate's (2009) ethnography of political speech in Tamil Nadu, for example, has shown how aesthetic forms associated with the ancient past could be mobilized to deepen political commitment in the present. Similar processes were under way in the Arivoli movement, even if its politics were somewhat different from those of the dominant Dravidian nationalist parties. By beginning from the present, then, we can understand how the very idea of "Arivoli" can resonate with a range of narrative structures from different perspectives, a resonance that serves to recharge and shape the present itself.

Some Village Views on Light and Knowledge

We saw how the founding members of the Science Forums draw on a global history of the Left. Their story is vitally connected to this history in concrete ways. Here, I would like to shift social locations away from the largely urban leadership, to look at how the idea of Arivoli has been viewed from the perspective of activist and nonactivist villagers in Pudukkottai. The progressive Left, or what Tamil speakers would commonly refer to as the "*iṭatu cārikaḷ*" (the Left lines) is, in fact, quite plural, as the Tamil words used to refer to it indicate. Moreover, villagers who are not at all politically active in the Left movement also have their own ways of narrating a connection between light and knowledge that resonates with a number of intertexts. The rural poor who made up the core group of volunteers in the movement drew on a wide range of narrative pasts to interpret their present actions, from Tamil literature to the twentieth-century linguistic nationalisms that have given the classical past renewed political salience. While we will have occasion to investigate how villagers' orientations to questions of literacy and knowledge are entangled in the broader Left movement, it is important to understand the degree to which global histories of the Left stand in a peripheral relationship to these other narratives of enlightenment in Tamil Nadu.

Most of the village-level literacy workers I interviewed claimed that the word "*aṟivoḷi*," a compound of the roots for "knowledge" (*aṟivu*) and "light" (*oḷi*), was coined in 1990 by Science Forum activists in Pondicherry as they were launching their Total Literacy Campaign. It appeared to most as a neologism. Some had heard of a publishing house by the same name and a few knew that "Arivoli" was the name of a famous orator on the public-speaking circuit. If many people I asked took the name Arivoli to be a neologism, they nevertheless found it to be a particularly apt word to use for the literacy movement. The name "Arivoli" was, in fact, already in limited use as a proper name given to boys in the wake of the pure Tamil movement of the 1930s. Led by the neo-Saivite philosopher Maramalai Adigal, this movement has had profound impact on the politics of the Tamil language because it encouraged people to search for names and words in Tamil that drew on non-Sanskritic, Dravidian etymology. As I was told by a village literacy coordinator in Pudukkottai who was aware of the word "Arivoli" prior to its use in the literacy movement, "It is a beautiful *Tamil* name," with emphasis as she said it on the name's etymological origins. "Arivoli" probably first arose as a purified, Dravidianized form of similar Sanskritic names like "Gnyanadeepam" or "Gnyanaprakash," which may have Buddhist or even Christian roots. While such Dravidian names were first used by those influenced by this movement only to de-Sanskritize south Indian culture, by the later twentieth century it had become very common for even marginally educated villagers to search for properly Dravidian names for their children. The purist ethos of the Tamil language movement now saturates the cultural world of Tamil Nadu, where Dravidian nationalist parties inspired by this movement have been in power for the last forty years.

It was, in fact, the Dravidian nationalist and rationalist movements of the mid-twentieth century that served as the most obvious pasts to draw on for village-level Arivoli activists. Led by the anti-Brahman social reformer E. V. Ramaswamy Naicker, or Periyar (the Great One), the movement calling for a separate homeland for the Dravidian people of south India drew very heavily on radical thought from Europe while playing a large role in recasting texts like the *Tirukkuṟaḷ* as sources for a secular Tamil past. Like some of the early leaders of the science movement, Periyar had traveled to the Soviet Union and had been greatly impressed with the progress he saw in what he took to be a society without caste or religion. A mass movement in its own right, the self-respect movement is responsible for popularizing the thought of many non-Indian scientific and social thinkers such as Rousseau, Voltaire, Marx, and Engels in the Tamil language through its journal *Kuṭi Aracu*. Even if there is no evidence that Periyar himself used the word "Arivoli" to refer to Enlightenment, his frequent denunciations of "*mūṭanampikkai*" (superstition) has been replicated in the discourse of scientific rationalism in the Science Forum activist and in the Arivoli Iyakkam, referring to that which obscures the light of knowledge. The European Enlightenment and its conceptual vocabulary of transparency and opacity has certainly served as an important model for the modernist imaginary across a range of similar movements.

Periyar also drew heavily from the vocabulary of revolution. His concept of *maṉitatarma* (human dharma) is in many senses also quite close to the Arivoli Iyakkam's emphasis on *maṉitanēyam* (humanism), emphasizing human self-determination as an ethical duty (Cody 2011). Periyar's rationalist self-respect movement for caste and gender equality lasted from 1926 to 1949 and was subsequently institutionalized as a political party that would not contest elections, the Dravida Kazhagam (DK). Periyar's legacy is also claimed by the major Tamil nationalist parties that have controlled the state legislative assembly since 1967. Many would argue, however, that the radical secular spirit of earlier Dravidian nationalisms has been dulled and pushed to the background of ethnic, linguistic, and caste politics. The DK nevertheless continues to maintain a high profile in the Pudukkottai region, and I had the opportunity to attend many public functions that were jointly organized by the DK and Arivoli Iyakkam village volunteers in their capacity as members of the Tamil Nadu

Progressive Writers Association. During my fieldwork, for example, Arivoli workers worked in tandem with members of the local DK chapter to celebrate Periyar's birthday in public events. On such occasions I was often asked to speak about possible intellectual connections between the man people call the "Voltaire of south India" and other movements for social justice in the United States. Within Pudukkattai's literacy movement there have been a number of secular "Arivoli Weddings," often across castes and celebrated without priests, modeled on DK self-respect weddings.[14] It is also through the DK that the first large network of village reading rooms was established in Tamil Nadu, again providing a model for Arivoli libraries as a place where villagers could meet, read, and discuss pressing political issues. But the cultural appeal of Arivoli goes well beyond Dravidian nationalist politics.

The Arivoli Iyakkam also draws from a deeper well of images and narratives that are more widely distributed among Tamil villagers. The equation between written language and light, or more specifically the power to see, has recognizable roots in Tamil literary and folk traditions. For example, in what is perhaps the most widely celebrated ancient Tamil text, the *Tirukkuṟaḷ,* the very well-known verses 392 and 393 read,

> Those called figures and letters, the wise declare,
> Are eyes to live with.
> (Eṇṇeṉpa ēṉai eḻutteṉpa ivviraṇṭum
> Kaṇṇeṉpa vāḻum uyirkku.)
> Only the learned have eyes—others
> Two sores on their face![15]
> (Kaṇṇuṭaiyar eṉpavar kaṟṟōr
> mukattiraṇṭu
> Puṇṇuṭaiyar kallātavar.)

These couplets from the subchapter on education are learned by heart by students in their formal schooling and they are featured in the front of public buses across the state. The verses were readily proffered to me by literary-minded activists in Pudukkottai's Arivoli movement when asked about the place of literacy and education in Tamil culture. The same lines are also used by activists in their mobilization efforts in order to shame people into joining the literacy movement, precisely because the *Tirukkuṟaḷ* carries such moral authority (Tamilcelvan 2004b, 19). The great poet Auvaiyar is credited with a very similar verse, "Numbers and letters are equal to eyes" (*eṇṇum eḻuttum kaṇṇenat takum*), which also serves as an ethical text used in primary schooling, emphasizing the virtues of literacy through the idiom of sight. In the case of Auvaiyar, the verse is taken from her famous *Koṉṟai Vēntaṉ,* a text used in traditional schooling that is itself arranged in alphabetical order to aid beginning students in their memorization of the Tamil alphasyllabary. These texts have been attractive to a range of modernizing social reformers, including the Dravidian nationalists, because of their largely secular character.

Texts such as the *Tirukkuṟaḷ* point back to pedagogical traditions that differ in significant ways from the literacy-as-enlightenment practiced by the Arivoli Iyakkam. However, these memorable texts circulate very widely across the Tamil-speaking world and have nevertheless been absorbed into the literacy movement's grassroots presentation of itself as consistent with Tamil educational traditions of the classical era. One might also assume that, because these are literary texts learned through formal education systems, they would not be available to villagers who would actually take part in literacy lessons, precisely because they had never gone to school as children. But the equation of literacy with eyesight was, in fact, also familiar to many villagers I spoke with across Pudukkottai District who had had little or no formal education and would not have come across these tropes through their own reading of these classical texts in school but rather through a differently formalized familial oral circulation. There is a certain continuity between these classical models of ethics and everyday formulations of progress and literacy, a point that has been emphasized by Anand Pandian (2009) in his book on the trope of cultivation and the practice of everyday ethics in rural Tamil Nadu. Images from the classical past intersect with twentieth-century politics and twenty-first-century activisms in ways that could not be anticipated.

For example, when I asked a group of Arivoli learners in the village of L.N. Puram the naive anthropologist's question "What does Arivoli mean?" I received the following response from a woman in her forties who had never gone to school:

> Arivoli means like an eye seeing [*oru kaṇterikiṟatu mātiri*] for those who can't read, that's all Arivoli means. If you don't know how to read, it means it's like an eye that cannot see [*oru kaṇteriyātuṉṉu arttam*]. Arivoli means, we'll read and that eye will see light [*kaṇṇukku ōḻikiṟatu*]. That's Arivoli [*atutāṉ aṟivoḷi*].

Without hesitating, this unlettered villager drew on the metaphor of an eye seeing the light and opposed literacy to the condition of being blind much like the sage Tiruvalluvar had done in his *Tirukkuṟaḷ*. She had done so without quoting the text directly. The *Tirukkuṟaḷ*'s figuration serves rather as an implicit intertext. I have received a large number of similar responses from learners and teachers alike. While prompted by a question that few people would ever ask themselves, such responses attest the degree to which the assimilation of literacy and knowledge with light and seeing is in the air, although this trope has undoubtedly been amplified through its use in the literacy movement.

The Arivoli concept's contemporary power in circulation, though propelled by central government funds and a robust activist network associated with the broader Left, therefore also rides on classical literary tropes and the polythetic traces of twentieth-century reformist projects, including Tamil nationalism, but also a more specifically Dravidian rationalism. It was through the forging of ideological ties to these resonant pasts that the Arivoli Iyakkam could legitimately claim to be a "people's movement" with tens of thousands of rural activists working for the cause in districts like Pudukkottai. It was the sheer scale of efforts like the Total Literacy Campaign in this district, which mobilized over 250,000 learners at its height that lends weight to the claim that the literacy movement is in fact a "second independence struggle."

"Arivoli" as Enlightenment, "Enlightenment" as Arivoli

I would now like to return to the Arivoli Iyakkam's urban leadership in the Science Forums in an effort to flesh out some of the conceptual connections that have been made across social barriers. Recall that from the perspective of the urban middle-class leaders who initiated Arivoli activism in the late 1980s and early 1990s, they were participating in a global movement. Connections to Tamil reformist nationalism and to literary tropes connecting script to the eyes are more strongly felt at the district level, especially among the rural Tamil-language literati, than in India-wide official ideology of the people's science movement. But certain new resonances, suturing the narratives of Tamil classicism and Dravidianist reform to those of a global vision of progress, have been forged through the course of nearly two decades of rural literacy activism. It was through the Arivoli movement that many came to think differently about the Enlightenment itself.

When I initially asked Dr. T. Sundararaman, one of the early leaders from Pondicherry whom many credit with coining the very word "Arivoli," about the origins of the idea and possible connections to Periyar's Dravidian rationalist humanism, he told me that it had not even occurred to him. He attributed the coining of the word "Arivoli" for the literacy movement to his wife, Sudha Sundararaman, a prominent feminist at the all-India level and general secretary of the All India Democratic Women's Association (AIDWA)—the women's wing of the Communist Party of India (Marxist). In contrast to Pudukkottai's literati activists and village learners, the urban intellectuals who had founded the Science Forums were much more likely to refer to models of literacy activism from other countries or to anticolonial and democratic struggles in India more generally. The European Enlightenment is easily invoked as a precedent by many urban activists in the Arivoli Iyakkam, as are the Russian Revolution and similar educational experiments in Fidel Castro's Cuba and Julius Nyerere's Tanzania. Sundararaman did eventually concede that there may be some broad affinities among these varieties of social critique and earlier Tamil nationalist claims to an anti-Brahman secularism, but he was quite weary of associating literacy and science activism with what he took to be an overly ethnicized vision of political action that would conflict with his universalizing claims to the Enlightenment project.

While discursive resonance with appropriate pasts may be cultivated for strategic ends by the movement framers, their vision of activism was only slowly influenced by their encounters with visions offered by subaltern activists and learners. Inspirational texts offered by the urban leadership were more easily incorporated by village-level activists than vice versa. Even those who write primarily in the Tamil language consistently sought to tie their work to revolutionary models inspired by events elsewhere, often in Europe. For example, a recent Tamil-language book documenting songs that were written in the service of Arivoli Iyakkam takes its title, "A Terrible Beauty Was Born" (*Pēraḻaku Piṟantatu*) from the famous poem by W. B. Yeats depicting the failed Irish uprising of Easter 1916. According to the author, N. Karunanidhi, Arivoli Iyakkam's Velur District coordinator, as well as a Science Forum leader and a school headmaster, the concept of Arivoli Iyakkam as a revolutionary idea and call for continuous change is purposefully open ended:

> The very words "Arivoli Iyakkam" made many think. Government officers would pronounce these words and make efforts to discern their meaning. They grumbled that there could even be a revolution within this movement. But the movement's friends were attracted by the very feelings captured by this word. The word's true bundle of meanings can be seen in the continuing Arivoli library and cultural movements taking place after the first Arivoli literacy movement. . . . The Arivoli movement serves as a base for many social works, movements for social change, and ongoing struggles. These struggles are all suitably joined, as part of the very meaning of the word "movement" [*iyakkam*]. "In proclaiming the French Revolution a magnificent terrible beauty was born."[16] Like this, through Arivoli a great beauty was born in Tamil Nadu. (2003, 27)

The author is very conscious of the phrase's extensional meanings for both government officials and volunteers, and he makes explicit use of comparisons to earlier revolutionary moments to argue for the global import of the movement toward enlightenment through literacy. I would particularly like to draw readers' attention to Karunanidhi's use of citation to explain and perform similarities between Arivoli Iyakkam and already available narratives of social change.

The line Karunanidhi quotes is attributed by a footnote to W. B. Yeats, but it has in fact been rendered to refer explicitly to the much better-known French Revolution, rather than to the original subject of Yeats's poem.[17] What is interesting for our purposes here is not so much the slippage between the Irish uprising and the French Revolution (from the original source of translation), but rather the desire on the part of the narrator of Arivoli's importance to attach *likeness* and perhaps even continuity to these events of social rebellion. "*Like this*, through Arivoli a great beauty was born in Tamil Nadu." The French Revolution can thus act as an explicit icon, a parallel case, in the cultural poetics of Arivoli discourse. The literacy movement can be understood in terms of its predecessor, an event that would be well known to an already literate audience. The author is clearly well aware of what he terms the "bundle of meanings" that are gathered in the Arivoli idea and seeks to exploit the possibilities of such bundling, specifically seeking to represent Arivoli as a source of perpetual movement and progress. The Yeats quotation shows how the Arivoli movement can be seen through the lens of the French Revolution, or any movement for progressive social change that has preceded it, for that matter. Prior revolutionary events could act as the ground on which the more recent Arivoli Iyakkam stands, and Arivoli could be seen as a translation of the original Enlightenment or prior revolutions into Tamil language and onto Tamil soil.

But the converse is also true as the discourse on enlightenment circulates, and this is a critical point lest we reduce this desire to find likeness as just another case of postcolonial mimicry, or a simple case of "vernacularization" (cf. Merry 2006). Appropriation quickly turns into *retrospective incorporation*. The word "Arivoli" can now, in the wake of mass mobilization, be used retrospectively to refer to the European Enlightenment itself in the Tamil-language cultural and literary press in ways that were not possible prior to the literacy movement. An example of such usage can be found in the science activist T. V. Venkateswaran's review article on the field of cultural studies in the March 2000 issue of the political journal *Putu Vicai* (New Force), which uses the word "Arivoli" to refer to the European Enlightenment in the context of explaining critiques of scientific reasoning. It is, in fact, through a proliferating literature on modernity and postmodernity in Tamil that the idea of Arivoli has come to be so closely associated with Enlightenment philosophy, in addition to the broader cultural influence that the literacy movement can be said to have had.

For rural activists who have taken to reading journals like *Putu Vicai* and books about modernism and postmodernism through their involvement with the movement, Arivoli acts as a lens through which prior similar events in India and elsewhere can be interpreted. It thus seemed perfectly natural for the village-level activist Neela, who had been reading about theories on modernity in books and journals that circulate among

Science Forum members, to state that she had just read somewhere that an "Arivoli Iyakkam" had already happened in Europe in the eighteenth century. The Enlightenment itself, then, can be rendered as a prior instance of what activists already know through their encounters with science and literacy activism. Note, however, that this sense of priority is temporal and not necessarily prior in the sense of being somehow more foundational in the eyes of village-level activists. The very act of retrospection can be understood as an agentive enlistment, preserving the philosophical priority of the present.

Failed Resonance: A Geography Lesson

This last example of a Pudukkottai villager learning about the European Enlightenment and its scientific rationalism through the lens of her own activism demonstrates a sort of circular motion of interpretation that serves to knit narratives together across contexts. Arivoli activism was full of such attempts at alignment that can cut across spatial and social divides. Discourses on Arivoli drew on different understandings and experiences of the past, and through the work of activism and reflection, these varied pasts can be made commensurate to a certain degree. But sometimes activists were struck with the extreme difference in orientations toward space and time that are both a product and continuing cause of social difference. To the extent that the Arivoli Iyakkam was a program associated with the state and with urban orientations to personhood, time, and place, it oftentimes failed to resonate with the villagers it sought to mobilize. Rural women who were subject to Arivoli's pedagogy often responded critically, forcing activists to rethink their orientations to enlightenment. I would therefore like to end this chapter with a few episodes excerpted from the writer S. Tamilcelvan's memoirs of his days as a literacy activist, titled *Iruḷum Oḷiyum* (Darkness and Lightness), in order to suggest what the experience of failed resonance and a rupture in the chronotope of national development might mean for the practice of the Arivoli Iyakkam.

Tamilcelvan was a leader in Tirunelveli District's Arivoli Iyakkam during the Total Literacy Campaign and Postliteracy phases of the movement in the 1990s. Today he is a prominent short-story writer and essayist, an activist in the Tamil Nadu Science Forum, and the president of the Tamil Nadu Progressive Writers Association. Tamilcelvan is from a middle-class background, hails from the small town of Pattamadai, and represents someone who dwells at the intersection of urban leadership and the rural grassroots. His thoughtful reflections provide an indispensable window onto the class contradictions that were made manifest through the practice of activism. He also shares his insight into what these contradictions might mean for attempts to foster enlightened citizenship among villagers by means of literacy activism. Throughout his book, Tamilcelvan describes events that lead him to reconsider his relationship to knowledge and to people. He had sought to teach people their place in world history and in the nation by writing pamphlets and speaking about the struggle for independence and the problems of contemporary communalist politics, only to find that his activism required him to learn much about his own place in relation to the world of rural marginality.

For example, on one occasion Tamilcelvan went to a village named Ayiraperi to oversee an Arivoli lesson in which the literacy teacher asked a group of villagers which district they were living in. Districts are the primary administrative units for development projects and tax collection within the state of Tamil Nadu. Much to Tamilcelvan's surprise, however, the students of Ayiraperi responded that they do not live in a district. The following is the excerpt in which he reports this encounter (2004b, 41):

> This was an Arivoli literacy circle run by Kandasamy, a very loving and committed volunteer. The students in this circle were all women. This is a conversation that happened between them that night at the lesson:
>
> *Kandasamy asked, "Which district is your village [ūr] in?"*
> *The students replied, "Our village is not a district."*
> *Then he asked, "Which subdistrict is your village in?"*
> *Again, "Our village is not a subdistrict."*
>
> Thinking perhaps they misunderstood the question, Kandasamy explained:
>
> *"So, you know there's Madurai District and Virudunagar District, right? Like that, which district are you in?"*

The students then said very clearly and patiently,

> *"Our village is not in any district. It's always here. The subdistrict is in Tenkasi. The district is in Tirunelveli. Do you understand?"*

> After the lesson I took a walk with Kandasamy and we talked with amazement about our lack of understanding. They had made us understand that the *town of Tirunelveli itself was the district.* The idea that Ayiraperi (their village) was located *within* the area of Tirunelveli District had not reached the people *even fifty years after Independence.*

This incident is of interest because of what it tells us about the middle-class activist's dilemma when faced with resistant villagers, and more specifically because of the idioms of space and time in which this epistemological struggle is conducted. Tamilcelvan was shocked at what he took to be the villagers' expression of their own marginality with regard to the state and to his own world of spatial experience. Their response raised the question for Tamilcelvan of whether they were really living as fellow citizens of an independent India if they had no meaningful experience of living *in* a district called Tirunelveli. He had assumed that they would also take for granted his approach to place. However, his was an approach to the categories of place that had been saturated, by virtue of his formal education, middle-class experience, and work as a postal employee, by state-centered principles of classification. In another passage meant to capture this social difference the activist tells readers that "the distance between us was much more than that between letters *ā* and *ī*." (2004b, 25).

Tamilcelvan's interlocutors were purposefully marking their social difference through the idiom of place. For these rural women learners, the district (*māvaṭṭam*) and subdistrict (*tāluka*) were distinct places in other towns. They appeared to resist the assumption that they were living *within* an encompassing government spatial unit known as the district. E. Valentine Daniel (1984, 61–105) has written extensively about the pragmatic meanings of the Tamil "*ūr*"—the word I have unsatisfactorily translated above as "village" but which could also be translated as "home" or "place." Daniel explains how a person shares substantial qualities with their *ūr*. The answer to the question of what is one's *ūr* also depends completely on the context in which such a question is asked.

An *ūr* must therefore be understood in contrast to the rationalized and abstracted government spatial categories that children learn in school: stable, bounded categories that cannot shift in the same manner according to the context of interaction (see also Scott 1998). A series of *ḳirāmam pañcāyat* (revenue villages) are bound within the *tāluḳa* (subdistrict), which is within the *māvaṭṭam* (district), which is in a state, and so forth. The villagers of Ayiraperi who had insisted that their *ūr* is not a district were using this idiom to argue that their village does not have that quality of being a seat of state power.

Using the activists' own language of geography, the villagers clarified their point. The Tamil locative case marker in Tamilcelvan's reported dialogue, "*eṅḳa ūr enta māvaṭṭattilēyum illai*" (our village is not *in* any district) points not only to a simple spatial location but to a much more profound distance. Tamilcelvan has interpreted the villagers' use of a spatial distinction between villages being *in* a district and the district being in the town of Tirunelveli as a social index, indicating a great epistemological disjuncture between him and his interlocutors. They had made him understand that the "district" is an office building in the town of Tirunelveli where the field of state power is centered. Theirs was an *ūr* that had perhaps been abandoned by the state and certainly did not share in the substantial qualities of a "district." Their *ūr* was enmeshed in a rather different regime of power. The villagers' orientation to place appeared to resist Tamilcelvan's attempt to teach them how to address the district administration with their grievances, the initial purpose for the activist's line of questioning. They had refused the very premises of such an act.

It is crucial to note that Tamilcelvan also interpreted this difference immediately within the frame of the Indian nation and state. How could they understand national issues if they did not even know their place in local administrative structures? Here, epistemology, a way of knowing place, has been tied to the questions of agency and belonging to the nation-state. It was the distance between Tamilcelvan and the villagers that brought into serious question the effectiveness of simply teaching them how to write a petition in order to ensure their full rights as citizens. These villagers would need to be taught a different sense of place and not only how to write in order to participate in modern citizenship. The Tamil Nadu Science Forum, in fact, has a slide show that they bring to villages precisely to socialize people to an objectifying Cartesian sense of space through satellite photos showing villagers the place of their district in the state, in the country of India, on the globe, and eventually, through diagrams, in the solar system and galaxy. From the activist's perspective, in order for learners to make demands on a government and to act as empowered agents, they first need to think in terms of a Cartesian spatial imaginary different from their own, and to think of themselves as having stakes in the forms of power connected to state institutions. Villagers would need to know themselves as living under an administrative unit known as a district. We can again glean a sense of the many-layered epistemological difficulties facing Arivoli activism.

What Dipesh Chakrabarty (2000) would call the "historicism" of the reformer's perspective becomes evident when the problem of multiple topographies is easily translated into a problem of multiple temporalities: "The idea that Ayiraperi was located *within* the area of Tirunelveli district had not reached the people *even fifty years after Independence*." The problem in Tamilcelvan's eyes was not just that they spoke as if they did not know that they lived in a district, but that they were living in a time outside that of independence. They had not yet been brought into the fold of national contemporaries who experienced freedom. They would have to be "educated into citizens" for Indian independence to be complete. Arivoli as a "second independence movement" would thus entail pedagogy as the unification of national space and time that would act as the interpretive ground for new forms of agentive social action. It seems that overcoming this first, epistemological gap between rural topographical imaginaries and state-centered delineations of space is precisely what leads to a greater exposure of a second, embodied-communicative gap requiring that villagers must learn to write. That is, they would need to be taught to think in terms of living in a district only to learn that they were not in a position, *yet*, as nonliterate members to make use of this fact until they could write a petition. The Arivoli Iyakkam has thus been invested in a project of cultural work that serves as a prerequisite to the task of teaching people the skills of literacy. It is a pedagogy that teaches people "the gap between membership and belonging," thereby redefining people's marginality as something *within* the state's field of power (Das and Poole 2004, 17). Through this encounter, however, Tamilcelvan was made very aware of the fact that he was also writing about villagers as full contemporaries, who despite their lack of formal education were already *supposed* to be fellow citizens of India.

Tamilcelvan becomes all the more critical of the gap between formal and substantive citizenship as he teaches villagers of their marginal place in the nation-state. The propensity for self-criticism among Arivoli activists is born of this realization that villagers are already supposed to be citizens, even when it is subsumed under the larger project of unifying the nation. It is the very desire for unity that brings heterogeneity into relief. Tamilcelvan's narrative construction of spatial and temporal difference within the frame of the nation, sparked by the interaction he witnessed between the Arivoli activist and the villagers of Ayiraperi, therefore also signals his recognition that such forms of difference are organized along the lines of gender and social class. The residents of Ayiraperi lived not far from Tamilcelvan's own home, but they appeared to live in different worlds because of who they were.

Reflecting further on the conversation about the village of Ayiraperi not being in any district, Tamilcelvan continues, "Only a week earlier in that same village I had spoken for half an hour about the importance of national unity.[18] Speaking to people who did not even know about the ideas of a district and subdistrict about nations and nationalism . . . made me feel ashamed" (2004b, 42). He was reproaching himself for giving a speech on national unity in the wake of violence between Hindus and Muslims in North India, for assuming that it would be of concern to the villagers of Tamil Nadu who were struggling for their own survival. The author turns this event into a parable about India's middle classes and the problems they foist on the rural poor without understanding that these are, in fact, the problems of a nation-state that is often quite distant from the concerns of Tamil villagers. The question of citizenship that had driven Tamilcelvan to go out into the villages of his district and teach his fellow Indians how to read and write in the Arivoli Iyakkam was turned back onto himself and his social class. Discussing a similar visit to another village in Tirunelveli, where an old man had asked him where he had been all these years if was he so excited about bringing national unity and literacy to everyone, Tamilcelvan writes, "I started to hate my pants and shirt. It occurred to me that I could have worn a *vēśṭi*. Even if I had come wearing a *vēśṭi* I could not have been one with him.

After forty years of powdering my face I could not just wipe my middle-classness off" (2004b, 19).[19] The "darkness" of ignorance in the title of his book *Iruḷum Oḷiyum* (Darkness and Lightness) turns out to be his own and that of his readership, not that of the villagers.

The Cultural Work of Chronotope Production

Historians of the subaltern studies collective have argued that the experience of state and nationhood among those at the rural margins is of a radically different order than that of those whose proximity to modern state power has rendered its ways of organizing the world as natural (e.g., Amin 1995; Chatterjee 2004; Guha 1983). In the episode above, we can see that, to the extent that Tamilcelvan's orientation to place and time had been coterminous with that of the state, the enlightenment project he had devoted himself to sat in tension with his desire to be "one" with subaltern villagers on their own terms. The rupture felt in the activists' narrative of progress is palpable: "we talked with amazement about *our* lack of understanding . . ."

Here, we confront squarely one of the major intellectual conundrums facing activists who engaged in the cultural work of Arivoli: producing autonomous subjects through enlightenment activism requires activists to recognize actually existing social conditions and cultural formations in rural Tamil Nadu. It is this fact that prompts Tamilcelvan to turn his criticism back on himself, his fellow activists, and his readers, if not to denaturalize state-centered categories of space and time completely, at least to delineate the limits of their hold on rural people's imagination.

If this realization was not to be incapacitating, it would have to serve as a means to develop a more expansive vision of progress that could incorporate such forms of difference within the project of Arivoli as Enlightenment. Indeed, despite their recognition of the limits of state reason, activists like Tamilcelvan nevertheless took the task of teaching the villagers of Ayiraperi that they live in Tirunelveli District to be a necessary step in the long journey toward unifying the nation, even as many in the Arivoli movement became increasingly critical of the Indian state as a result of their work. But it is only when we return to the perspective on Arivoli offered by village-level activists that we can appreciate the real depth of the contradictions that unfolded as result of the literacy movement's project to create autonomous subjects by tying their sense of self to larger social formations such as the nation-state. When Tamilcelvan's fellow activist and progressive writer Neela says that "we need to run this movement according to the qualities of this soil," it is precisely to argue for a different orientation to the project of Enlightenment itself, one that let the qualities of the *ūr* confront the instrumental rationalities of district governance. Such a method would ideally never take for granted the end point of Arivoli, but always use the experience to speak back the work of projecting an as-yet unattained future.

In this chapter I have therefore dealt with the production of chronotopes in at least two, interrelated, ways. First, we have been concerned with the claims being made on behalf of literacy, such as the underlying claim fueling activism that mass literacy would unify a national space and time. To claim that Tamil villagers must become literate to enter the imagined community of the modern nation-state is to claim that they must adopt a new vision of sociality. People must be taught to think in terms of an affiliation to this large-scale spacetime, connecting villagers to their fellow citizens. The second kind of chronotopic action of interest concerned the ways in which the Arivoli Iyakkam formulated its self-image through discursive links to the past, and especially to other, comparable movements such as the struggle for Indian independence. We can moreover observe how this second project—that of racinating the literacy movement in the history of a place to produce a sense of continuity—is entailed by the primary project of producing autonomous subjects through the unification of a nation-state spacetime.

Activists in the Arivoli Iyakkam quickly realized that their task could not be that of imposing perfectly new senses of place, time, and personhood. Such a form of cultural domination would too readily contradict the premise that people must make themselves, and it would undoubtedly fail from the start. While part of the role of activism was to make people feel ashamed of aspects of their lifestyles that are deemed anachronistic, the Arivoli Iyakkam also drew from what Reinhart Koselleck (2004) would call the "space of experience" to inform their vision of the future. The movement's task was to cultivate and elaborate those aspects of peasant life that would fit into their model of modernity. My analysis has therefore focused on the forms of reflexivity that arise in such a project when the chronotopic politics of modernization conflict with the equally strict requirement that the subject of modernity must forge herself. The production of a rural modernity that sat at the core of Arivoli pedagogy forced a heightened self-consciousness on the part of activists of their role as epistemological and ethical mediators, sitting between competing visions of knowledge and of the good life.

People like Tamilcelvan, Sheik, Neela, Karuppiah, and their colleagues in the literacy movement took on a responsibility to produce specific pasts that could be enlisted for their work, and the question of how to build an affective connection to history and locality was interpreted differently depending on the social positioning of the activist. Learners in the Arivoli movement also had their own understandings of the connections among light, knowledge, and literacy. In the analysis of Arivoli efforts, we must therefore move beyond Marx's notion of a "time-honored disguise" that would somehow hide the true intent of the modernizer, or rather understand the degree to which such a mask would, in fact, shape its wearer's understanding and experience of the drama at hand. Once chosen, the "borrowed languages" that serve to root the modernizing project in a time and place do more than impede the forward motion of history. The available means of invoking Enlightenment often raised new questions about the very project they were meant to serve. This last argument about the power of narrative and social praxis to produce reflexivity on the part of activists is a thesis that will be developed in depth over the course of this book.

2

Feminizing Enlightenment

The Social and Reciprocal Agency

Like many efforts to remake the world, the Arivoli Iyakkam led to social changes that no one had expected. Over the course of the Total Literacy Campaigns, activists and bureaucrats were not only amazed at the scale of what the rural district of Pudukkottai had been able to achieve; they were equally surprised at who was participating and leading the way in many villages. Contrary to widespread fears among founders of the Arivoli Iyakkam that it would be very difficult to compel women to meet in public spaces for the purpose of holding literacy lessons, it was men who turned out to be more recalcitrant learners.[1] Leaders of the movement speculate in retrospect that men were more fearful of being embarrassed about their illiteracy in public (Athreya and Chunkath 1996, 177). Perhaps the initial apprehensions of urban activists also tell us something about widespread stereotypes regarding rural life. In any case, by the time I began my fieldwork, the literacy movement had all but given up on trying to attract men to their classes. The Mahalir Arivoli Iyakkam (women's

Enlightenment movement) of the early 2000s focused almost exclusively on women. Reflecting on nearly two decades of activism, many whom I had interviewed and befriended in the Arivoli movement during this last campaign would claim that the simple fact of creating a new form of public space for women in villages had a greater impact on social life than the spread of literacy itself.

By the mid-1990s, Pudukkottai had already become known among liberal and Left circles in India because of how the Arivoli Iyakkam mass-literacy program had taken on the character of a rural women's movement. The charismatic district collector during the Total Literacy Campaign, Sheela Rani Chunkath, featured prominently in a number of well-publicized efforts to focus on women as agents of rural development and social change. A venture to train women in the once frowned-upon act of bicycling and to provide bicycles for Arivoli teachers through government subsidies is the best known among the district's achievements during this period. Several thousand women learned to cycle through this program, irrevocably changing orientations to space and mobility in the countryside. Another innovation of the Arivoli Iyakkam, also attributed to Chunkath, was to enable Dalit women to take out leases from the government to work on their own granite quarries in an area where they had previously worked as bonded laborers under male quarry owners of the dominant Maravar community.[2] After her term as the collector of Pudukkottai, Chunkath would help shape global development strategies, serving as one of India's official representatives at the United Nation's Fourth World Conference on Women in Beijing in 1995. She is also remembered fondly by many in Pudukkottai. "Sheela Rani" has since become a common name for girls in the district's villages.

The manner in which the Arivoli Iyakkam combined grassroots literacy activism and feminist development politics through a joint state-NGO effort is emblematic of a broader shift away from state-led development.[3] As a result of this convergence, many initiatives in rural India straddled what was once a much wider gap between development work and social movement politics. As we have seen in the previous chapter, it was only through such a hybrid initiative that the nonparty political Left could gain such a wide appeal in the Tamil countryside.

Scholars like Aradhana Sharma (2008) have noted, however, that what was once a critical feminist model of development has, in fact, been absorbed into a broader neoliberal restructuring of the rural economy.[4] Participating in the new development regime focused on women has often meant the adoption of discourses of economic "self-help" and entrepreneurship. Whereas past adult literacy efforts that were fully state run, like the Farmers' Functional Literacy Project of 1967–77, sought to impart literacy skills to men as a technical means to help the spread of green revolution technology, the Arivoli Iyakkam was designed to reshape women's very orientation to development.[5] In this regard, my ethnography of Arivoli Iyakkam activism among women enters into conversation with analyses of feminist politics in a context where renewed interest in gender and "empowerment" has become intimately tied to the privatization of development functions (John 1996; Kapadia 2002; Sharma 2008). Such hybrid programs face competing pulls from a politics that would demand a greater role for the state in redistribution, on one hand, and the attractions of a discourse on the grassroots "empowerment" of women as agents of development, on the other hand.

In this chapter, however, I pursue the seemingly much more basic questions of *how* women were targeted in activism and *why* it is that women participated in programs like the Arivoli Iyakkam in the first place. I seek to understand the very process of mobilization from the perspective of activism. The promise of becoming literate, and especially of learning to sign one's name so as to escape the stigma of being a "thumbprint," provides some explanation for why the movement was attractive. The material gains and sense of dignity offered by self-employment in the quarries, easier access to microcredit loans, and the simple thrill of riding a bicycle also go some distance toward explaining why women participated. But I would argue that these motivating factors do not exhaust the possibilities, and they tell us relatively little about how the Arivoli Iyakkam was able to attract and mobilize women in particular. Although I do not intend to provide a definitive answer regarding the primary motivation causing women to take part in the literacy movement and its associated activities, following this line of questioning allows analysis to define more clearly the models of agency and gender that have developed in attempts to empower women. What did "empowerment" mean to bureaucrats, activists, and other villagers? More specifically, what were the presuppositions about gender, agency, sociality, and personhood undergirding such attempts at "empowerment"? How might we devise a means of thinking about mobilization otherwise than through the received logics of "empowerment" at the heart of contemporary development efforts?

Models of Agency in Practices of Mobilization

Scholars working in a range of contexts have argued that women are attractive targets of small-scale development aid because they are widely perceived to be more docile. The literature on microcredit goes so far as to show how efforts to "empower" women through the formation of self-help groups in Bangladesh, for example, in fact target women in particular because they are supposedly "more submissive than men" (Grameen Bank worker, quoted in Rahman 1999, 69). Such strategic adherence to gender stereotypes belies the feminism that microcredit banks claim to be promoting, and on closer scrutiny seems to have more to do with economic logic.[6] How, then, can we begin to read attributions of docility differently?

At the outset, more work needs to go into understanding the very models of agency that are employed to mobilize women in development efforts such as the Arivoli Iyakkam. The literacy movement used several different idioms in which to articulate its vision of progressive change, ranging from familiar feminist critiques of the social construction of gender to more indigenist attempts to recuperate "traditional" notions of women's power. Tracking shifts back and forth between idioms of agency tells us much about the sleight of hand that allows earlier feminist critiques of economic exploitation to be folded back into the ongoing construction of gender stereotypes. But in this chapter I ultimately argue that the Arivoli movement was, in fact, successful to the degree that it developed a third mode of social action: what one might call "reciprocal agency," through which women paradoxically participated in a movement designed to foster a sense of autonomy out of a sense of obligation, or duty, to activists themselves. By paying attention to modes of initiating social action that cannot be reduced to a universalist understanding of individual agency nor to assertions of traditional feminine virtues, we can perhaps understand better how women are mobilized by development programs that can also lay claim to being social movements.

Much of what is at stake in the difference among models of women's empowerment has to do with differing models of sociality itself. I have noted in the previous chapter how much of Arivoli Iyakkam activist labor was devoted to encouraging people to think and act in terms of large-scale social formations that would transcend the worlds of villages, castes, and kinship. To this end, activists commonly invoked an all-encompassing vision of "society," referring to the form of consciousness they sought to produce as a "*camūka pārvai*" (social perspective). But what was at stake in these efforts is not just a matter of encouraging people to think in relation to larger scales of belonging. Building a *camūka pārvai* just as importantly entails a new understanding of what it means to belong to this more inclusive group. Everyone, men and women, belongs to this "modern social imaginary" as contemporaries on equal terms (Taylor 2004). A number of authors have noted the manner in which the modern concept of society has replaced divinity as the ontological ground of human existence in post-Enlightenment thought, at once natural to humans and instituted by humans.[7] It is this relation between the social and the question of human agency's power to institute a particular vision of the social that is forced into the foreground when thinking about an activism that invokes the concept of society in the name of women's "empowerment." Such a vision of society was important for activism largely to the degree that it could be worked on as a field of action, once made aware of itself. To develop a *camūka pārvai* was to be made aware of one's capacity to change the world in which one lives. It was to be responsible to large-scale, *gesellschaftliche* modes of indirect relation that could be apprehended only through forms of theoretical reasoning, and it is ultimately to become a historical actor. As such, this form of social consciousness was intimately connected to the very process of becoming literate in the Arivoli Iyakkam. Instructing people to think through such abstractions was no easy task, however, and this particular form of cultural work in Arivoli activism was often supplemented by other visions of empowerment.

In the process of inculcating such a social perspective among their fellow villagers, activists faced problems that demonstrate how contradictions in post-Enlightenment thought reveal themselves with particular clarity in postcolonial contexts. The conceptual vocabulary available for this exercise in abstraction, building a *camūka pārvai* (social perspective), is tied precisely to those regimes of filiation and sociality, frequently rendered as "community," "caste," or "sex" in a range of discourses, that the encompassing concept of "society" was meant to overcome. That is, the abstracted concept of society contends with existing forms of sociality and existing vocabularies of belonging. In the words of Sudipta Kaviraj (1997, 92), writing about a related set of issues around the ideas of public and private in postcolonial Calcutta, "concepts do not enter an empty unmarked conceptual space. They have to affect the operation of established practices and their implicit conceptual structures." There were both established practices and established conceptual structures similar enough to the Arivoli Iyakkam's version of a social perspective to pose a problem of disambiguation for activism—a problem of which version of society, or *camūkam*, was actually being imagined and instituted. Analysis must therefore not only take the details of a variety of feminist practices seriously but must also elucidate the variegated textual fields into which discourses on women have inserted themselves in order to assess their political significance.[8]

In response to problems posed by the work of abstraction required to develop a "social perspective," another strategy developed to motivate women's participation in the Mahalir Arivoli Iyakkam was to emphasize the virtues of Tamil womanhood, such as women's putatively superior power (*shakti*). This model of agency also depends on a certain form of reification characteristic of the ongoing construction of a tradition. Insofar as the construction of women's power (*shakti*) was developed as part of a self-conscious strategy of mobilization, this process also tended to force new reflections on the part of activists concerning those aspects of Tamil womanhood and sociality that are conducive to "empowerment." When shifting attention to how learners in Arivoli articulate their own perspectives on mobilization, however, we learn that village women did not necessarily respond directly to abstract calls to inhabit a social perspective on gender or to embody the virtuous qualities of *shakti*. Women took part in the Arivoli Iyakkam in response to calls from particular people: activists and volunteers, who were either from their own villages or from neighboring villages, people who might well be asking them to perform according to the abstract models of agency I have just outlined.

This insight into the personal quality of address allows us to revisit vexing questions of agency and docility from a different perspective, that of *reciprocity*. Signatures and microcredit loan repayments in this idiom, for example, might be conceived of as return gifts from groups of villagers to activists, even if these gifts nevertheless act to build a new relationship between village women and large-scale structures of power. Reciprocal agency is a form of social action that is not about personal choices, indirect relationships to the abstractions of social theory, or individual desires; nor is it about adherence to tradition, some preexisting community, or the constraint of desire. Rather, this form of agency is essentially interactional and collective, unleashing social forces that are immanent in the field of activist mobilization, and not reducible to the binary trap of freedom versus cultural constraint. But this formulation, too, remains quite abstract at this point in my narrative. Let us turn to a thicker ethnographic narrative to give flesh to these claims. I will begin with attempts to build a social perspective, then move on to a description of the ways in which the virtues of Tamil womanhood were employed in the movement, before returning to this last argument regarding reciprocal agency.

Learning Gender: The Social as Malleable

One day I accompanied the Arivoli Iyakkam activists Neela and Ramalingam to the village of Tuvarappatti, just outside of Pudukkottai Town, for a "gender awareness training" session that they had decided to organize as part of the Mahalir Arivoli Iyakkam. They had chosen this village for their training session because Ramalingam had already been working with many of the young women for nearly one year. The Arivoli Iyakkam office, in conjunction with the rural development office, had already established a tailoring training center in this village. The young women whom Ramalingam had recruited to join the tailoring program, and who would now attend the gender awareness training, were all in their late teens and early twenties. They had all joined self-help groups to contribute the money they earned doing tailoring work to a collective bank account. After one year these groups would be eligible to apply for a loan to buy sewing machines of their own. None of the trainees had gotten married yet. Most had gone to school until the tenth standard, though at least two among them had dropped out of school much earlier and were thus not completely at ease with writing. The reason for their meeting that day, however, had little to do with literacy or training in practical skills. The training session, Neela explained to me, was rather meant to give "*viḻippuṇarvu*" (consciousness) regarding "*peṇkaḷōṭa cūḻnilai*" (women's situation).

Ramalingam had already asked the local Arivoli volunteer, another young woman from this village, to have the trainees assemble by the panchayat office by ten o'clock in the morning. The panchayat office was housed in a medium-sized concrete building sitting next to a temple of the god Vinayakar in the center of the village, next to a dry water tank. By the time we arrived, five of the trainees had already gathered at the office and the volunteer told us that the others were on their way. The training was to be held inside the office, which had a large central room. While waiting for the rest of the trainees to arrive, Neela and Ramalingam started to prepare. They had put up an Arivoli Iyakkam banner that had been painted by Karuppiah for the occasion and they also nailed a poster they had taken from the literacy office to the wall. When everyone had arrived, Ramalingam asked the trainees to sit in a circle on the floor of the unfurnished room. He began the session by introducing Neela, whom only some of the women had met before. I had already met all of them through earlier visits to the tailoring center. He then asked all the attendees to introduce themselves by telling us their names, how much schooling they had had, and what work they did, so that Neela could get an idea of whom she would be talking to. While one of the young women was attending college in town, most responded, "I'm simply at home," implying they had no formal jobs.

After introductions, the first activity of the training session, led by Ramalingam, consisted of getting the trainees to talk about the different varieties and amounts of work men and women are expected to perform. He began by distributing white chalk to everyone. He then asked them to draw a giant circle on the concrete floor of the panchayat office. Having drawn a circle the trainees were then asked to draw and number twenty-four tick marks around the edge. These would represent the twenty-four hours of the day. Ramalingam then divided the young women into two groups. One group was to use red chalk to divide the day into activities that women do, including all forms of work, rest, eating, and so on. The other group would do the same for men. They were asked to divide the clock using their chalk and write out what each chunk of time was normally devoted to. The young women worked on this task for a good fifteen minutes, discussing among themselves what they did over the course of the day. Their fathers and brothers served as reference points for what a typical man's day would look like. For the sake of simplicity Ramalingam had asked them to focus on a typical farming family, because having to take into account people who went to work in town, still a minority even in this village that is close to Pudukkottai, would bring in unneeded complications. Once they had finished their respective time maps, Ramalingam and Neela called for their attention and began a discussion.

Neela began by asking the trainees who had mapped a typical man's day to walk everyone through their map. The day began quite early with manual work in the fields such as plowing or supervising transplanting, followed by some time at the local tea shop reading the newspaper and discussing politics with neighbors. After a late breakfast at home men often took a nap during the hottest part of the day. They would then do some lighter work in the fields such as shifting irrigation patterns by damming sections of irrigation ditches to assure an equal distribution of water. This was followed by more social time at the tea shop in the evening and an early bedtime.

The other group was asked about their day next. The typical woman's day, once mapped in this manner, clearly consisted of much more work and much less time socializing. Women's days started earlier than men's with the fetching of water from the local well. This was an especially arduous task in this village where all the nearby wells had run dry and where a government-supplied public faucet connected to a water tower worked only for one hour in the morning. They often had to cook both in the morning and in the evening, in addition to helping out in the fields. Women would also be doing some sort of housework, such as peeling tamarind pods or winnowing rice, while the men slept in the middle of the day, and then again well into the evening after many of the men had gone to sleep. These were the times during which women socialized, while also working. All this did not include the fact that they were also always responsible for younger children, a constant task that the young trainees also mentioned in their report. Although the young women seemed genuinely surprised at the difference in time spent working once quantified, when asked why it was this way, they unanimously responded that it is simply because "we are women and they are men."

This response gave Neela the opening she had been looking for. She proceeded to ask every one of the young women who had gathered to describe when they first began to sense that they were different from their brothers and the boys around them. Responses from the trainees all tended to focus on late childhood and early adolescence. For example, one of the women said, "I used to be free like the boys to go out and play. There was no difference. Then after I became of age [referring to her first menstruation], my mother told me that I had to stay away. After that I was not to go out, I had to help her with cooking at home."[9] Others remembered how they would be sent out to graze the goats while their brothers were allowed to play cricket with their friends after school. Another sign of difference that the young women remembered was when they were first told by their mothers or fathers that they should be "*veṭkam*" (shy) in front of boys, "or others will talk." Neela then asked them about other differences, such as the practice of men and boys eating before the women and of women eating in the cooking area rather than out in front on the veranda like men. Neela had been writing a list of everything the young women had said regarding differences between boys and girls that only became apparent later in childhood and into the adolescent years.

She repeated the list, and then, using a distinction that has been foundational for a number of feminist visions of agency, at least since Simone De Beauvoir's *The Second Sex* (2011 [1949]), Neela proceeded to try to explain that these differences were in fact socially constructed rather than natural. She asked everyone what the word "*pāliṉam*" (sex category) means, "*pāliṉam eṉṟāl eṉṉa?*" The word *pāliṉam* is a compound of two roots: *pāl,* the root used to refer to gender classification in language or to sex, and *iṉam,* the Tamil equivalent of the Sanskrit *jāti*, which can be used to refer to any natural kind or category, though it is often used with reference to caste, especially in official contexts requiring "pure" Tamil forms. Like caste or any natural kind (*jāti*), such as plant or animal varieties, villagers would normally refer to the "*peṇ* (female) *jāti*" in everyday colloquial speech. However, *pāliṉam* as the word for sex category would have been familiar to most of the trainees from school or from any number of official forms or applications, such as those they would have had to fill out in order to join tailoring class, for example. One of the trainees responded that *pāliṉam* is the "difference between men and women" (*āṇkaḷ peṇkaḷ vēṟpāṭu*). Neela then clarified saying that the differences they had all been listing were in fact "*camūka pāliṉam*" (social sex category, or gender), adding the modifying word *camūka,* an adjective meaning "social," as Nila was trying to use it in this context.

Neela was marking a very important conceptual distinction using a word, *camūka,* the adjective form of *camūkam,* that in other contexts might *also* have referred to caste or more broadly to community.[10] Official forms or even everyday talk might refer to someone's *camūkam* just as one might refer to one's *jāti* or *iṉam.* However, Neela was using this adjective in the different sense of referring to the social, a sense of this word that the trainees who had gone to school would have been familiar with from their "social science" (*camūkaviyal*) classes, for example.[11] Once again, we can see in this encounter the layered epistemological difficulties facing Arivoli activism. The very efficacy of Arivoli activism relies on wresting words from the vocabulary of caste and community—relational and "natural" forms of belonging that presuppose no choice or exertion of will—in order to invoke a more universalizing principle of "society," something that everyone belongs to equally, once realized in its highest form, and that can potentially be remade. This is what activists mean when arguing that people must develop a "*camūka pārvai.*" To think in terms of being a member of a *camūkam*, in this sense, is to transcend restrictive, historically contingent, and for that reason arbitrary, contexts and interests.

The differences that the trainees had listed between men and women, Neela explained, were the product of a social situation (*camūka cūḻnilai*). "*Pāliṉam*" on the other hand, refers to differences in our body, she told them. "So, for example, it is because of your *pāliṉam* that you menstruate. But it is because of your *camūka pāliṉam* that you do the amount of work that you do." Neela went on to argue that gender norms had in fact changed over time. She used the example of women now riding mopeds and scooters, whereas in the past, in their mothers' generation, women would not even have ridden bicycles. Ramalingam then spoke and reminded them of the great changes that had occurred in the district as a result of the Arivoli Iyakkam's earlier efforts. Neela asked the young women to give some more examples of their own to illustrate the distinction. The young women who had gathered for the gender awareness session illustrated that they were well aware of recent historical changes and listed other examples, such as the fact that it was now possible for a woman to become the chief minister of the state or even prime minister of India. But they showed no signs that they had been convinced that this sort of historical change turns on the conceptual distinction between *pāliṉam* and *camūka pāliṉam*. It would take a more prolonged exposure to the feminist discourse on gender for this distinction to carry the weight it did for seasoned activists like Neela. Nevertheless, the distinction had been drawn and the young women who attended certainly came away with a vivid mental map, an objectification, of the different labor regimes to which men and women are disciplined to accept as normal.

With this lesson, Neela and Ramalingam began to draw the meeting to a close. They asked the local volunteer to lead the group in singing a song that was written down in the Mahalir Arivoli Iyakkam handbook that they had distributed to the trainees.[12] The first lines go as follows:

> Fear, shyness, devotion, and modesty, these are mere words of ingratiation.
> Is this a woman's duty? To be just a thing like a desirable parrot?
> (Accam nāṇam maṭam payirppu ākiya coṟkaḷ veṟum pacappu
> Iccai kiḷiyāy pōkap poruḷāy iruppatu tāṉā peṇ poṟuppu?)

In this, the most recognizably feminist song in the Arivoli corpus, the four classical virtues of Tamil womanhood—*accam, nāṇam, maṭam, payirppu*—are not celebrated; they are held up as empty ideals.[13] The time for these norms of social identity has passed, the song suggests. They are but hollow form. The young women sang along, and after thanking Neela and Ramalingam for their presentation, started back to their homes.

Much like the consciousness that everyone needs for total literacy described in the last chapter, Neela and Ramalingam described their intentions with this meeting to be a giving of "*viḻippuṇarvu*" (awareness) and a "*camūka pārvai*" (social perspective). The exercise in mapping gendered work schedules consisted of promoting what Bourdieu (1977) would call a "synoptic view" of everyday life, objectified in chalk so that it could be held up for critical reflection. It is important to note that such a totalizing perspective, as if from outside, is by no means restricted to social scientific practice. Such means of objectification are also used by activists in political practices that seek to critique the naturalization of gendered divisions of labor, as we have just seen. This strategy consists of breaking with experience to argue that what Neela referred to as "women's situation" can in fact be transcended and changed. Their presentation was premised on the potential for a relationship of equality to men in the universalizing terms of humanism, which I would argue is a product of their intellectual formation in the science movement. The promise of transcending restrictive social contexts fits in neatly with the promise of transcendence through scientific knowledge of the natural world that has long been promoted by the Tamil Nadu Science Forum.

What was at stake in the familiar distinction between sex and gender that Neela tried to impress on these young women is a particular model of agency.[14] To understand that gender is socially constructed, Neela argued, was to understand that the differences the young women had listed were not inherent, but rather open to change through the exertion of a subject who has been made aware of her freedom and power to engender change. This theory of agency relies on what scholarship has identified as an understanding of autonomy that ignores the ultimate reality of the very social processes through which gender and agency are constructed, or other modalities of freedom and self-making (Mahmood 2005; Mohanty 1991; Povinelli 2005). This variety of activism, in which the abstract "social" is invoked as a generalizing term, must nevertheless encompass the particular social formation of subjects. Apart from explicitly feminist critiques of gender, literacy pedagogy was more broadly intended to act in similar ways, to wrest subjects from restrictive contexts, while denying the more concrete social relations that would define the pedagogical encounter from the perspective of learners. This is a transcendence premised on a notion of individual personhood as some quality that exists somehow prior to the particular social relations that bind one to others. This is not a self that is the *product* of accumulated transactions, specific relations to kin, to affines, to the qualities of the soil of one's village, to the local deity, or more generally to one's *camūkam* in colloquial uses of the term.

But developing an ethnographic critique of the normative liberal individualism that sits at the core of many modernizing movements and feminist projects presents anthropology with a particular set of problems. Many of the alternative models of personhood that previous generations of anthropologists have developed to account for the conduct of rural social life in Tamil Nadu have tended to draw either on an Indology that would paint the Indian villager as the mirror opposite of an (already reified) egalitarian individual (e.g., Moffat 1979) or on a mode of ethnosociological analysis largely derived from McKim Marriott's (1990) argument that Indian persons are best understood as "dividuals," made up through transactions of "coded-substances."[15] Since this time, work on the contested quality of caste relations and on the effects of violence in molding ethnic identity has certainly opened the field to more politicized approaches to the Tamil person (Daniel 1996; Kapadia 1995; Mines 2005; Pandian 2009). Studies of colonial governmentality and its modes of reification have also inspired new approaches to the postcolonial social life of bureaucratic categories of sociality and personhood (Dirks 2001; Scott 1999). Anthropology can no longer point with the same ease to some coherent Tamil "culture" as a means of explaining what are, in fact, overlapping and competing models of sociality and personhood that are already at play in villages, even prior to interventions like the Arivoli Iyakkam. Although the young women who attended the session described above certainly are, in some meaningful senses, the product of accumulated transactions and of specific relations to kin and to gods, they are equally produced through their intensive engagement with the categories of a governmentality that has sedimented itself in the practices of everyday life in rural Tamil Nadu. We have seen, for example, how the ubiquitous categories of "*camūkam*" or "*iṉam,*" through which people speak of social formations, are used in official survey forms that the young women from Tuvarappatti would have been used to filling out or even administering themselves. The use of such terms and ideas to identify people in official contexts must also certainly affect the pragmatic uses of these terms in other contexts.

To continue and move beyond this earlier work, I am seeking to develop ethnographic accounts of the very processes of entextualization that allow categories like "*camūkam*" to circulate and rearticulate with a number of discursive formations, ranging from everyday speech about castes in a village, to government surveys and textbooks, and on to progressive feminist attempts to inculcate a "social perspective" on sex and gender. New values for such concepts are produced at every step of this process, through the very act of recontextualization, which is not to say that concepts are empty or infinitely malleable. To speak of "*camūkam*" as the imaginative means by which one can learn to inhabit an enlightened consciousness is certainly different from invocations of this category in explanations for why a young woman should marry one person as opposed to another, for example, even if there is a certain stickiness to the concept such that the latter usage sometimes bleeds into the former. Following Bakhtin, we can see how, as it circulates, "each word tastes of the context and contexts in which it has lived its socially charged life" (1981, 293). It is through the very interplay of past contexts of use and new attempts at rearticulation that we can understand the difficult epistemological work of Arivoli Iyakkam's cultural politics. I now turn to investigate the ongoing stickiness and rearticulation of a few other key concepts in the discourses on gender and Tamil culture, concepts that are more closely identified with womanhood itself. In the following cases we will see how it is the very aura of tradition that adheres to the concepts at hand that is attractive to Arivoli activism.

Of *Shakti* and *Kōlams*: Objectifying and Praising Tamil Femininity

If the four classical attributes of "fear, shyness, devotion, and modesty" mocked in the Arivoli Iyakkam song above are not qualities of Tamil womanhood that activists found appropriate to the movement's vision of progress, what are the qualities attributed to women that *were* valued in such a movement, and how did activists go about fostering these qualities? Among the most ubiquitous concepts associated with femininity that were positively valued and taken up in Arivoli Iyakkam activism was that of feminine power, or *cakti* (henceforth I will use the more familiar Sanskritic form, *shakti*). Women's putative greater capacities for self-sacrifice and social service are, in fact, also connected to this broader concept of feminine power. As in the SUTRA women's organization in northern India described by Kim Berry, symbols of *shakti* have been harnessed to an imagination of national development in the Arivoli Iyakkam to craft a "hybrid feminist discourse" (2003, 87). Idioms of agency that celebrate women's virtue in the literacy movement consisted of a recuperation of "tradition" for modernist ends. In order to understand exactly how the literacy movement harnessed and objectified womanly virtues associated with the Tamil tradition, let us turn to a brief description of a typical outreach exercise in the Mahalir Arivoli Iyakkam.

One evening, early on in my fieldwork, I accompanied Murugan, an older man who worked closely with the literacy movement as a fieldworker in the rural development office, to a relatively remote village in the southern part of Pudukkottai District. On the ride out from town in a government-owned jeep, Murugan explained that we would be visiting self-help groups for two reasons that night. One was to determine what these women might be able to produce for sale at the government-owned handicrafts store in Pudukkottai. He explained how some groups make pickled limes and mango, some make craft items, and some just buy a cow and sell the milk. Recently there was a big drive to teach self-help groups how to make and market their own bath soap. He explained, "I'm from a village myself, so I understand what works and what doesn't. It's my job to give them motivation, and to teach them how to sell it. The development office will give them the supplies and training." The second reason for our visit was to encourage these groups to start holding literacy lessons at least once a week when they met as a self-help group. He told me how his office had been working very closely with the literacy movement in recent years and that members of self-help groups would all need to know how to sign their names in order to secure a loan. They would also need numeracy skills that they could learn through the literacy movement.

On arrival we met with a group of twenty women who had recently formed a self-help group. After introducing himself, Murugan proceeded to introduce me to the group as a researcher from the United States who had learned to speak Tamil. He told them, much to my surprise and dismay, that I was going back to report to my advisers at the university on their "progress" (*mun̲n̲ēr̲r̲am*)[16] and on the development of literacy and women's progress across the district. As he was talking, the local Arivoli Iyakkam volunteer handed him a notebook that served as an attendance roster for the group. She also showed him their account book, explaining that each member of the group had been diligently contributing fifty rupees per month and they were ready to ask for a loan. Murugan looked down at the book and said, "I see your group's name is 'Jhansi Rani.'[17] That's a very good name." He then looked over the rest of the book very quickly, saying, "OK, OK, OK," and looked up at the group. Murugan started asking the group questions about their economic ambitions. They appeared eager to apply for a bank loan, but remained unsure about the prospect of starting their own business. Murugan suggested they try making pots to sell at the store in Pudukkottai because they were from a part of the district that is well known for pottery.[18] When they replied that plastic had replaced pots for carrying water, he explained that the development office hoped to revive the tradition of using simple disposable teacups made of clay. He explained how they have to help build a market for these things by telling them about self-help groups in North India that had begun selling traditional village jewelry on the Internet. The women he was talking to would never have used computers, but they might well have heard of the tremendous business opportunities that are available through computer communication.[19] Seeing that the group remained skeptical, he said they might want also to think about producing homemade soap, and that they should discuss this with their local Arivoli volunteer and with local NGOs that were similarly engaged in microcredit projects.

But, he said, they would all have to learn to read and write before starting a business like that. He told them how he had noticed a few thumbprints in the group's attendance book and that the bank they hoped to secure a loan from would find this unacceptable. They would also all need to learn how to handle money and hence work on their numeracy skills. He then handed the group a stack of literacy primers, with the title "*Shakti*" written in bold on the cover, and told the volunteer to make sure that they start lessons, at which point he invoked the virtues of womanhood, not the four classical virtues, but a related set more amenable to Arivoli activism:

> Women know how to measure just enough masala and salt to make food taste just right. You know how to draw beautiful *kōlams* [rice flour designs], how to keep your house and gardens clean. Women work harder than men and they save money for family needs. So you can easily learn to read and write. Truly, women's power [*cakti*] is limitless. . . . I came from a very poor family in Ramnad and it was all due to the strength [*cakti*] and toil [*uḻaippu*] of my mother, who raised my sisters and me, that I now have a government job. This is why I work for women's equality [*camam*] to men.

In Murugan's speech and actions, we can see many of the major themes that characterize a form of activism that is "hybrid" in several senses. First, the work of literacy activism is tied to that of promoting a microcredit-based development strategy, one aimed more at alleviating poverty through local entrepreneurial initiative than at engendering critiques of structures of economic distribution. The work of enumerating populations and training these women to think in terms of how they could "help themselves," for example, seems like a rather far cry from the sorts of radical politics that motivated the founders of the Tamil Nadu Science Forum, discussed in the previous chapter. Second, and more important for the questions I pursue in this chapter, we can see how "working for women's equality to men" entails an invocation of their difference from men, insofar as Murugan argues that "women's power [*cakti*] is limitless," allowing them to work harder than men and to lead a more disciplined domestic life. Here, Murugan draws on a discourse that attempts to fuse aspects of the feminist critique of male dominance with qualities of womanhood that are widely taken to be traditionally Tamil.

The *kōlam* that Murugan had mentioned in his little speech was among the symbols of women's capacity to maintain domestic discipline and auspiciousness that were often used in Arivoli activism. These rice-flour designs, often complicated, repetitive, and maze-like, can be found in front of the doorway of just about any South Indian house in the morning. Women draw *kōlams* every day at the crack of dawn. Through the course of the day they disappear as people walk in and out of the house. *Kōlams* are not in themselves particularly sacred, although they may be drawn in front of offerings to deities for worship on certain ritual occasions. On collective festive occasions such as the village temple festival, and in the Tamil month of *mārkaḻi* (December/January), women often draw more elaborate designs that include bright colors. Insofar as they are not drawn if there has been a recent death in the household or some other *tīṭṭu* (serious pollution), these quotidian products of embodied, feminine craft can be interpreted as signs of domestic auspiciousness and of the power of women to maintain auspiciousness.

Self-help groups would be recruited to draw *kōlams* for any literacy movement event or even for special Arivoli celebration of public holidays like Deepavali or Independence Day. However, Arivoli *kōlams* operated a little differently than their quotidian models. An everyday skill that is usually taken for granted as "what women do" was revalorized by virtue of being tied to the end of proclaiming women's capacity to participate in development through self-help groups and literacy lessons. The *kōlam* pictured below (figure 2) is typical of Arivoli *kōlams* in its incorporation of the National Literacy Mission's emblem around the edges, bringing the state home, as it were. The Tamil text below the design, also made from rice flour, reads "Arivoli House." At the center of the *kōlam* are two women.

Figure 2. An Arivoli *kōlam* drawn by activists and learners in front of a volunteer teacher's house as part of a mobilization drive in Annavacal, Pudukkottai District.

The medium of the *kōlam* itself and the mode of life it is connected to are an important part of the message. Part of the performative power of Arivoli *kōlams,* for the outside observer as well as for the Arivoli literacy activist, is also a product of the historicist imagination and the objectification of tradition. It is derived from the very use of a quintessentially traditional and feminine everyday craft of domesticity to deliver literacy as a universalizing Enlightenment and liberation, celebrating the coexistence of dual temporalities and the palpable tension thereby produced in a distinctly modernizing mode. Consider the following lines of a song sung at many Mahalir Arivoli Iyakkam mobilization functions: "*kōlam pōṭum kaikaḷukku āṉā pōṭuvatu kaśṭamā?"* (Do the hands that draw a *kōlam* find the letter "A" difficult?). Using an argument very close to that Murugan had been using with the self-help group, the song both proclaims difference (the verse aimed at men is about tractors) and argues that it is *through* their embodied skills that women can be incorporated into the world of literacy and into the Arivoli movement.[20]

In their attempts to localize the drive for women's empowerment, activists were aligning ideas about tradition and womanhood in a modernizing fashion familiar from studies of nationalism (Chatterjee 1989; Sarkar 2008). Drawing on the texts of anticolonial nationalism in Tamil Nadu, especially Subramanya Bharathi's early twentieth-century nationalist devotional poetry, Arivoli activists often invoked women's "*cakti*" as a resource in building a modern India. Activists frequently sang Bharathi's songs of praise to *tamiḻttāy* (Mother Tamil) and *pārata mātā* (Mother India) at Mahalir Arivoli Iyakkam meetings. Both an Indian nationalist and a devotee of the Tamil language itself, as embodied in the feminized character of *tamiḻttāy* (Ramaswamy 1997, 194–204), Bharathi had proved to be especially important for those who would localize discourses on radical Enlightenment. Neela and Karuppiah, for example, often discussed the gender politics of Bharathi's poetry in their room in Alangudi, trying to reconcile what they had learned through their exposure to the feminist movement with his celebration of women's virtues as a "*pattiṉi*," a wife whose fidelity is exemplary.[21] In this idiom of agency, it is by virtue of their womanly qualities, and their *difference* from men, that women were argued to be the true leaders of national development.

The "feminine virtues" of self-sacrifice and productivity, that are effects of women's *shakti,* were also taken up by activism. In a quote prominently displayed on the "Mahalir Arivoli Iyakkam Volunteers Handbook" and on Arivoli office walls, for instance, Mohandas Karamchand Gandhi asserts women's centrality to the health of family and nation, "A man's education will be of use only to him. But a woman's education will be of use, not only to her family, but also to her whole people."[22] It is women's putative selflessness that makes their education particularly important to the familial and national good in a nationalist discourse that imagines the Indian nation itself in feminine terms as *Bhārat Mātā* (Mother India) (Goswami 2004; Ramaswamy 2001, 2003). In the idiom of cultivation, it is women's productive powers that must be unleashed through literacy, as in the equally prominent verse by the Tamil poet Bharathidasan, written in large letters on the outside walls of the Arivoli Iyakkam office in Pudukkottai: *kalvi illāp peṇkaḷ kaḷar nilam* (Women without education are saline earth). Education is the ingredient that would allow women to properly fulfill their roles as producers, using what Leela Dube (1986) has identified as a ubiquitous South Asian trope identifying womanhood with the productive earth.

These invocations of women's greatness naturalize certain gender ideologies in the service of "empowerment." But activists' use of such idioms did not consist of simple tactical deployments of an already existing tradition. Such uses of select tropes associated with womanhood should be interpreted in terms of the continued constitution of tradition in feminine terms, and under conditions of an encompassing modernizing ideology. Tradition in this idiom is not an obstacle in the race to become modern, but rather serves as a resource in a future-oriented project of development. This is how women's purportedly traditional virtues make them more appropriate leaders than men in the new development regime. Discourses on women's empowerment circulated across a cultural field fraught with tensions and unresolved contradictions, rearticulating with a range of interdiscourses. We might say that the Arivoli Iyakkam movement as a whole was fundamentally ambivalent about how it framed the question of women's agency—whether it celebrated women's virtues or denaturalized gender distinctions in the service of equality. The broader self-help-group movement that provided the immediate context for Arivoli mobilization in the 2000s also sat at the conjuncture of a number of discursive regimes, including science activism, international feminism, Indian and Tamil nationalist discourses on the "woman question," and neoliberal models of entrepreneurship.

Investing in *Shakti*

Late in the 1990s, in the wake of the first phases of the Arivoli Iyakkam, nongovernmental activist organizations, including the Tamil Nadu Science Forum, organized a number of self-help groups. International private banks, such as the Mumbai-based ICICI Bank, later followed the lead of NGO activity and government development programs in organizing their own microcredit self-help groups among village women, recognizing that they can provide a better rate of return than individual loans made to (predominantly male) farmers. Over the course of the 2000s the rural self-help-group movement expanded exponentially. Some Arivoli Iyakkam workers needing supplemental income while government honoraria were not forthcoming, like Neela, were also beginning to be employed by banks to organize groups and to maintain accounts. Several thousand groups had formed in Pudukkottai District with hopes of receiving small loans for the ostensive purpose of starting a small business. Even if it is not clear that these "microbusinesses" generated any serious income, it appears that as result of joining these groups, women were sometimes more likely to control parts of the household economy and that they would borrow from the self-help group's fund rather than going to the local money lender.[23] These bank groups, in addition to those organized by the literacy movement itself and by various NGOs, formed the target population for the first phase of the Mahalir Arivoli Iyakkam.

We must place the Arivoli Iyakkam's adoption of the *Cakti* (Anadamurthy and Harikumar 2001) literacy primer for some six months in 2003 at this moment of conjuncture.[24] Although the *Cakti* primer was eventually replaced in the second phase of the Mahalir Arivoli Iyakkam on the grounds that it was too difficult for use as an initial primer, a quick look at the *Cakti* literacy primer will help make more sense of the aesthetics and even the disciplinary techniques of a rather neoliberal feminism. This idiom of activism incorporates both a critique of dominant gender paradigms and an emphasis on women's *shakti* as keepers of domestic and national health. Both idioms of agency that I have outlined above can be used in the service of a turn toward empowerment understood as increased financial responsibility. The first word one learns to recognize in *Cakti* literacy training is "money." Using an ostensibly Freirean critical pedagogy of generative words to promote critical thinking—to be explained in detail in the following chapter—this primer has replaced criticism of the class order prominent in the earlier *Aṟivoḷi Tīpam* primers designed by Science Forum activists with a language of making-do and saving money. Lesson plans combine literacy training with narratives that emphasize women's equality, the importance of saving money in a self-help group, and the virtues of environmentalism, sanitary living, and household economic planning—in which the *woman* is in charge. These sorts of materials often present a rather negative view of working-class men as prone to drink and unnecessary expenditure. Lesson 7, for example, on "savings" (*cēmippu*) and "expenditure" (*celavu*), depicts a woman keeping track of family income and expenses while her husband and daughter look on. It is they who must learn from her how to manage financial life in the new economy. The story below the picture ends with the moral, "Savings are good for the house and the nation" (*cēmippu vīṭṭukku nāṭṭukku naṉmai tarum*).

By lesson 12 in the *Cakti* primer, literacy as training for entrepreneurial leadership in a microcredit group reaches its most explicit form. There is an exercise in which the learner is asked to rate herself on her "leadership qualities." This practice of abstraction in which one's "thriftiness," "honesty," "virtue," and "family management" skills among others are to be rated and calibrated into a scale of four divisions, ranging from "none" to "some" to "good" to "very good," is precisely how banks and development agencies would rate women for creditworthiness and efficiency. Through literacy pedagogy women would ideally also learn to subject *their own lives* to such calibration. This exercise exhibits the general pattern of using literacy lessons as a context for self-objectification. But the social identity presented for inhabitation here is not only that of citizenship but of a distinctively gendered, neoliberal variety of citizen, able to care for her family and self and to measure her success along a rational scale of values provided by the book.

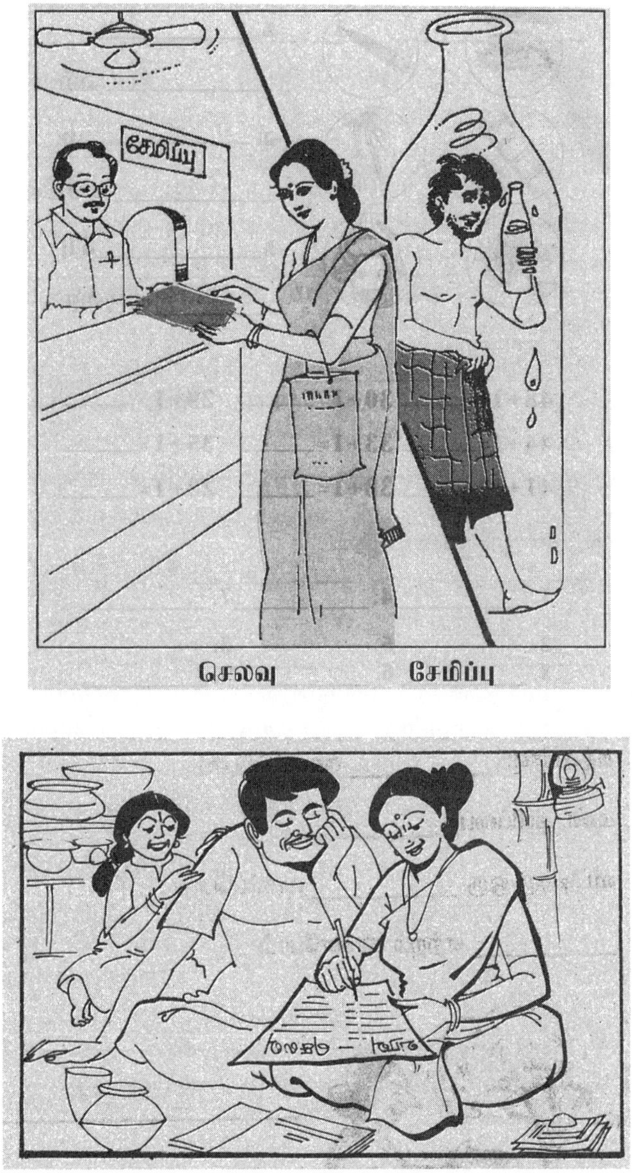

Figure 3. Lessons from a revised version of the *Aṟivoḷi Tīpam* primer (A) and from the *Cakti* primer (B) depicting women's responsible savings habits. Reproduced with permission from the Tamil Nadu State Resource Centre.

Such operations on the self have been discussed by scholars under the Foucauldian rubric of "neoliberal governmentality" (e.g., Ferguson and Gupta 2002; Sharma 2008). These scholars emphasize the productive role of techniques that would regulate conduct by calculated means that cut across the domains of society, the state, and the family. Akhil Gupta (2001), for example, has provided an ethnographic account of how these modes of self-regulation operate in the context of the Integrated Child Development Service Programme in villages in the North Indian state of Uttar Pradesh. He describes visits by government officers much like Murugan's visit that I have described above. Gupta also accounts for subtle modes of resistance by villagers to disciplinary attempts made in this development program. While the villagers in his account claim that the arrival of a child-care center marks an exciting change in their village and they have become accustomed to visits by state officials looking over the attendance rosters at this center, it is not at all clear they have internalized the ideals of child care that the program has promoted. Similar reactions could be found among those who were participating in the Mahalir Arivoli Iyakkam in Pudukkottai. There is little evidence that learners in the movement had effectively taken up these forms of self-measurement and self-government any more than they had the first lessons of the *Aṟivoḷi Tīpam* primer aimed at inducing class consciousness (which I describe in detail in the next chapter). It is not because literacy primers attempted to create neoliberal, feminine subjects that we can assume that such subjects had in fact been created in rural Tamil Nadu. In order to account for how self-help groups did nevertheless meet and hold literacy lessons, even if the actual content of these primers might not have been taken up as the authors had intended, I would now like to turn the learners' perspective on the Mahalir Arivoli Iyakkam.

Reciprocal Agency: Mobilization in Response to a Call

The Arivoli Iyakkam and the larger self-help-group movement that it had both begun and then relied on for recruits in Pudukkottai successfully created conditions in which a need was being felt among most women for at least minimal literacy. According to the district literacy office, between 2003 and 2006 over ten thousand women had participated as learners in the Mahalir Arivoli Iyakkam in some fashion or another. To this degree, Neela's claims in the previous chapter are correct: that when put in positions where they would be made to feel ashamed of leaving a thumbprint, people will understand the need to learn to sign their names. But how was this need to learn to sign one's name articulated by the women who had joined self-help groups and literacy classes in the Mahalir Arivoli Iyakkam?

An answer to this question began to emerge for me only when I met with a group participating in the Mahalir Arivoli Iyakkam's first phase in the village of L.N. Puram, just five kilometers down the road from where I was living in Kovilpatti. This group had first been organized by Neela in her capacity as an ICICI Bank self-help-group coordinator. I had already met this group once before at the beginning of their literacy lessons eight months earlier, and I had come to know the local volunteer teacher, Hemalatha, quite well through Arivoli Iyakkam meetings in Alangudi and Pudukkottai Town. This group began as a self-help group and had already received a loan to start a small business even though not all of them knew how to read and write. They had been preparing mango pickles from their own trees and selling them at the local store. The group, named "Mother Tamil" (*tamiḻttāy*), was in the process of trying to market their pickles on a larger scale. By the time of my second visit with the group, they had all learned how to sign their names. They were among the most motivated literacy groups I met with during my fieldwork.

My visit first began with the local volunteer asking learners to show off their newly acquired skills. The group claimed to have finished the whole *Cakti* primer within six months, a feat few other literacy groups could boast of. They had been using the *Aṟivoḷi Tīpam* primer simply to practice reading and writing the script. When I asked them which primer they preferred, they seemed rather indifferent. Perhaps they were not used to such questions regarding preference. Then one of the learners told me that the *Cakti* primer was difficult because the reading passages were very long and the script was written in a small font. *Aṟivoḷi Tīpam* was better, she said, because the words were fewer and bigger. This was a consistent complaint I had heard about *Cakti,* and it is for this reason that the primer was eventually abandoned by Pudukkottai's literacy movement. Even when pressed by my questions, however, these women expressed indifference about the content of either primer.

I then started asking them why they joined the literacy program. Again, I had asked the question in such a manner that did not seem particularly interesting. Hemalatha again asked them why it is important to learn to read and write, but no one responded.

It was only when I asked one of the more talkative learners, whom I will call Cintamani, about her education prior to joining the literacy group that she gave me a sense of why she had joined in the first place. She had gone to school for a couple of years as a child, but said that she had forgotten everything since then. The following is from a recording of this conversation:

> C: Then once I joined the group, so Arivoli came right? So then, OK, it became important to sign my name [*ceri ḵaiyeḻuttu pōṭa vēṇṭiya vanticcu*]. Before that, our signature was useless.
>
> F: So you wouldn't sign before?
>
> C: We would sign [*pōṭuvōm*]! What would we sign for [*etuḵḵu pōṭa pōṟōm*]? Who would call us to sign our names [*nammaḷai yār ḵaiyeḻuttu pōṭa ḵūppiṭuṟāḵa*]? After we joined the group, only then we learned how to sign well. After Arivoli came [*atuḵḵu piṟpāṭu aṟivoḷi vanticcu*] I read and write a certain amount. I only read Tamil script. I don't read too much.

For Cintamani, it was the "call" to sign her name that seems to have motivated her sense of the importance of literacy. She explains her need to sign and her own actions as a response to this call. She has thus given us a sense of how a context has been created in which more and more women feel the need to learn how to sign their names, if not necessarily to become fully literate. But Cintamani was also telling me something more.

No one had ever bothered to call these women before in this fashion, and it was the call itself that seemed to matter to her. The Tamil verb that Cintamani had used, "*ḵūppiṭu*," which I have provisionally translated as "call," could just as well be translated as "invite." It is the word that one would employ when inviting a guest to a wedding, for example, or when a woman is "called" by her natal family to return home for a festival. To "*ḵūppiṭu*" someone in this fashion is actually to put them in a position of obligation. It can be done most effectively by someone of relative social proximity, like Neela, who had "called" or "invited" this group to come to sign their names so that they could open an account. Neela was probably more successful with this group than Murugan had been with the group described above, for example. Neela lived nearby and she had been working with this group for over a year. Cintamani and her fellow group members had taken it as their duty to respond to her invitation (in addition to economic incentives).[25] In describing the formal invitation to join a self-help and literacy group and to sign her name in this fashion, Cintamani was in fact drawing on a language of reciprocity common to other domains of life.

As I talked to Cintamani and the other learners in L.N. Puram more that evening, they repeatedly spoke of a "*kaṭṭāyam*," a responsibility—literally, a "tying"—binding them in a relationship to the bank and to the literacy movement. For example, another group member said, "We have a *kaṭṭāyam* to put our signatures and to deposit [*kaṭṭu*] money at the bank." The bank would give them loans and the literacy movement would give them primers and training. It was their responsibility to reply; they would sign their names, return money, and so fulfill the obligations of a relationship. Just as woman is "tied" (*kaṭṭu*) to her husband and his family in marriage, these women had entered into an unequal relationship of exchange. The very same verb, *kaṭṭu*, to bind or tie, is used to refer to the acts of depositing money (*paṇam kaṭṟatu*) and to be given in marriage (*kaṭṭikkoṭukkiṟatu*). These are both relationships of mutual obligation. Writing about "mutuality" in the caste-based division of labor in a Tamil village, Diane Mines describes lower-caste families as "'attached' or 'tied' (*kaṭṭu*) to certain [upper-caste] families" such that they have certain "responsibilities (*kaṭṭāyam* or *poruppu*) to those families or to the *ūr* [village] as a whole" (2005, 64).[26] This model of mutual or reciprocal responsibility contrasts with other modes of exchange, such as "*tāṉam*" (from the Sanskrit *dān*), through which faults or inauspiciousness can be transferred to service castes (ibid., 68–69; Raheja 1988).[27]

The women who had gathered for literacy class that evening had used this very language of unequal reciprocity, which is by no means limited to talk about caste or marriage, to talk about how they now had a "*kaṭṭāyam*" to sign their names, to pay (*kaṭṭu*) money into the collective account, and to attend literacy class. Other such responsibilities that would be called *kaṭṭāyam* might include fulfilling your community duties by performing certain rituals at a temple festival, or fulfilling your wifely duties to your husband and his family, for example. Any labor that must be done in response to such a call might be called a "*kaṭṭāyam.*" To break a *kaṭṭāyam* is to sever a relationship, such as when Dalits refuse to play their ritual role in temple festivals (a common mode of protest in Tamil Nadu). While not socially equal in any respect, these types of reciprocal relationships do not emphasize absolute subordination or the transfer of negative qualities as a *tāṉam* might (Mines 2005, 79, 99). The *kaṭṭāyam* is nevertheless quite different from the sort of agency exercised by a sovereign subject such as that imagined in the gender-awareness session that Neela had led among the younger and more highly educated women of Tuvarapatti.

Cintamani and her fellow group members had talked about writing their signatures on an official form using this language of unequal but reciprocal binding, and I would argue that women feel the sense of obligation or responsibility to respond more than men. Men somehow did not feel bound to respond in the same way when called, especially in a world where a certain "bullish" resistance to authority is so highly prized (Pandian 2009). While men certainly feel a sense of *kaṭṭāyam* in numerous contexts, they had not responded to Arivoli's calls to participate out of a sense of *kaṭṭāyam*. When I asked Karuppiah about why men had been difficult to mobilize as learners, he responded by telling me that men have "head weight" (*talai kaṇam*), meaning that their sense of self-importance is stronger than that of women and that they are less likely to listen to others. He and others who had worked for a long time as activists would often remark that there was something about the very newness of the public events carried out in the Arivoli Iyakkam that women responded to in a way that men did not. Having been socialized to respond to an invitation, but never invited to sign their names, the L.N. Puram self-help group found the fact of being directly addressed as members of a group and not as someone's wife or mother quite significant. Women also probably had more to gain in terms of social power by responding, but the sense of responsiveness at the root of mobilization seems to me to resist interpretations that would focus either on rational self-interest or appeals to traditional values. Nor does the idiom of "docility" quite capture what was happing in the Arivoli Iyakkam.

As I have already mentioned, the very fact of holding Arivoli group meetings in public spaces was constantly invoked by villagers, especially women, when asked about changes that have come about as a result of the movement. Much of the Arivoli Iyakkam was really about occupying public space in response to a call from trusted activists, illustrating the degree to which social-movement politics work through affective connections (Goodwin, Jasper, and Polletta 2001; Staiger, Cvetkovich, and Reynolds 2010). Neela had become a "big sister" to the women of L.N. Puram and so could not be ignored when she asked them to hold lessons and to sign their names. The Mahalir Arivoli Iyakkam was indeed founded through categories of governmentality that had taken on dimensions that could not be anticipated through a simple theory of governmentality. In the words of Partha Chatterjee describing a different struggle among slum dwellers, "the categories of governmentality were being invested with the imaginative qualities of community, including its capacity to invent relations of kinship, to produce a new, even if somewhat hesitant, rhetoric of political claims" (2004, 60). One of the less noticed effects was the fact that a whole generation of women can now sign their names, even if they can do very little else by way of reading and writing.[28]

Concluding Reflection on Interpellation and "Self-Help"

Interpellation was effective in the Arivoli Iyakkam primarily because it could invoke this sort of sense of responsibility among women only when a fellow villager whom members of a self-help group had come to know quite well over the years, someone like Neela, was doing the calling. Perhaps "interpellation" is not even an appropriate term to characterize women's responses to being repeatedly called in such a fashion. Arivoli activism derived power through a form of address that is structured somewhat differently than Louis Althusser's (1994) classic model of interpellation. In his essay on ideology, Althusser develops an important argument about the capacity for state ideologies to be reproduced through the production of docile subjects across a wide set of social domains, ranging from the family, the church, the trade union, on to the political party. In this limited sense, he anticipates Foucault's argument about the socially dispersed nature of what would later be called "governmentality," and he helps us understand how state power is inscribed in ritual behavior, extending deeply into the realm of the "private." But Althusser's most powerful and memorable image of how such modern subject formation operates at a quotidian level is that of an anonymous policeman calling someone on the street. The person who has been so hailed, or "interpellated," turns around, recognizing that it is he who has been called, and it is indeed the fact that interpellation is speech addressed to a stranger that makes this example of an imaginary identification with the state so powerful.

In contrast, Arivoli worked precisely through modes of address that are more fundamentally mediated by direct interpersonal relationships, often through idioms of kinship, and not by impersonal agents of the state as in Althusser's classic allegory. Neela had been cultivating a relationship with the L.N. Puram self-help group over the course of years, coming at least once a week by bus to visit, chat, and share meals with these women. Murugan's visit to the self-help group in which he extolled the virtues of Tamil womanhood would probably not have had the effect of binding women to the movement, unless he was someone they had come to know and to feel obligated to. Successful hailing of this sort is built over time, through repeated visits and not through the logic or even the emotional pull of a quick speech given by someone who has just arrived by jeep from Pudukkottai Town. Even when calling people to work for the betterment of abstractions like "society," or when encouraging women to draw an Arivoli *ḳōlam*, Arivoli volunteers had begun to realize that women were, in some deep sense, responding to them as known people and fictive kin, and not necessarily as representatives of a social movement or government program.

Tamilcelvan is among those intellectuals of the Arivoli movement who had come to understand how his activism worked through such direct personal relations of reciprocity. Such an understanding, he explains in his memoirs, could come only when he had begun to question his own presuppositions about personhood and social action by learning from those he sought to mobilize. "Through their very life-breath, these villagers melted the impurities in our [his and his fellow activists'] hearts, without having learned the trickery of the world we had learned to inhabit" (Tamilcelvan 2004b, 24). Tamilcelvan, whose method had once been to make "thumbprints" feel guilty for not participating in the story of national progress "and to use that feeling" (18, see also chapter 1), learned through experience that the women who attended Arivoli classes did so for a very different reason:

> It was only through visiting again and again and developing intimacy with villagers that I understood: they joined Arivoli without a single guilty feeling in their hearts. They came to study only because our Arivoli volunteers came day after day to call on them, and our Arivoli volunteers themselves had become children of the village [*ūr*]. It was only after a very long time that we understood that people were coming to lessons, out of the kindness of their hearts, to help *us*. (24–25)

The Arivoli Iyakkam managed to mobilize tens of thousands of villagers because these women were responding to a call from young activists, who had become like children of the village, by attending lessons. We can see here that the "help" being given is to the activists themselves, not from some "self" that exists prior to the relationship that had developed through repeated calling in this fashion. The gap between the Arivoli Iyakkam and the villagers it sought to educate that activists consistently commented on had as much to do with senses of personhood and social action as it did with senses of place and time.

But it is not only the literacy movement that attracted learners through such hailing. Women are increasingly bound in a new relationship with a wide range of bureaucratic institutions, including the state, banks, and other NGOs, through direct personal relationships. We can thus also appreciate the degree to which governmentality and statecraft, in this context, worked through the devolution of calling/inviting functions perhaps more than through the dissemination of literacy primers like *Cakti*. This was a devolution of the capacity to establish "*kaṭṭāyam*" to people in institutions (banks and state development bureaucracies) that operate at an extravillage and even extraregional level. It was the *fact* of being called rather than the content that seemed to matter to most women in the Arivoli Iyakkam. Massive social changes are thus wrought through accumulated acts of personal hailing, but the more specific capillary power to form liberal, self-measuring subjects remained underdetermined and relatively thin at the ends. We will now turn to see how more radical visions of empowerment were equally subject to underdetermination in the practice of literacy pedagogy. It was through this sort of self-help group and this very sense of obligation that Karuppiah, whom we met in the previous chapter, was eventually able to organize literacy lessons in the village of Katrampatti, just across the fields from his home.

3

Labors of Objectification

Words and Worlds of Pedagogy

Karuppiah conducted literacy lessons in the Dalit village of Katrampatti a few nights every week for about one year. Lessons were held outside, under a dim streetlamp by the side of a dirt road in the center of the hamlet. Some of his students were women he had known well his whole life as workers in the fields and as fictive kin. Some had only recently moved into the village after marrying one of its residents. Many of the older women remembered Karuppiah as a boy, from working on his family's rice fields. He was one of the few from the caste-Hindu settlements who would come play with their children, often receiving punishment at home for spending so much time with Dalits. He was a "*tampi*" (younger brother) to most of the women who attended classes. It was through literacy lessons that he hoped to develop a new relationship to them.

Although Katrampatti sits just across the paddy fields from Karuppiah's village of Kovilpatti, social conditions in this colony were quite different. Most of the women toiled as daily-wage earners in the surrounding fields, while many of the men worked as fishmongers in the market or for one of the musical troupes that play at weddings in the nearby town. All of the women in Katrampatti above the age of twenty-five, and a few below that age, were unable to read or write. The majority of the younger women and men had gone to school at least to the lower-secondary level; but a number had failed the important tenth standard exam and then dropped out of school to work in the fields or to find jobs in town. There is a clear generational divide in literacy skills because more children are now going to school. Dalit hamlets such as Katrampatti nevertheless felt left behind in comparison to the progress that caste-Hindu villages had experienced in the last decade.

The literacy lessons that Karuppiah conducted in Katrampatti, however, were very different from the style of schooling that children undergo. Karuppiah used the Arivoli Iyakkam's methods devised for adult education. This critical pedagogy had been adopted from the *Pedagogy of the Oppressed* (1970) first developed by Paulo Freire, the Brazilian philosopher and educational adviser to the World Council of Churches. In the Freirean method used by the Arivoli Iyakkam, literacy is not reduced to an ability to decode and employ written script. Literacy is instead taken to refer to the development of self-aware human subjects. Written language is a means used in this broader developmental process. True literacy, for Freire, is synonymous with the work of what he calls "*concientização*" (1970, 67), a cultivation of one's awareness, humanity, and freedom. Tamil activists working in this tradition use the term "*viḻippuṇarvu*" (awakened consciousness) to capture this quality that is to be developed through adult literacy education. Such enlightened persons would be made aware of their position in a larger social system, more free than they were before to reflect on social facts, and contrastively, on themselves as agentive subjects. It was through Arivoli lessons, for example, that Karuppiah expected to discuss issues of class oppression with the women he had known until then as lower-caste neighbors, workers, and extended kin.

Lessons in Katrampatti began at night as the women finished cooking and eating their dinner, after a day's work in the fields. Karuppiah would tell the children of the hamlet to go call their mothers, aunts, and sisters, and he would sometimes need to go down the street to each house himself, pleading with learners to attend. He would then wait for everyone under the streetlamp at the end of the street near the now-abandoned public television room. Some of the older men of the village would also sit on the front verandas of houses at the end of the street and chat with Karuppiah while chewing tobacco, betel leaf, and areca nut. A couple of households in Katrampatti had been given free television sets in exchange for their votes in the previous election, and apart from simple exhaustion, the temptation to fall asleep in front of a movie at home or at a neighbor's house proved too strong for many to resist. Those ten to twelve women who did attend fairly regularly did so mainly out of a sense of obligation that they should reciprocate the affection that Karuppiah alone would show by crossing the fields, not to call them for work, but simply to talk, sing songs, and conduct lessons. Some of the older women questioned their very capacity to learn to read and write. They attended primarily because Karuppiah had asked them to.

Arivoli classes always started with friendly chatter about the day's work and with questions about the health of everyone's family. My presence as an ethnographer studying, not only literacy in Arivoli Iyakkam, but also Tamil culture, often prompted Karuppiah to ask one of the women to sing a folk song so that I could record it. He was as keen as I was to collect these songs, knowing that younger generations were not very familiar with them. The women of Katrampatti are known to be better singers than their higher-caste counterparts in Kovilpatti, and it had become a matter of pride to maintain this reputation. Often, before lessons began, I would play the song recorded at the previous lesson back to the assembled group. They were happy to hear their voices on tape, although somewhat surprised that I should want to bring these recorded songs back with me to share with others. Karuppiah often said with deliberately overstated enthusiasm, "Your voices are going all the way to America, so sing well!" and everyone would laugh.

On one such occasion, Govindammal, one of those who had gathered for the lesson, asked, "Where is that? Is America near Delhi?" To this, Chitra jumped in, "No, it's out past Sri Lanka." The three young women from Katrampatti who helped Karuppiah during lessons rolled their eyes at their mothers' ignorance of geography. Karuppiah had a different reaction. He saw this line of questioning as an opportunity to teach them about the world outside the village and about science. He explained to the group that America is on the other side of the earth, and that when it is daytime in Katrampatti, it is nighttime over there. He looked at his watch, seeing that it was nine thirty at night and said, "Frank's mom and dad are just waking up and having their morning meal now. For them, it's morning!" This started a whole discussion of how that could possibly be, which lasted for some fifteen minutes. Karuppiah tried to show them how the movement of sunlight around the earth works, using a cricket ball under the streetlamp. But many of the women remained unconvinced. He then promised that he would bring in a globe from the Tamil Nadu Science Forum office in Pudukkottai Town, and the group turned to practicing their signatures. One week later, Karuppiah organized a demonstration in front of the temple gate that was attended by the literacy group and their children. Using a flashlight, he showed them where the United States is and explained how the sun's light moves around the earth to produce daylight on one side of the globe when it is night on the other side.

This little event illustrates Arivoli Iyakkam activists' style of propagating scientific reasoning in the context of literacy lessons. Karuppiah's demonstration also shows the degree to which lessons about written language and a broader pedagogy of scientific objectification had been fused in the movement. In later stages, literacy primers were used to give explicit lessons in geography, environment, and physical science. But even in these initial stages of literacy training, Karuppiah would seize on learners' curiosity about a fact they had previously never considered, and use this curiosity as a means of teaching them about their place in a world that had been newly objectified for their contemplation.[1]

Although the emphasis on scientific objectivism had been more greatly elaborated in the South Indian avatar of Freirean thought than in other contexts, this sort of exercise does extend an important phenomenological theme at the center of Freire's theory of consciousness and freedom: subjects understand themselves to be agents through processes of objectification. Drawing on a tradition of Hegelian dialectics, and citing Jean-Paul Sartre, Freire elaborates, "The world which brings consciousness into existence becomes the world *of* that consciousness. . . . Thus men and women begin to single out elements from their 'background awareness' and to reflect upon them. These elements are now objects of their consideration, and, as such, objects of their action and cognition" (1970, 82–83).[2] In the vignette recounted above, it is the earth itself, and its movement around the sun, that are meant to be the objects of reflection. The "world," both as a physical object and, as we will see shortly, as a set of social relations, once objectified as a world *of* consciousness, may then become an object of action.

Like the globe standing in for an objectified world, the Arivoli Iyakkam emphasized the use of particular *written words* in literacy lessons to refer to the world of social relations so as to alter learners' sense of subjectivity. It was not only in science demonstrations but in their theoretical orientation to language as well that the literacy movement was invested in the objectification of the world. In fact, writing has often served as the paradigmatic tool for this sort of modernist self-abstraction and distanciation. In sketching the structural contours of what he calls the "'modern' mythical practice" of writing, for instance, Michel de Certeau explains, "This is a modern Cartesian move of making a distinction that initiates . . . the mastery (and isolation) of a subject confronted by an *object*" (1984, 134, emphasis in original). Activist leaders in the Arivoli movement frequently cited Freire, when he describes this very process of subject formation as a "reading and writing of the world." Their pedagogy was therefore performed as a means of imparting literacy as a medium of objectification, and as a tool in the humanization process. Although Karuppiah started reading Freire seriously only while teaching these lessons, it was through his fifteen years of training as a member of the Tamil Nadu Science Forum and the Arivoli Iyakkam that he had already internalized this pedagogical methodology. In Katrampatti under Karuppiah's tutelage, written words, much like the globe he had shown his students, were designed to function as the triggers for this dialectic of objectification, subjectivization, and reflection in the performance of a dialogical pedagogy.

Writing, Objectification, and Freedom

How has writing become a primary sign of the modern and of the very ability to abstract from the immediacy of experience? Jacques Derrida (1976, 1988) has drawn attention to the manner in which writing is commonly thought of as a species within the general category of communication that is peculiar in its capacity to break with the context of its enunciation and thereby to represent a subject in absentia. He went further to explain that it is precisely this quality of writing that has led it to occupy a problematic role in a philosophical tradition premised on the metaphysics of presence and in models of communication founded on logocentric theories of meaning. But it is precisely this apparent freedom from determining context that makes writing the most appropriate medium for the exercise of subjective autonomy in the mythology of enlightened literacy.

The performative effects of writing are not wholly reducible to immediate contexts of production because written language is always subject to recontextualization, reproduction, and mass circulation.[3] This facet of language is manifest most obviously in the visual and tactile materiality of writing, and in the technologies of mass production associated with print, even if it is inherent to speech as well.[4] In fact, it is only through this lens of writing that speech appears as stable and excessively localized. As a "modern mythical practice," then, writing serves as both a model of, and a means to autonomy from, embodied experience. Writing, in this narrative, breaks the bonds of textual authority and appears to encourage reflection on one's self as a person because of the way it "separates itself from the magical world of tradition and voices" (de Certeau 1984, 134). In the Freirean system followed by the Arivoli Iyakkam, written language is how one separates one's self as a subject from the perception of "reality as dense, impenetrable, and enveloping . . . by means of abstraction" (Freire 1970, 105). Writing is the primary means by which one objectifies the world by "naming" it, "reading and writing the world," and mediating an abstraction of one's self from it. If objectification is a ubiquitous social process, taking place in ritual behavior or in everyday gift exchange, then it would seem that there is a particular type of objectification leading to the forms of critical social reflexivity that are valued by activists (see also Keane 2003, 422–23).

The Arivoli Iyakkam pedagogy based on this "modern mythical practice" used written language and pictures to spark oral dialogues on issues that are of concern to the movement's learners, people who were among the most socially disadvantaged and economically exploited in the countryside. Both written words and their accompanying drawings acted as what Freire calls "codifications," aspects of learners' lived reality that had been artificially decontextualized so as to encourage reflection. So, for example, the first written word one learned in the Arivoli Iyakkam is the Tamil word for "land deed," and this word was intended to act as a spark for critical discussions of land tenure. This is a form of objectification that was meant to have liberating effects. "As they separate themselves from the world, which they objectify, as they separate themselves from their own activity, as they locate the seat of their decisions in themselves and in their relations to the world and others, people overcome situations that limit them" (Freire 1970, 99). According to this pedagogy, the object presented before the thinking subject produces awareness not only of the object itself; it produces the conditions in which the subject may reflect on herself as a subject contemplating an object, enabling action and self-knowledge. In the Hegelian language favored by Freire and his followers, this theory of education argues that it is through processes of textual objectification that consciousness is externalized and turned back on itself so as to understand the true location of agency. But what did the movement make of alternative orientations to written language, knowledge, and learning? Are all forms of written language use equally suited to this project? What does this process look like in more concrete terms?

In previous chapters, I have already begun to analyze the privileged place of mass literacy in the logic of developmental democracy and space-time unification. Here, I address these questions about language in more detail through an examination of the specific pedagogical means by which literacy lessons attempted to extract subjects from their everyday orientations to the world. I also examine some of the problems raised by the movement's adoption of such a theory of language and personhood. First, the movement had to contend with different orientations to language and textuality that are deeply embedded in existing Tamil pedagogies. In the attempt to develop a radical pedagogy suited to awakening adults' sense of their own agency, the Arivoli Iyakkam used models of personhood and language that map only partially onto those that obtain among the movement's villager learners. Learners themselves provided a critique of the primers and pedagogy through questions they asked about the poetics of Tamil learning traditions and about how written language becomes memorable and meaningful. But there were also contradictions *within* the theory of literacy as enlightenment that were exposed through literacy lessons and the activism that surrounded them. The very modernist valuation of written language's capacity to mediate an abstraction from concrete realities, for example, tended to occlude the stubborn fact of literacy as a technique of the thoroughly socialized body. For anyone who has observed an adult literacy lesson it becomes quite evident that the capacity to read and write is not simply a mental or cognitive one. It requires physical training. The socialized human body is the existential ground on which any knowledge of language must be built. This was a lesson in the phenomenology of knowledge that was also imparted primarily by learners in the movement and learned by activists when facing the limits of their theory of language and liberation.

My investigation of pedagogy requires particular attention to a zone of overlap between theories of language and subjectivity that have served as models for activism and those that have influenced more scholastic approaches to questions of agency, consciousness, and textuality. A degree of shared ground presents certain difficulties for any ethnography that would

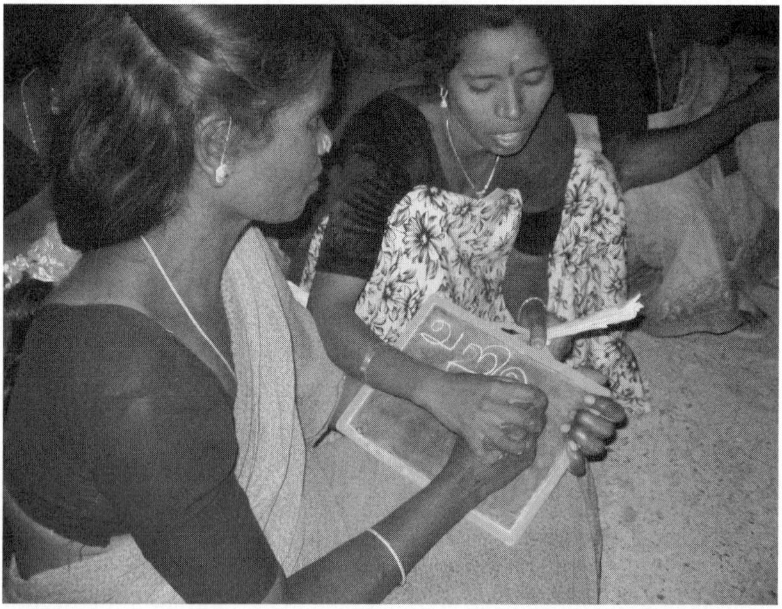

Figure 4. Embodying enlightenment: a young activist helps a fellow villager learn to write the word "Arivoli" (the light of knowledge). Photograph by the author.

seek to interrogate philosophy and social theory with contradictory facts and understandings gathered from "the field." In this case, Hegelian and Marxian philosophies of liberation had profoundly shaped orientations to language among literacy workers in rural Tamil Nadu. Nevertheless, activists' encounters with plurality in ideologies of language and subjectivity, made salient in the pedagogical encounter itself, do provide opportunities for points of critical interrogation. These points are extended through an ethnography of reflexivity regarding language and the contradictions of literacy as enlightenment among activists themselves, developed at greater length in the following chapter.

Dialectical Pedagogy in the Tamil Country

Paulo Freire's pedagogy has influenced adult education projects across the globe, and it has made an especially strong impact both on grassroots movements and on government policies across Latin America, Africa, and South Asia.[5] Whereas much of the research on Latin American literacy projects in the field of education has been concerned with whether this method actually induces progressive social change (e.g., Bartlett 2005; Gottlieb and La Belle 1990), work on Freirean projects in Nepal examines how they often have unintended consequences because of how they interact with different conceptions of gender and agency (Ahearn 2001; Leve 2007). The Arivoli Iyakkam's adoption of Freirean pedagogy in Tamil Nadu therefore involved a process that can be seen as the "localization" of a transnational project of critical literacy into a vernacular cultural world, similar to the way in which Sally Engle Merry (2006) conceives the localization of global human rights discourse. This pedagogy encourages a questioning of the power relations that are reproduced through existing local institutions of formal education, for example, while struggling to universalize a model of literacy-as-freedom. The lenses of "localization" or "vernacularization," however, might obscure the manner in which some basic premises of the Freirean pedagogy were constantly being reshaped through interactions with existing traditions of education and literacy and through contradictions within the project itself. Liberation and enlightenment are indeed widespread goals, pulling people to learn to read and write; but they remain goals with qualities that cannot be predetermined.

Analysis must therefore be attentive both to explicit theorizations of language commonly found in Tamil Nadu and to concepts presupposed in social action to understand how this dialogic pedagogy interacted with other conceptions of language and learning to produce novel forms in the course of activism.

To understand the new conjunctions that emerged in the application of Freirean methods in the rural Tamil context, and how the method itself was rethought, we should first examine how this model of education came to the villages of southern India from Brazil. Activists and academics first introduced Freire's style of adult literacy lessons on a small scale in a few Tamil villages in the 1970s. Siddhartha, one of the early leaders of this small, experimental movement, was a student of Louis Dumont in Paris, where he was first exposed, not only to structuralism and phenomenology, but also to radical student politics. In a 2005 essay, he recalls how he and his fellow activists in the South Indian leftist student movement, known as the "Free University," made Freire's thought known in India:

> [We] worked till the early hours of the morning to type onto stencils what was a pirated edition of Paulo Freire's classic *Pedagogy of the Oppressed*. By the end of the next day the first hundred copies of the book had rolled off the cyclostyling machine and were made available to discerning Indian readers. We had got a hold of the pirated book from the Philippines, a good many years before the Penguin volume was to appear in the local stores. At that time Freire's ideas on transformative education and political change made for heady reading, particularly to those of us who were young, angry and idealistic. (Siddhartha 2005, 84)

Through the course of 1980s, these pirated copies of Freire's books were copied and distributed through student groups and Left activist networks across South India. Paulo Freire also visited Bombay and Bangalore in the mid-1970s, where he met with a number of activists from the KSSP who would then develop his critical pedagogy in Kerala's literacy program. Several of his books have since been translated into the Tamil language.[6]

The founders of the Science Forums in Pondicherry and Tamil Nadu had been a part of this student network. They were especially attracted to Freire's critique of what he calls the "banking" method of formal education, in which knowledge is simply "deposited" into students rather than being co-constructed with teachers through critical dialogue. It was Dr. S. Madasamy, a former professor of adult education at Madurai Kamaraj University, who was among the most ardent Freireans in this group, leading him to design the Arivoli movement's literacy primers and teaching methodology along the lines of the Brazilian's critical pedagogy. Through the course of his career, Madasamy followed not only Freire's work but also Julius Nyerere's experiments in Tanzania and the educational policy of revolutionary Cuba. He explained the attractions and difficulties of developing the primers to me when I interviewed him in Chennai: "We took from Freire the idea that literacy is a 'reading and writing of the world,' and that learning to read and write is a way of raising consciousness [*viḻippuṇarvu*]. But this process is not so easy. We had to learn how to fit that into a Tamil context [*tamiḻ cūḻnilai*]." The introduction of this method into a Tamil context clearly raised a number of difficult issues, most of them the result of a rather different approach to language and learning that remains hegemonic in Tamil Nadu.

The theorist of education Krishna Kumar (1986, 2005) has argued that the "textbook-centered curriculum" in many Indian schools has colonial roots that continue to shape the perception of pedagogy as a civilizing process. Modern Tamil-language standardization efforts and purism have inherited these colonial structures of education and use them to somewhat different ends. Research in Tamil schools by R. Aruna (1999), for example, reveals harsh inequalities in the treatment of different Tamil dialects in relation to textbook-style written language, which favors high-caste linguistic forms, known as "*centamiḻ*" (high or refined Tamil) in the development of literacy skills. Standard written Tamil draws on an archaized literary language prized in schools and public culture for its refined beauty, its "*cemmai*," a quality that distinguishes the language of education from the "*koccaittamiḻ*" (vulgar Tamil) of lower-caste villagers. Tamil formal schooling systems therefore emphasize the unifying power of a standardized written language as a mode of social reproduction separate from the world of speech and everyday practical experience. To learn to read and write in school is also to learn a different and more highly prized variety of Tamil.[7] It is to become a more cultivated person, not necessarily through critical reflections on social life but through the internalization of a hoary tradition that reaches back into the ancient past.

It is these understandings of the function of literacy that the Arivoli Iyakkam sought to define itself against, precisely because language in this system does not mediate a dialectic producing human subjects and a world they are able to change. Language is, instead, a means of reproducing social domination and "depositing" information in schools, according to activists. In the words of Sundari, a literacy activist I came to know well in Pudukkottai, "In school they only memorize with the goal of passing [exams]. Even those holding advanced degrees are unable to talk about any other subject or to relate their education to their lives. But Arivoli is about many things. . . . We teach them about politics [*araciyal*]. Teaching literacy is only one side; we also give them awakened consciousness [*viḻippuṇarvu koṭukkiṟōm*]." Like Madasamy, she emphasized the politics of consciousness-raising as something that distinguishes Freirean and Arivoli literacy from that taught in schools. In teaching literacy as a means to cultivate a sense of agency, the Arivoli Iyakkam therefore found itself in opposition to dominant orientations to written language. This opposition, in turn, raised the question of what it meant to import a globally circulating philosophy of literacy-as-freedom if the very subjects of freedom in rural Tamil Nadu often hold different orientations to written language and perhaps to the question of freedom itself. The dialogical method served to raise these questions regarding the models of language and subject formation that underpin Freire's very philosophy of education. It is to this contradictory pedagogical process and to the production of reflexivity in the practice of education that we now turn by means of a return to the literacy lessons Karuppiah conducted among the women of Katrampatti.

"Reading and Writing the World" in the Village of Katrampatti

The nighttime Arivoli Iyakkam lessons in Katrampatti typically began with talk, stories, or a basic science demonstration like the one described above. Sometimes Karuppiah would discuss some article he had read in the newspaper that day and ask the women about their opinions on the topic at hand. Then, after ten or fifteen minutes of such discussion and singing while waiting for everyone to arrive, accompanied by some less focused talk about the day's work or some other local news, Karuppiah would shift frames and say, "OK, shall we begin the lesson now?" He expected the more important forms of dialogic pedagogy to take place in the literacy lesson itself. The first sounds one heard when the Arivoli literacy lesson had officially begun in Katrampatti, as in other villages in Pudukkottai, were "*paṭṭā . . . pa, iṭṭ, ṭā . . . paṭṭā.*" Following the Freirean method, the teacher started with a familiar word, in this case the noun, "*paṭṭā*" (land deed). The word itself was supposed to spark conversation. After talking about the object named by the word, the teacher would then break that word down into constitutive sounds, corresponding to the letters (ப,ட்,டா) (*pa,ṭ,ṭā*) in this case, and then she or he would reiterate the word. This was done while either pointing to the word as spelled on a makeshift blackboard or pointing to it in the *Aṟivoḷi Tīpam* (Lamp of Enlightenment) literacy primer book. Learners were told to write the word out themselves with chalk or with their fingers in the dirt, and then to repeat it orally.

In the first phases of literacy training, Arivoli lessons were centered on the meaning of words. They might be said to be lexicocentric. The meaning of literacy as a liberating critical consciousness was designed, in the lesson primer, to be established through words and pictures, well before learners were expected to know the whole of the Tamil alphasyllabary. The first *Aṟivoḷi Tīpam* primer in a series of three, which were designed to be taught over the course of one year, focuses exclusively on learning individual words. It is only in the later primers, which few study groups go on to master, that sentences and short stories are introduced. The hope is that learners will come to share the same orientation to words from the very beginning of their education, a proper alignment to text in which written words are liberating windows onto a new world shared by teachers and learners. It was in this early moment that the pedagogical process already ran into productive difficulties. To apprehend the precise nature of these difficulties, I first describe the text of the primer as it was meant to be taught, and then move on to a description of issues that arose in the Katrampatti literacy lessons.

Teaching from the Lamp of Enlightenment

Karuppiah had learned his pedagogical techniques through training programs held regularly at the Arivoli Iyakkam headquarters in the collector's office and at subregional training camps held by the Tamil Nadu Science Forum.[8] In these training sessions volunteer teachers like Karuppiah were taught by "master trainers" from the literacy movement that words in this pedagogy are a weapon (*āyutam*) in grasping and eventually changing the world through the production of awakened consciousness (*viḻippuṇarvu*) and a corollary self-confidence (*taṉṉampikkai*). Teachers were thus expected to socialize learners to this very orientation to written words in relation to selfhood, in addition to teaching how to read and write the words themselves. Literacy as greater self-understanding was also inevitably tied to nation building and "a social perspective," as discussed in the previous chapters. Training sessions for volunteer teachers, held about once every two months, emphasized Arivoli's philosophy not only that literacy is a functional tool that can be used for immediately given ends, but that it is mainly about developing self-awareness and an attitude that the learner can change things for a better future.

The front cover of the *Aṟivoḷi Tīpam* primer that was used in the Mahalir Arivoli Iyakkam depicts the Pudukkottai district collector teaching a group of women how to read and write. The state, as patron of enlightened education and empowering knowledge, is thus physically represented in this cover photo. Yet in the very structure of the *Aṟivoḷi Tīpam* primer one can find traces of the struggle to inject revolutionary pedagogy into a government development program. The first pages of the primer were designed by activists to tell a different story of class struggle. The Science Forum literacy activists who designed the *Aṟivoḷi Tīpam* primers for adult literacy chose the word *"paṭṭā"* (land deed) as the first word to teach, because it is easy to spell and, more important for the authors, because it refers to the document that separates those who own the means of production in this agricultural area from those who do not. The learners in Arivoli tended to fall into the latter category, and that is very much the point: to make this social category explicit as a platform for discussion. Not surprisingly, land deeds are a subject of much concern in rural Tamil Nadu, especially for landless laborers like those in Katrampatti who made up the bulk of Arivoli's learners, and for many of their volunteer teachers as well. Most petitions made to the local administrative offices, for example, concern land deeds in some form or another, and the document itself would seem to stand as a material testament to the power of inscription over people. The choice of the word *"paṭṭā"* in Arivoli's first lesson is emblematic of the movement taken as whole. It might promise both a radical critique of extant unequal social relations as mediated through property, while simultaneously binding the promise of freedom to a state-regulated variety of writing.

This pedagogical technique uses what Freire calls a "codification" of the lived experience of the learner, made clear and distinct as an object of consciousness, so that it might be "decoded." "Codifications are the *objects* which mediate the decoders in their critical analysis. . . . In the process of decoding, the participants externalize their thematics and thereby make explicit their 'real consciousness' of the world" (Freire 1970, 114–15, emphasis in the original). Codifications can take the form of words, longer texts, pictures, or songs. Codification in the case of the literacy primer takes the form of what Freire calls a "generative word" and an accompanying picture. The word "*paṭṭā,*" (land deed) had been plucked from a naturalized discourse to be brought to the level of an explicit consciousness-*of*. The very experience of deprivation is supposed to be objectified and abstracted from everyday life, detached as a text, so as to be available to explicit critical reflection, an act of recontextualization. The strategy is to entail a novel relationship between the learning subject and an objectified social world, which has been represented for reflection.

The word "*paṭṭā*" is followed in the literacy primer by another generative word, or "codification," the verbal root and command form "*paṭi*" (read). A large drawing of a man holding a land registration document accompanies these words. He stands in front of abundant fields, which presumably belong to him by virtue of the very document named in writing (figure 5).[9] After introducing the word, first by means of the drawing, and then by spelling it out, and finally sounding it out syllable by syllable, the volunteer teacher was expected to continue the first lesson by asking what a land deed is. Teachers might then ask what types of people have a land deed and who does not. Discussion is then supposed to move on to the topic of why not everybody possesses a land deed.

The second lesson in Arivoli Iyakkam presents a contrast, inviting the learner to compare it with the first. In this lesson, the words "*paci*"

Figure 5. The first page, lesson 1, of the Aṟivoḷi Tīpam literacy primer used in Pudukkottai District in 2004.

(hunger) and "*maṉitaṉ*" (human being) are accompanied by an illustration of a visibly poor family with an empty dinner plate and an empty water pot (figure 6). The man's ribs are showing, and both he and his wife look distressed. The world of the laborer depicted in the second lesson is supposed to act in a manner that would invoke a contrastive reality, by pointing back to the first lesson. The simultaneity of unequal landownership and

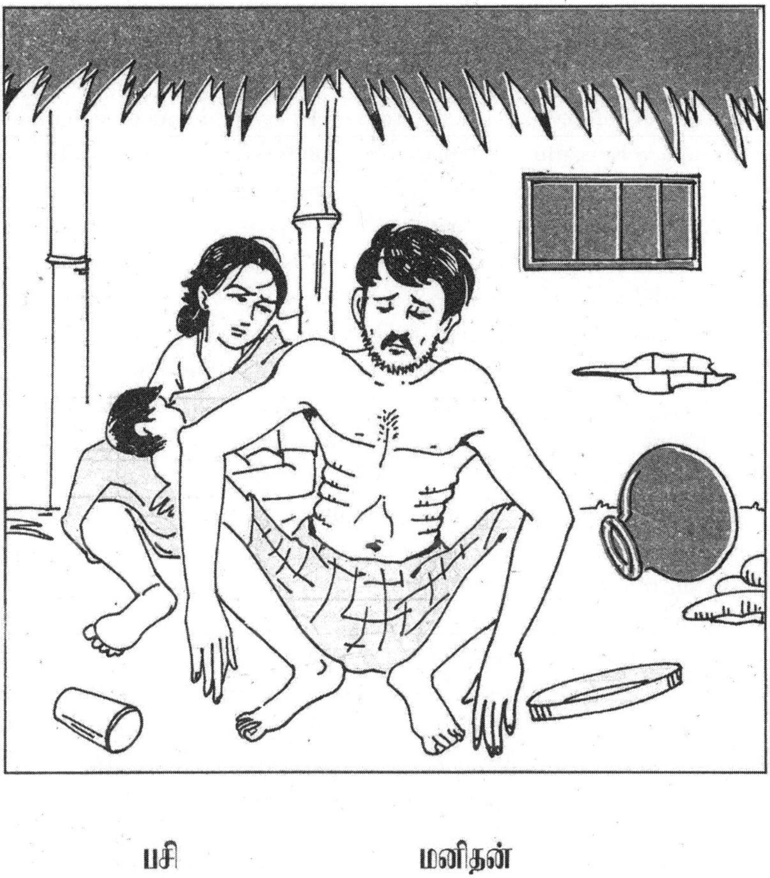

Figure 6. The second lesson of the Aṟivoḷi Tīpam literacy primer used in Pudukkottai District in 2004.

a hungry humanity is made visible in the picture and the text, implying a causal connection.

Truly literate subjects, in the Freirean sense of literacy envisaged by the designers of *Aṟivoḷi Tīpam*, would be subjects who would take an explicit evaluative stance in response to these words and pictures as objectifications. More accurately, they would have to take a stance on the very lived reality referred to and objectified by these codifications. One must "name the world" in order to produce one's self as a free subject. Freire elaborates, "The world—no longer something to be described with deceptive words—becomes the object of that transforming action by men and women which results in their humanization" (1970, 67). Deceptive words, which would enforce a silence regarding relations of domination, naturalizing euphemisms, must be replaced by problematizing authentic appellations. In naming the world, the learner realigns her relationship to it such that "the world" becomes something "out there" that is subject to understanding and change. "Humankind *emerge* from their *submersion* and acquire the ability to *intervene* in their reality as it is unveiled" (109, emphases in the original). This is the process of humanization at work in the naming process. Freire's philosophy of education works within a theory of transcendence also insofar as it is founded on the figure of the ultimately free subject, and premised on the possibility of true correspondence between the word and the world.

This narrative of liberation is logocentric, but not in Derrida's (1976) sense of privileging speech over writing. This liberation pedagogy works on the opposite assumption that writing embodies the promise of freedom more fully than speech. The Freirean pedagogy adopted by the Arivoli Iyakkam is logocentric in Derrida's much more generalized sense of a semiotic in the service of a meaning that would transcend, or exist somehow prior to, phenomenal sign activity. The concrete form of written language is supplementary, not to speech, but to a "writing of the world," as the praxis of a pure subject. It is this promise of transcendence that makes it very difficult for Freire to address what is specific to written language or even language in general. It is the human that stands at the center of this system, and the socially specific forms of written language in use are always subordinate to the forms of world-disclosing textuality attributed to "the word." The "word" exhibits a freedom from context, which allows for what Paul Ricoeur (1991) would call a "distanciation" productive of a "world," on the one hand, and a correspondingly freer subject of self-understanding, on the other, one who can act on this world. Written words are key to liberation and to the humanizing project in this tradition of thought precisely because of their capacity for world-disclosing meaning, which can transcend any particular context of enunciation.[10]

What had been circulated in South Indian activists' photocopying and distribution of Freire's works is not only a pedagogical method but also a whole orientation to words as world-disclosing texts, derived from this philosophical tradition.[11] The pedagogy, if it was to work, must hit an already sore mark, an invocation of discontent and personhood assumed to be there but submerged so as to "rehumanize" the subject (Gottlieb and La Belle 1990). But this performance was also meant to entail a radically new frame in which learners are treated as extracted subjects who are free to discuss what seemed natural prior to the pedagogic encounter by means of written words as textual generators. In fact, the felicitous performance of this pedagogy would demand a strong negation of those social regularities that are lived as natural by learners. Such a desired uptake by learners was not so easily achieved.

The Rough Texture of Lessons

For the women who came to Arivoli lessons in the village of Katrampatti, the choice of words used to introduce literacy appeared for the most part arbitrary. It is true that the letters used to spell "*paṭṭā*" (பட்டா) employ no curved lines and they were therefore easy to draw in the dirt or on a small slate while sitting under the dim streetlight. Although usually very tired after a long day of work, the women of Katrampatti dutifully wrote the words "*paṭṭā*" and "*paṭi*" over and over again, two or three nights every week for a month. They did so while sounding out the word and then the syllables as they were told to by Karuppiah. They persisted in their literacy exercises while the chalk piece sat uncomfortably in their hands. The learners' children, many of whom were learning to read and write at the nearby government school, would be anxious to jump in and help. But the revolutionary discussion of property relations never quite happened.

Every time Karuppiah tried to inject politics into the first literacy lessons, asking them what a *paṭṭā* is, and why only some families have one, the learners would change the subject or joke sarcastically. A favorite retort I heard in Katrampatti and elsewhere was "Why? Are you going to give us one?" This reply marks difference between teachers and learners, but in the case of Katrampatti, it took on added meaning because of the caste difference between Karuppiah and his pupils. He belonged to the landowning Kallars, and the students belonged to those who work for his family. On a few occasions I witnessed in other villages, when the attempt at Freirean dialogue was extended beyond learners' patience, I heard students respond to the questions about land deeds with an exclamatory, "I've never even *seen* a land deed!" effectively telling the teacher to drop the subject. When responding like this, learners were questioning, not only the choice of generative words, but more important, the very presuppositions of the generative word technique as an extractor of subjects from objects. These are presuppositions that would have to be shared for the performative effect of "naming the world" to work. The Katrampatti group refused to play along with the Freirean script, in which they perhaps perceived a degree of condescension in being asked about a document they could never hope to have. In fact, many Dalits in the area would much rather leave the rural agricultural context altogether, and move to a city where their caste would have less bearing on their lives (many of the young men of Katrampatti have done just that). The connection between this written noun and a whole set of social concerns regarding landownership, class, and caste inequality was difficult to establish.

Although the Dalits of Katrampatti were often critical of how they were treated as poor laborers who were dependent on landowners for work, and as members of a caste that faces numerous forms of discrimination and abuse in their everyday speech, the context of a literacy lesson did not easily lend itself to the discussion that the framers of Arivoli had hoped would take place. Karuppiah was in the role of a teacher, and attempts to build solidarity across the teacher-learner divide on this particular topic seemed inappropriate. Furthermore, the Katrampatti learners' everyday complaints about the village labor regime would more often be expressed to outsiders in terms of specific employers' obligations to them not met, rather than in the terms of an abstracted, generic criticism of land tenure.[12] It was the latter form of critique that many in the Arivoli Iyakkam's leadership—and the many volunteers who, like Karuppiah, thought of their work in political terms—hoped to generate through the discussion of land deeds.

Karuppiah was the eldest son of one of the women's traditional Kallar employers in the village, adding an extra degree of awkwardness to the question of property ownership. While Karuppiah's caste background may have shaped the learners' response, I must add that I observed similar responses among several literacy groups composed of Dalit workers in which the teacher was also a Dalit woman and in a very similar socioeconomic position as the learners. The lack of uptake on the part of learners, if not necessarily peppered with defiant sarcasm, is common across many contexts. Many teachers and coordinators have confirmed the widespread nature of this reception of the Arivoli text. I have also sat in on many Arivoli literacy classes in which the volunteer teacher did not even try to initiate a Freirean dialogue on the topics of land deeds and hunger. Most teachers confirmed my observations in Katrampatti and elsewhere, reporting to me how students would ask why they are learning these words when they would rather start by learning how to sign their own names.

Dalits in Katrampatti were most likely to frame their complaints of caste domination and exploitation in terms of access to local power structures connected to the village temple. Having won access to worship at the popular Nadiyamman temple in the 1960s, the Dalit community in Katrampatti and in neighboring villages had, by the 1990s, begun to demand representation on the temple board of trustees. The community had also begun to demand that they be given rights to sponsor a day of worship and a free lunch for devotees, as the other caste communities have in the past two decades.[13] They worked for the temple and felt that they should be allowed to sponsor worship there. However, the caste-Hindus of the main settlements surrounding the temple had always roundly refused to grant these rights to the Dalit community. While I was in the field, there was talk among Dalits of protesting this form of casteism by refusing to play their ritual roles during the festival season, a common mode of protest in Tamil India. A number of Dalit-specific rituals traditionally held around the temple on other occasions had already ceased to be performed in the years immediately preceding my fieldwork period.

Another, more subtle mode of articulating public narratives that would question the legitimacy of upper-caste domination was through storytelling and songs. As with the songs that have been collected in Chingleput District by Margaret Trawick (1986, 1991), songs and stories told by Dalit women in Katrampatti had come to define the very mythological world in which the goddess Nadiyamman lives.[14] While the songs that Trawick analyzes contained veiled metaphors that then circulated in a wider social sphere, in Katrampatti it was through the narrative of how Nadiyamman became a goddess who favored the Dalit community, as exemplified in stories surrounding the temple, that the residents of Katrampatti questioned aspects of the caste order. Dalits claim that Nadiyamman herself is a fellow Dalit. This was a claim that some caste-Hindus begrudgingly agreed to, because it is the only authoritative origin story for the goddess, but that others find impossible to accept, because it places their very caste dominance at risk. But such stories about gods were not easily taken up by activists who would seek to cultivate a distinctively secular-humanist form of agency. It was only when activists encountered failure in their more radically humanist critical endeavors that they began to take up folklore as a resource for critical literacy pedagogy, a move I discuss in the following chapter.

If the learners were skeptical of learning through codifying their lived experience, why did they turn up for literacy lessons at all? I have already noted that the learners from Katrampatti had come to lessons largely out of a sense of obligation to Karuppiah, a young man who had made the effort to invite them personally before every lesson. But learning to write one's own name was also among the most compelling reasons pulling people to participate in the literacy program. We have already seen in the previous chapter how a sense of obligation and the act of learning to sign one's name were connected in the context of self-help groups. This particular form of literacy offered immediate satisfaction, and served as a basis for learners to associate literacy both with the fulfillment of a duty and with the self-confidence so valued in Arivoli discourse. It is also the basic form of literacy that could be developed in these early stages of pedagogy that is most clearly connected to notions of empowerment, citizenship, and self-representation as literate interaction with the state, a topic I take up in greater depth in chapter 5. The next step in lessons after learning to sign one's name would be to learn to spell the names of their respective villages. This often happened, as it did in Katrampatti, in parallel with the "*paṭṭā, paṭi*" lesson.

In Katrampatti, where the learners were relatively patient with Karuppiah's political intentions, it took months of "*paṭṭā . . . pa, iṭṭ, ṭā . . . paṭṭā*" before they even broached the subject of land for a cremation ground they had long been demanding of the village panchayat, a request that required possession of this very document whose name they had been reciting and spelling out incessantly. That discussion eventually did turn to this topic of great importance to the learners in the context of a literacy lesson, after nearly four months of effort, was in fact a major political breakthrough. That this discussion arose, however, and that the learners were eventually persuaded by Karuppiah to file a petition to the district government, is not concretely linked to the use of *paṭṭā* as a generative word. Karuppiah learned about this problem through more personal conversations with learners at the beginning of lessons, before moving on to the primer. It was also through discussion with other villagers from Katrampatti that this problem took on salience as a topic to be addressed through petitioning. The decision to take action, and make a demand for land through writing, did not immediately arise out of the generative word techniques of the primer. This decision was made, instead, as a result of the new social form of the literacy group that had been enabled by the Arivoli Iyakkam. In other villages, where the teachers were not already well known to the learners, I have heard of villagers turning hostile when talk turned to politics, even to the point of physical threats against Arivoli activists.

Other than the difficulties of persuading learners that generative words could successfully make them agents, Karuppiah faced another basic challenge. Unschooled, but not ignorant of how schooling works, the Arivoli learners of Katrampatti often wondered why Karuppiah kept going on about land deeds when he was supposed to be teaching them to read and write. The Freirean pedagogy demands attention to experience so that one may break with it, to treat it as an object for reflection. However, this break with experience is not an obvious value for the learners. Literacy was, to them, mainly about signing your name on documents and learning to read the signs on buses. The learners of Katrampatti were in a position where they had perhaps learned to be ashamed of being "illiterate," but they were not convinced that a group discussion of land deeds would amount to anything worthwhile. It was, in fact, the learners who made a demand for what is known in state development circles as "functional literacy." They wanted to learn how to sign their names and how to write the name of their village. Teachers were left with no good response to the questions students ask them, and quickly moved on to the more immediate, though still difficult, task of teaching the letters that make up the learner's names and the generative words. After encountering this resistance to engage in a discussion along the lines intended by the primer's structure, Karuppiah quickly dropped his questions invoking general class conflict and focused on teaching the script.

"It Just Won't Stand in My Mind"

Rajalakshmi, known to everyone affectionately as "Bappi," was, in her midfifties, oldest among the Katrampatti learners and the leader of their work group in the rice fields. She was regarded as one of the most knowledgeable and skilled singers of work and religious songs in the area and has always been very fond of Karuppiah. Rajalakshmi had worked under his family for her entire married life, ever since moving to Katrampatti from another nearby Dalit hamlet. When he was a child, Karuppiah would spend much of his free time at her house in the Katrampatti colony, and he had grown up with her own children. Her daughter and her two sons had all completed their basic schooling in nearby village schools. They had all three moved to the metropolitan city of Chennai, in an effort to escape rural poverty and the everyday injustices that come with being a Dalit in a farming community. While Rajalakshmi had never set foot in a school, her husband, Velan, was an elderly man who had developed a voracious reading habit with only two years of formal schooling. He had spent much of his life working on plantations in Kerala and as a daily-wage worker in the fields of Pudukkottai. The two of them lived alone and received their children once or twice every year for Deepavali or the local temple festival.

Rajalakshmi seemed very unsure that she would ever be able to read and write, and I suspect that she participated in the lessons in large part because of her fondness for Karuppiah. Although she eventually did learn how to sign her name, she often complained, like many of the older women in Arivoli lessons, that she could not see properly and that it was difficult to make out differences between letters. Rajalakshmi could not afford eyeglasses and she refused offers made by Karuppiah and others to help her buy a pair. But vision was not her only problem. There was also something about the way they were learning the script that she found difficult to retain. She complained of memory problems, even though she had managed to retain hundreds of songs and even epic stories that she would share with the youngsters of Katrampatti in the evenings. In Arivoli lessons she often said, "I just can't seem to remember [*maṉacile nikkamāṭṭeṅkatu*]"; literally, "It just won't stand in my mind." To this Karuppiah would reassure her, "Keep saying it while reading it over and over, and then it will stick in your mind [*tiruppittiruppi collikkiṭṭē paṭikkaṇum. appatāṉ maṉacile patiyum*].” Sometimes he would joke affectionately that if she learned to write these words by heart then even her eyesight would improve.

During lessons, Rajalakshmi also often asked, “When are we going to learn *āṉā āvaṉṉā īṉā īyaṉṉā?*” referring to script in alphabetical order and poetic form as she knew it was learned in school. “Do you have a book that will teach us that?” Other women in the group began asking similar questions.[15] Like everyone else, Rajalakshmi was accustomed to the sound of children reciting their lessons from school. The school-aged children of Katrampatti would do so in small groups on the front verandas of houses in the mornings before school and again in the evenings. It was up to the older children to help the younger ones, many of the parents being unable to contribute. Rajalakshmi was curious as to why learning to read and write should be so different for them in Arivoli lessons. She and her fellow learners all knew that among school-going children, one first learns the sound *a* spoken as “*āṉā,*” followed by the contrasting lengthened *ā*, which they would have heard as “*āvaṉṉā.*” They had never heard children recite, “*paṭṭā . . . pa, iṭṭ, ṭā . . . paṭṭā!*” These are conventions learners appeared to be aware of and very used to as part of their sonic linguistic environment, if not in control of so as to be able to produce and decode writing.

The first Tamil letter learned in contemporary schooling is *a* (அ), although children learn it through common pedagogic speech as “*āṉā.*”[16] The “*ṉā*” acts as a poetic postfix, attached to all the phonemes in oral recitation of the script. This postfixing allows students to string the alphasyllabary along, against a stable and repetitive sonic background. The following sound, “*ā,*” is rendered orally as “*āvaṉṉā,*” such that the difference between a short vowel (*kuṟil uyireḻuttu*) and a long vowel (*neṭil uyireḻuttu*) is marked in oral recitation, not by the sonic temporal length of the root vowel in question, but rather by the insertion of the syllable “*va*” after the always-elongated vowel and a corresponding slight lengthening of the following consonant, “*ṉ.*” The vowel series, consisting of short-long oppositions between five vowels and two diphthongs when heard in school or when children are reciting their homework, would sound like, “*āṉā, āvaṉṉā, īṉā, īyaṉṉā, ūṉā, ūvaṉṉā, ēṉā, ēyaṉṉā, aiyaṉṉā, ōṉṉā, ōvaṉṉā, auvaṉṉā.*”

What Rajalakshmi was invoking, with her seemingly simple questions, is in fact a system of vowel organization dating back to Paninian linguistics, as well as the very sonic background of poetic form, from the Tamil *aricuvaṭi* pedagogical tradition of recitation.[17] These are both parts of a structured pedagogy that drew attention through parallelisms to the sound of language itself (Jakobson 1985), so that it could "stand" in the mind. The poetic form of classical Tamil language learning is deeply intertwined with the production a virtuous subject (Raman 2010). This pedagogy is also, however, relatively devalued in pedagogical orientations that focus primarily on connecting words, through the referential function of language, to a "world" to be understood and eventually changed. As Sundari, whom I quoted earlier in this chapter, said, "In school they *only memorize* with the goal of passing [examinations]. Even those holding advanced degrees are unable to talk about any other subject or to *relate their education to their lives*" (emphasis added). It was precisely this kind of education that Arivoli sought to avoid. In any case, standardized exams are irrelevant to these adult learners.

The teaching of literacy in formal schooling traditionally begins as a mnemonic oral exercise, like the vowel series I have reproduced above, not unlike the English "A-B-C" song. These sounds are then made to correspond to a written alphasyllabary, in a movement from sound to grapheme. It is only later that a teacher exposes learners to meaningful words, as in the following sequence:

> "*āṉā*" corresponds to அ (*a*) in the word, அம்மா (*ammā* [mother])

The Tamil word *eḻuttu,* which is usually translated as "letter" in English, in fact means something closer to phonemic sound in the Tamil grammatical tradition derived from the *Naṉṉūl,* and taught in schools today.[18] In theorizing what he calls "the dimension of orality in Tamil literature," Kamil Zvelebil thus describes five distinct levels of sign activity in verbal art, beginning with sound (*eḻuttu,* phonetic/phonemic), then moving to form (*col*, morphosyntactic), and then moving on to the meaning (*poruḷ,* semantic) dimensions of language use and to higher linguistic units of prosody (*yāppu*) and rhetoric (*aṇi*) (1990, 135). Tamil textbooks and literacy lessons in school are organized precisely in this order. Having built up their phonological knowledge, and then a basic vocabulary of written words, students go on to learn rhyming songs and a series of lexical substitutions introducing words proper to written literary genres of Tamil. This process both socializes them to the exalted register of *centamiḻ* and prepares them for the higher levels of learning and meaning.[19] It is in this manner that learning language is connected to the broader cultivation of virtue in Tamil medium schools.

Karuppiah was at first ill equipped to answer Rajalakshmi's question as to why they were learning things that appeared completely different from the sounds they were used to associating with the learning of written language. This is because he had been taught, for years in training sessions for teachers, to focus first on the referential *meaning* of the words being taught, and then on the shape of the written script itself. Arivoli was meant to be a form of social action that was fundamentally different from learning in school, where repetitive memorization through recitation dominates pedagogy. Arivoli also marks a shift away from the learning of written language as introduction to, and social immersion in, the poetic genres of ancient Tamil, focusing rather on the communicative, or referential, function of language to describe the world. Freirean literacy pedagogy for adults was guided by a different sense of virtue and it had reordered the relations among sound, grapheme, and reference accordingly. Instead of building an embodied poetic knowledge, it followed a progression beginning with the word as vehicle of reference, moving to a graphic representation of the alphasyllable, ending with a depoeticized oral rendition:

> [பட்டா] (*paṭṭā* [land deed]) begins with ப (*pa*), which sounds like "*pa*"

What is at stake in this difference is not just a reordering of the alphasyllabary according to ease of writing as opposed to placement in the mouth. (ப [*pa*], with its three straight lines, is easier to write than அ [*a*]). What is also important is the insertion of a reference and script-centered language ideology into a larger pedagogical field dominated by the poetics of oral mnemonics, even in the teaching of writing.

It is for this reason that the Arivoli Iyakkam method of teaching the Tamil script would not "stand" in Rajalakshmi's mind. Rajalakshmi's question had exposed these referential and script-centered visual biases of Arivoli's pedagogy, which are tied to the very philosophy of language and subjectivity tacitly underpinning the Freirean system.[20] The question was also grounded in a complex frame, tying written language back to the context of formal schooling and to even broader dominant orientations to textuality, which the Arivoli Iyakkam cannot so easily escape (cf. Bate 2010; Raman 2010; Venkatachalapathy 1994). Again, a certain sociological realism on the part of learners, experienced as familiarity with semiotic form in this case and calibrated to different expectations of written language, appears as resistance to the project of raising a liberated consciousness.

The pedagogical techniques employed in the initial stages of the Arivoli learning sequence presupposed the importance of what is being referred to by the generative words, in a radical separation from school learning, which is often disparaged as "rote recitation" learned only in order to pass examinations. While the designers of the primer had also paid a great deal of attention to the shape of the visual inscription of language, choosing letters that are very simple to trace, the embodied sonic discipline involved in socialization to written language had largely escaped attention as a pedagogic issue in these early stages of literacy education. The initial *Aṟivoḷi Tīpam* primers used to learn the script through words, while still in use during the time of my fieldwork, had begun to be criticized, both within Arivoli and without, on pedagogical grounds.

Karuppiah eventually started referring to the script using the more common spoken forms he had learned in his own schooling during lessons in Katrampatti.[21] "*Pa, iṭ, ṭā*" became "*pāṉā iṭṭaṉṉā ṭāvaṉṉā*" two months into their lessons. But the overall structure of lessons remained intact as they studied the first *Aṟivoḷi Tīpam* primer. When I asked Karuppiah about the reaction of learners to the Arivoli style of education, he responded both with humor and a little frustration that what is in fact needed is a complete change in formal schooling itself. He recalled how he, as a child, found very little connecting what he was learning in school to the world around him. He saw the same thing happening in his own daughter's education. "There is no relation between what kids memorize in school and life itself." This was the gap he felt Arivoli must work to bridge, though he and many others in the movement have come to the conclusion that new methods must be developed such that Arivoli's pedagogy could fit more neatly with textual forms, such as songs and stories, that learners were already familiar with. I will describe the turn in Arivoli to folklore, and to narrative forms and speech genres associated with Tamil village life, in the following chapter. Here I must merely emphasize the point that a recognition of disjuncture between different orientations to words and to written language had been born of activist practice, such as the lessons in Katrampatti I have described.

The Social Production of Reflexivity

So far this chapter may appear to have reiterated common and long-standing themes in the study of literacy. Written language is often connected to abstraction and objectification in opposition to an embodied orality. In the narrative of "restricted literacy" (Goody 1968), the qualities of orality I have described in the practice of Tamil schooled literacy would appear as a residue that resists transcending an immediate context. The ideological turn in literacy studies, however, exemplified in the work of Shirley Brice Heath (1983), Brian Street (1984, 1993), Brinkley Messick (1993), Bambi Schieffelin (1996, 2000), and what has been called the "new literacy studies," provided anthropology with tools to understand this apparent division in a more sophisticated manner—as the product of an unequal encounter between conflicting ideologies of the written word—so as to better appreciate a plurality of literacies.[22] It is this insight that has allowed for a preliminary comparative investigation of Tamil schooled literacy, as a system with its own logic. But the encounter between these different orientations to written language, now placed firmly in the realm of an ideologically mediated practice rather than that of technological determinism, remains fundamentally unequal insofar as "alternative literacies" are consistently framed by researchers and educators alike as deviations from a globally circulating norm.

The norm of what I have been calling "enlightened literacy" has as much to do with emancipatory theories of the modern subject as it does with an explicit theory of writing per se. The written text, in this theory of literacy, is important insofar as it is the privileged site for the exercise of abstraction and objectification of the world in the cultivation of a freer subject, aware of her capacity to change the world. Insofar as written language has been prized as the perfect vehicle for this kind of intellectual abstraction in the post-Enlightenment world, literacy has been systematically misrecognized as a mental activity commonly associated with silent reading and writing.[23] The very fact of writing as an embodied, mediating, material system of signs and social power is thereby obscured, even in many of the most sophisticated analyses of the public sphere (e.g., Habermas 1989).[24] The Arivoli Iyakkam was faced with the difficulty of developing a pedagogy that could internalize this tension between written language's promise of freedom and the fact of literacy being a skill requiring socialization of the body to a dominant habitus. Their search for an adequate method led to the emergence of a certain reflexivity regarding the roles of sociality, embodiment, and linguistic form in shaping the politics of literacy.

Rather than narrate a simple failure of the Freirean system of codifications to deliver on the promise of raising consciousness among learners, I would like to conclude this chapter by asking how interactions with existing systems of education, literacy, and sociality served to reshape some of the very premises of this critical pedagogy. Although grounded in a teleological, developmental narrative of humanization, the Arivoli Iyakkam's pedagogy had also set the conditions for its own questioning. The conditions for reflexivity regarding heterogeneity in orientations to written language and implicit theories of pedagogy and subjectivity were built into the movement's pedagogy in several ways. First, the centrality of dialogue in Freirean thought ensured that a student's reaction to the pedagogical encounter, like Rajalakshmi's question about learning the script, for example, must be given a response. The requirement that literacy lessons speak directly to the world of learners in the Arivoli movement forces a recognition that schooled literacy was, in fact, a part of their world, even if someone like Rajalakshmi had never set foot in a classroom. Her question had forced Karuppiah not only to open his teaching style beyond the parameters of the primer but also to articulate more sharply, for himself and to certain degree for the learners, the logic behind the type of pedagogy he had been employing. He had perhaps even caught a glimpse of the limits of Freirean pedagogy in his own explanation.

The second means by which a certain reflexivity is produced through activist practice has to do with the volunteers themselves, and more specifically with their social positioning in relation both to their fellow villagers, who would be learners in the movement, and to the globally circulating norms of enlightened literacy. Arivoli Iyakkam village activists mediated between competing visions of language, sociality, and agency, enabling them to articulate a critical perspective on either side. For example, people like Karuppiah were unusually well positioned to understand the politics of reciprocal agency that would paradoxically serve as the engine for a project that seeks to use literacy to spread personal empowerment. He and Neela also stood in a relationship to their learners that allowed them to understand the limits of the models of personhood and language that had been projected onto the structure of lessons.

In order to develop a better understanding of how senior activists in the Arivoli Iyakkam reflected on why and how lessons had taken an unexpected turn, let us end this chapter by returning to Sundararaman, one of the architects of the movement. When I asked him about the influence of Freire, he explained that lessons actually worked for reasons that were not directly connected to the specifics of Freirean technique of subject production through objectification.

> We were obsessed when making our primers on another dimension of it, which was the Paulo Freirean dimension. So we were looking at the pictures, and conducting dialogues, how you will be able to structure dialogues around the pictures. And how to make it liberating and what word we would start with. So we started with the word "hunger" and we were very thrilled with ourselves for doing that. That was our set of concerns. We were very bothered about messages regarding poverty and exploitation. . . . So we didn't quite understand, we were so obsessed with the Paulo Freirean pedagogy.

Sitting in his Pondicherry apartment, Sundararaman recalled his experiments with generative words and codifications in the Arivoli Iyakkam campaigns with a sort of fondness for youthful naïveté, and with the distance of someone who has moved on to other things. The struggle he and his fellow activists had had with government development officials to start with words like "land deed" and "hunger," motivated by a deep faith in the revolutionary potential of Freire's pedagogy of naming the world, seemed a little misplaced in retrospect. But he told the story of their experiments with such techniques of liberation, not so much as a failure, but more as a process of learning about the relationship between ideas and practices of political pedagogy.

> Paulo Freire's . . . original concept of how you get into a dialogue with their life situation never really took place. That *concept* of empowerment never really happened. Empowerment happened in this campaign. And it happened in a very, very big way. There is enough unquestionable evidence of that. But it happened not because of the way the book was transacted. It was transacted horribly. But it happened because of the *kalajatha* [street drama], it happened because of the organization, because of all the groups, because of the meetings. It happened because of who we were, so it happened. Empowerment happened. Not quite the way Paulo Freire imagined or even how we would recount it to ourselves at that point of time.

The distinction between the "concept of empowerment" and the historical process of empowerment itself that Sundararaman makes is worth pondering for just a moment, in order to think about how such a distinction can be made in the first place and about why one appears to have happened while the other did not. Following the Freirean method, the Arivoli Iyakkam designed its primers around the idea that one could develop a concept of empowerment that would grow out of a guided dialogue between teachers and learners about issues like land tenure and food scarcity. These social issues, once objectified in writing and in drawings, would trigger reflection and new conceptualizations of empowerment and possibility among learners and also teachers. Similarly, street plays that would represent to an audience their own social situation, now available for reflection, would allow them to think critically about what they once took for granted. Literacy lessons or street plays might then be seen as means to the end of developing a concept of empowerment.

What Sundararaman and many like him had realized through their own reflections on activism is that the very fact that lessons and street plays happened in the manner in which they did was seen as a form of empowerment by those who participated. The Arivoli Iyakkam was successful to the degree that teachers and other activists were able to rethink the primacy of the "concept" of empowerment and instead focus on this process of mobilization. Sometimes this meant that reading and writing took a back seat to other activities. The realization of what we might term a more processual understanding of empowerment also meant, however, that the meaning of literacy and the role of language itself had also been rethought. A group of activists sought not necessarily to prioritize other modes of producing a sense of empowerment as much as they sought to rethink empowerment through written language, by tying it more closely to the social pragmatics of narrative speech. It is to these efforts that we now turn.

4

Search for a Method

The Media of Enlightenment

By the time we arrived in the village of Mayakkurichi a large group of people had already gathered in the main square around two young Arivoli Iyakkam volunteers who were standing under the diffuse light of a streetlamp. The women and children of the village were sitting on the ground in a circle. The teenage boys and men were all standing a few meters behind them in the darkness, or sitting on the verandas extending from nearby houses, forming an outer ring. No one noticed as Karuppiah and I walked up after leaving our motorbike under a banyan tree off to the side of the square. They were all listening attentively as the young woman in the center read aloud from a thin pamphlet. She shouted in Tamil, "I'm no longer willing to live as a doll in your doll's house [*pommai vīṭu*]. I've had enough of this life!" I immediately recognized these words as the final lines of the Arivoli Iyakkam's adaptation of Henrik Ibsen's *A Doll's House*, which I had read before at the main office back in Pudukkottai. After a short moment of silence, the crowd broke out into applause. The Arivoli volunteers then proceeded to ask the assembled audience what they thought of the story and whether it was right for Nora to have left her married home. They received a very wide range of responses, some negative but many sympathetic, all from the women who formed the inner circle of listeners. The men of Mayakkurichi stood in the shadows, watching and listening to the discussion from afar.

This public performance of the nineteenth-century Norwegian playwright's text had been organized by volunteer teachers as part of the Makkal Vacippu Iyakkam, the "people's reading movement." Since the mid-1990s, when this mode of activism began, a whole generation of villagers had come to empathize with Nora's dramatic struggle and eventual disillusionment with married life through such public recitations. In the words of Tamilcelvan, who was part of the group of writers who worked to translate this play and other stories, "The flesh and blood of Ibsen's letters, written over one hundred years ago, were brought back to life in the very soil of our villages. Toiling villagers came to know world literature through the teardrops they wept for Nora" (2004b, 83). Although no one was crying at the performance of *A Doll's House* that I had just caught the end of, the Makkal Vacippu Iyakkam did, in fact, mark a moment when "world literature" was brought to the villages of Tamil Nadu in way that it had not circulated before. Other well-known stories that were translated, adapted, written up into pamphlets, and read aloud in hundreds of villages across the state include simplified versions of Victor Hugo's *Les Misérables* and Leo Tolstoy's "How Much Land Does a Man Need?" But it should not be terribly surprising that texts from the European canon were used in this fashion by the Arivoli Iyakkam. This was, after all, the "Enlightenment movement." The people's reading movement also borrowed from modern Tamil fiction as well as folktales, and these textual traditions too had to be bent and reshaped to fit the vision of enlightenment propagated by the literacy movement. What was really at stake in the development of materials for the reading movement was therefore not only a matter of translating classics of modern English, Norwegian, Russian, or French literature into a new language.

The Makkal Vacippu Iyakkam's true significance lies in the search to devise an innovative genre of modern literature, or, more precisely, what Walter Benjamin would call a new "function . . . within the literary relations of production" (1978, 222). The artists who worked in the movement developing these texts and modes of performance were already aware of extant traditions of reciting epic texts like the *Ramayanam* aloud in villages and they had become more aware of the role of recitation in schooling through their earlier efforts. They were also trained in the critical traditions of socialist realism that are espoused by the Tamil Nadu Progressive Writers Association, to which most of them belonged. However, the mode of literary production they had adopted for this form of activism consisted neither of a continuation of existing modes of storytelling, religious or otherwise, nor of a simple importation of realist genres that had already been formulated elsewhere. The context of Arivoli Iyakkam activism demanded something new: a literary practice that would be adequate to the movement's pedagogical goals of raising critical consciousness of wider social realities while adhering to the space of experience and textual habits that defined the world of villagers. This was to be a literature for, and of, the rural poor of Tamil Nadu. The search for a method in the Makkal Vacippu Iyakkam therefore provoked engagement with some of the most vexing questions facing politically engaged artists anywhere in the world.

In the present chapter, I explore how the search to develop a new social function for literature in the people's reading movement speaks to these broad questions about the mediating roles of literary genre, performance, and language more generally in political activism. Whereas the beginning phases of Arivoli education, discussed in the previous chapter, consisted of a relatively unreflective insertion of Paulo Freire's pedagogical method into the Tamil context, the Makkal Vacippu Iyakkam represents a more creative moment in pedagogical design, when activists and authors devoted sustained consideration to their methods and to the social dimensions of language in pedagogy. Looking back on the failures of the earlier Arivoli Iyakkam primers to elicit the intended reactions among students in the movement through "generative words," for example, their designer, Dr. Madasamy, told me, "The early primers were too heavily loaded with messages. Be it the intellectuals who were so concerned with raising consciousness or the government officials who just want to transmit development plans. None of them thought of the *linguistic or cultural work* involved. It was as if we just picked out words from a dictionary! That had to change." Over the course of the Makkal Vacippu Iyakkam, Madasamy, Tamilcelvan, and their colleagues came to devote a great deal of thought and care to the problems of textual habitus and linguistic performance, beyond the level of words and "messages." Language had ceased to act as a window onto social reality or as a simple means for the transmission of knowledge, as it was conceived in Arivoli's introductory pedagogy. Language came alive, and instead became a productive element of social reality through reading aloud.

Literature in the Service of Activism

The literacy movement was remarkable for its capacity to mobilize creative writers and dramatists in the Makkal Vacippu Iyakkam. Artists from regions across Tamil Nadu came together to translate literature from around the world, to transpose classics of Tamil fiction into a different linguistic register, and to collect and collate folk tales and proverbs. Once collected and transformed, these texts were published as small pamphlets for reading in villages. Many earlier efforts had been made to translate texts from the European canon into Tamil, most notably by the modernist master Pudumaippithan (2000, 2002, 2004), who also revolutionized the language of Tamil fiction in the 1930s through his experiments representing regional spoken dialects in his own short stories. Prior efforts had also been made among Marxist authors to mine Tamil textual traditions for critical social thought, such as N. Vanamamalai's (1966) attempts to trace a history of materialism in Tamil folklore and literature in the 1960s and '70s. But the Makkal Vacippu Iyakkam was the first movement of its kind to draw on these earlier efforts in the service of making a modern literature specifically designed for people who had limited or no formal education.[1] It was this ambitious project of creating a new genre of village literature that provoked a set of practical, aesthetic, and political questions that earlier efforts had never confronted.

The first problem faced by writers working in the Makkal Vacippu Iyakkam concerns the wide gap, mentioned in the previous chapter, that separates most forms of written Tamil from that which is spoken by villagers. Tamil has often been characterized as a "diglossic" language because of the formal and ideological differences between what is considered to be the "high" literary variety and the "low" language of everyday speech (Britto 1986; Ferguson 1959).[2] Although similar distinctions exist in many languages, the high variety, known as *centamil̲* (refined Tamil), is especially revered in Tamil Nadu, in part because of twentieth-century nationalist efforts to "purify" the Tamil language of Sanskritic and English vocabulary. Bernard Bate (2009) has recently shown how *centamil̲* became the language of a new Dravidian politics marked by the rise of a modern oratorical aesthetic that harkens back to a glorious Tamil past. The learned speakers of the Dravidian movement brought this language to the stage for the first time in the mid-twentieth century, and parties like the DMK have since enforced its value through regimes of schooling and public culture that are saturated with the values of ethnolinguistic nationalism instantiated in the use of *centamil̲*. Everything else is generally considered to be *ḵoccaittamil̲* (vulgar Tamil) or *ḵoṭuntamil̲* (broken Tamil), especially the varieties spoken by villagers in places like Pudukkottai.

The writers who participated in the Makkal Vacippu Iyakkam decided, in contrast to the writers of the Dravidian nationalist movement, that composing and teaching using the standard written varieties that had been shaped by this language ideology would not only be difficult—most villagers are not very familiar with *centamil̲* vocabulary or its grammatical rules—it would also reinforce a form of cultural hegemony that denigrates the very language spoken by learners in the movement. The maintenance of a diglossic hierarchy within language offended the Marxian political sensibilities of the authors of the Makkal Vacippu Iyakkam, despite their broader sympathies with the populist struggle against caste domination and with the socialist ideals professed by major Dravidian parties. In their literature, the Arivoli writers therefore sought to represent verb endings, vocabulary, and expressions as these are spoken by the learners themselves and not as they would be taught in schools, where *centamil̲* is the only register worthy of writing. Village speech patterns would thus provide the basic material of literature, and even Tamil short stories used for the movement would have to go through an "intralingual translation" (Jakobson 2000, 114) process as they entered the field of village literature.[3] Speech would have to be rendered in writing, and written Tamil itself would be remade in the process.

The second major issue that arose in the search to create a literature for the movement had to do with the act of reading itself. There was already a fairly long history of experiments with rendering spoken Tamil in modern fiction, by the *Maṇikkoṭi* group of the 1930s, for example, and more recently in Dalit literature of the 1990s, where even the voice of narration is written in regional and caste dialects.[4] Most of these authors had also been critical of the Dravidian nationalist efforts to impose archaic literary norms onto modern prose. But existing forms of writing in which spoken language is represented were all expected to be read silently, a habit that expanded greatly in the early twentieth century around the novel, and which continues as the norm among middle-class readers of all sorts of texts today (Venkatachalapathy 1994, 2012).[5] The Arivoli authors, on the other hand, were seeking to design pamphlets for rural workers to be read aloud in large groups. Like the oral performance of *A Doll's House* described above, Makkal Vacippu Iyakkam readings were to be something like a dramatic performance, where one or two volunteers or neoliterate learners would animate a text and an audience would listen. The activists would then ask questions and engage in a dialogue with villagers about the story. Speech would therefore have to be reduced to writing, as described above, only to reenter the sphere of orality in recitation.

Reading in the Makkal Vacippu Iyakkam was a public event, not a private act of silent consumption. For authors of the movement who were themselves accustomed to participation in the public sphere through silent reading and writing, this shift to an aural, performance-based form of writing required innovative modes of narration for reading aloud, a strategy that had never been pursued before in the realm of modern creative fiction. In the words of Tamilcelvan, "Developing reading materials to read aloud in villages for villagers themselves demanded that we create a new language. Whole books would have to be grasped through the ear" (2004b, 76). It is in this regard that writers in the movement would have to reconsider the role of literature in the formation of a public sphere. Reading literature aloud with the aim eliciting discussion at the reading event forced writers out of their previous assumptions about silent intellection, and hurled them into new engagements with the history and materiality of language.

In their search for a literature adequate to this task, the writers of the Makkal Vacippu Iyakkam would eventually turn to practices of reading and storytelling that are as firmly rooted in the villages they sought to transform as they are in the forms of modern prose that these writers had been trained to read and produce. They would have to relearn the narrative arts from villagers themselves, and the classics of world literature, as they were reshaped for oral storytelling, would become unmoored from their roots, their origins irrelevant to rural listeners. The aura surrounding "high" art that led authors to bring literature like *A Doll's House* to Tamil villages would hold only for the authors themselves, for example, not for those they sought to engage in critical conversation. As villagers were brought into the world of books, they would eventually become authors themselves, joining Ibsen and other modern masters in supplying narrative materials for the Makkal Vacippu Iyakkam. In the words of Benjamin (1968, 232), describing Soviet efforts of the 1920s in his famous essay on art in the age of mechanical reproduction, in the creation of a worker's literature "the distinction between author and public" would eventually lose its "basic character." The struggle to create a literature that would dissolve existing hierarchies within language, as well as the boundary between authors and readers, in the Makkal Vacippu Iyakkam in fact resonates in interesting ways with some of the classic debates in Marxist literary theory for reasons that are both historical and ideological. I now turn to the literary theory that artists and activists of the Arivoli Iyakkam actually engaged with to understand these resonances in more detail, before returning to the reading movement's history and practice.

The Progressive and the Real

The Tamil Nadu Progressive Writers Association (Tamiḻnāṭu Muṟpōkku Eḻuttāḷar Caṅkam) is the forum where intellectuals of the Arivoli Iyakkam first developed their theories of aesthetics, language, and politics. This organization, which was founded in 1975, is closely affiliated with the Communist Party of India (Marxist), and their desire to create a literature in the service of revolution reflects the Leninist-Stalinist orientation of this party. The Tamil Nadu Progressive Writers Association now boasts approximately ten thousand members in districts around the state, and their aesthetic and political principles have remained remarkably consistent in their defense of socialist realism.[6] We have already begun to get acquainted with the thought of the president of this association, S. Tamilcelvan. He and other well-known writers of the Left who participated in the Arivoli Iyakkam put themselves in the difficult position of working closely with government bureaucrats in the context of this NGO-based mass social movement in the service of what they would sometimes jokingly refer to as "revolution on the government tab." But it was not only the middle-class leadership of the movement and widely recognized artists who were involved in the progressive writers group. Most of the serious full-time Arivoli activists I knew in Pudukkottai were active participants, whether they were published writers or not.

In cities, towns, and villages across Tamil Nadu, meetings of the Tamil Nadu Progressive Writers Association provided the context for critical discussions about literature and films, as well as more general debates on key political issues. In the small, agricultural market town of Alangudi, about six kilometers from his village, for example, Karuppiah rented a small room on the rooftop above a small groundnut warehouse that served to house the local branch of the association. Next to the entrance to this room was a sign announcing its occupant to be an "Arivoli artist." It was here that he and Neela met with other like-minded rural intellectuals from nearby villages. On almost any evening, at about six or seven o'clock, a small group of men and women would gather on the terrace next to this small room to chat after the day's work had been done, while children from the houses next door periodically climbed up to the rooftop terrace to look on. Those who dropped by included local schoolteachers interested in talking about literature and younger neighbors who came to talk about the latest film or to share poetry they had written. Some of the better-known published authors in the local branch had jobs in Pudukkottai Town, working for NGOs or in government offices. They would come by about once a week or so.

What these people from a range of backgrounds all had in common was an interest in the relation between the arts and society and a commitment to Left politics. The latest Tamil films, for example, would be analyzed in terms of how they depicted social problems such as caste or

Figure 7. Karuppiah and Neela in the room where members of the Tamil Nadu Progressive Writers Association and their friends would meet in the small town of Alangudi. Photograph by the author.

gender domination, and whether they could be read as taking a "progressive" (*mur̲pōḳḳu*) stance on these issues. Short stories published in the weekly literary magazines were subject to the same style of critique. This was the stuff of everyday debates and discussion. Once a month, the official Alangudi branch meeting would be held on the terrace just outside Karuppiah's room, where members of the association would discuss upcoming regional meetings and plan events such as the yearly all-night art festival they organized at one of the main crossroads in Alangudi. When any of the authors in this branch published a major work, the association would organize both an official book-release function to celebrate, as well as a more intimate critical reading-group meeting to address flaws in the work. I was also recruited to give presentations to the local branch, both on my Arivoli research and on important books in the English-speaking academy that had not been translated into Tamil. When Jacques Derrida died in 2004, for instance, I was asked to participate in a group discussion on the influence of his work, which was made known to those who participated primarily in the form of secondary interpretations in the Tamil literary press. The progressive writers group of Alangudi, therefore, acted as an important point of circulation among a wide range of people and ideas, introducing rural Tamils to the wide world of Left thought and especially the aesthetic concerns of Marxism.

Throughout the course of the Arivoli Iyakkam, it was the Tamil Nadu Progressive Writers Association that also served as the intellectual center for thinking about how to devise a new literature for the rural poor. It is in this context the authors of the movement would have to wrestle with the question of how literary theory relates to activism, and more specifically what it means to create a literature grounded in "realism" (*yatārttavātam*) for Tamil villagers. For example, I once went with Neela to a regional meeting of the progressive writers in the city of Tiruchchirappalli and we listened to the president at the time, Arunan, as he warned his fellow writers and activists not to "fall under the spell of language's power to intoxicate [*moḻiyiṉuṭaiya māntīka caktiyiṉ mītu eḻuttāḷarukkuḷḷa mayakkam*]. . . . The progressive writers must defend realism from such influences," he continued, "and assure that social problems are represented as problems in literature to give new inspiration to our Left social movements, not as beautiful stories to entertain and beguile." Neela was deeply sympathetic to this line of argument. The task of activists in the Makkal Vacippu Iyakkam, and more broadly in the literacy movement, as she explained to me on the long bus ride home after the meeting, was to reconcile the defense of realism with the needs of the movement. "So many of these high modernists [*atinavīṉavātikaḷ*]," she said, "they think that art is for art's sake, or for their own self-aggrandizement. But all these trends and styles, they do nothing for the common people. How will these stories help in giving consciousness to people? Even I find it difficult to read them," she continued, with that curious mix of humility and self-confidence that I had already come to appreciate over the course of our long afternoon conversations at the room in Alangudi.

Villagers like Neela and Karuppiah had, in fact, come to the question of socialist realism in literature through their activism in the Arivoli Iyakkam. It was when they joined the literacy movement as young adults in the early 1990s that they were first exposed to the progressive writers movement. This is also around the time when Neela took up her vocation as a writer, which she saw as part of her broader activist project. Her first book, *Pāmara Taricaṉam* (A Darshan of Common People) was published in 2002 with help from her friends and colleagues at the Tamil Nadu Progressive Writers Association, and it consists of a series of essays reflecting on the people she had met in villages across Pudukkottai as an activist in the literacy campaigns. Through these essays, many of which had been published before, and through poems and short stories written in the Left literary journals, Neela eventually entered the larger Tamil literary world. She now publishes regularly in the literary journal of the CPI(M), *Cemmalar* (Red Blossom), as well as in more popular weekly magazines like *Āṉanta Vikaṭaṉ* (Happy Entertainment), which is not political and is widely read in middle-class homes around Tamil Nadu. I learned through our long chats in Alangudi and through weekly visits to her home nearby that Neela credits her mother with turning her into a writer, because she was a great storyteller even though she never attended school. Neela often felt the burden of representing the voice of women and the rural poor at literary meetings, even those of the Tamil Nadu Progressive Writers Association, the organization that claimed to be writing for this class of people through their commitment to socialist realism.

What writers like Neela would often refer to as the other "*icaṅkaḷ*" ("isms"), like surrealism, expressionism, symbolism, and postmodernism, are commonly criticized in progressive writers circles precisely for their elitism, their distance from the concerns of common people, and what is taken to be their incompatibility with the will to use literature in the service of politics. I had first learned about these critiques of avant-garde literatures through meetings at the Alangudi room, where this was a very common topic of conversation, and through some of the regional progressive writers meetings I attended with Neela and Karuppiah. But it was only after immersing myself in the theoretical literature published by the Tamil Nadu Progressive Writers Association, especially the proceedings of their triannual state-level meetings, that I came to understand the deeper history of their antagonism toward literatures that focus too heavily on the form of language itself, at the expense of providing narrative criticism of social reality.

The core intellectual framework drawn on by this group of writers is indebted to the theory of socialist realism developed by the Hungarian Marxist philosopher Georg Lukács. In a series of polemical essays published in the 1930s while he was living under Stalin's auspices as an exile in Moscow, Lukács developed a forceful critique of the European literary avant-garde, accusing them of a "fetishistic dismemberment of social reality," with their focus on internal psychological states and experimental modes of narration at the expense of portraying the world of social relations realistically in its "totality." In a passage that is often quoted and paraphrased by leaders of the Tamil Nadu Progressive Writers, for example, he writes, "If literature is a particular form by means of which objective reality is reflected, then it becomes of crucial importance for it to grasp that reality as it truly is, and not merely to confine itself to reproducing whatever manifests itself immediately and on the surface" (2001 [1938], 1037).[7] Developing a theoretical framework based on the critical distinction between the immediate surface of experience and a deeper objective reality that is available for reflection by the politically tendentious author, Lukács went on to denounce the high modernist turns taken by many of his fellow Marxists. It was this very argument warning of the "intoxicating" power of linguistic form that was being echoed in the speech Neela and I had heard in Tiruchchirappalli.

The well-known and influential All-India Progressive Writers Association had already been established in the 1930s, under the leadership of the Urdu writer Sajjad Zaheer, well before the Tamil group.[8] Earlier efforts to produce a Left literature in Tamil in the *Kalai Ilaḳḳiya Pe̱rumaṉ̱ram* (Literary Arts Forum), associated with the then-undivided Communist Party of India, may also have served as models (Sivathamby 1978, 43). But it is perhaps because of rivalries among political parties of the Left and the ongoing Soviet influence on the CPI(M) that the Tamil Nadu Progressive Writers Association eventually took up the Lukácsian literary theory of socialist realism as their own, with only small gestures toward Indian antecedents.[9] In any case, a canon for the Tamil progressive movement was assembled by drawing on Lukács's narrative, including his celebration of Balzac and Tolstoy, Soviet socialist realist classics such as Maxim Gorky's *The Mother*, which is widely read by association members in translation, as well as earlier Tamil social reformist authors, like the revolutionary nationalist poet Subramanya Bharathi. This is the history of progressive literature that the activists working with the Arivoli Iyakkam like Neela have in mind when demanding that a literature for the movement must be adequate to the task of social critique.

Over the course of the Makkal Vacippu Iyakkam, however, the authors of the Progressive Writers Association found that the forms of realism that they had been taught to use in their own writing had been developed though literary genres, such as novels and the short story, that were largely irrelevant to the unlettered villagers they hoped to address. More specifically, these genres were not up to the task of being read aloud. They would therefore have to rethink realism altogether in their search for a village literature. Whereas these authors had always tacitly assumed a model of engagement based on private readership and public discussion of literature and politics, the literacy movement forced them to reconsider their very techniques. The textual production of a public would still be mediated by print in this context, but it required a language that oriented itself toward forms of embodied performance and aural uptake. This is precisely the kind of "linguistic and cultural work" that Madasamy argued had been neglected in the Arivoli Iyakkam's early primers, and it is a question that had not been anticipated in the theories propagated by the Tamil Nadu Progressive Writers Association.

Activist writers eventually drew on the previously existing practice of reading stories aloud in villages in a language that was easy to recite in their search for a method. Tamilcelvan explains this strategy in his memoirs in the following manner: "There is a tradition in our villages of reading the stories of Vakramadithan, Alli Aracani Malai, and Nallathangal aloud and singing from books written in large type. The Arivoli Iyakkam took up and recovered that tradition by giving it a new shape" (2004b, 76). The writers of the Makkal Vacippu Iyakkam therefore drew on this practice of reading aloud and inserted their own stories, many of which were drawn from the realist canon they were familiar with. But, as I hope to show in the following pages, this was not simply a case of "new wine in old bottles," to invert the familiar metaphor. Something more complex and more interesting was at stake in the effort to lend a new social significance to reading aloud. To leave the analysis of the Makkal Vacippu Iyakkam at the level of form and content would be to miss the new languages and novel social relations of performance that emerged through these experiments in "recovering" a tradition.

It is in this regard that Benjamin's (1978) orientation to thinking about the "author as producer" is helpful insofar as it demands that we focus on what he calls the "position" of the work within the "social relations of literary production," instead of limiting evaluation to whether a work takes a critical "attitude" to the social world. Writing in the context of the realism debates of the 1930s—the very same set of arguments that had led Lukács to develop the theory of realism that would serve as the aesthetic philosophy the Tamil Nadu Progressive Writers Association—Benjamin thought that the question of literature's political content had been artificially counterposed to that of its literary quality, or its form, by his fellow Marxist theorists, including Lukács. He argued, instead, that attention to "literary *technique* provides the dialectical starting point from which the unfruitful antithesis of form and content can be surpassed" (ibid., 222). Paraphrasing Marx's well-known argument that philosophy had thus far only interpreted the world instead of changing it, Benjamin also believed that a wholly "new language" must be constructed in the creation of a literature adequate to the task of socialist politics: "no technical renovation of language, but its mobilization in the service of struggle or work—at any rate, of changing reality instead of describing it" (1999, 733). The question would then no longer be whether a story was critical at the level of linguistic representation, or what is oftentimes glossed as "content," but rather how an act of storytelling itself fits within and transforms social relations of cultural production.

In what follows, I argue that this is a position that some of the progressive authors of the Makkal Vacippu Iyakkam who were previously concerned exclusively with questions of critical realist content would eventually come to take. They did so, not necessarily by reading Benjamin, but through their own search for a literature that could be used in the service of activism. They did so in pursuit of that elusive ideal of "unifying theory and *praxis*" (Jay 1973, 4) that is shared across a wide swath of thinkers working in a Marxian tradition that includes both the literary debates of 1930s Germany as well as those of 1990s activism in Tamil Nadu. For writers like Tamilcelvan, for example, who were first committed to questions of realist literature as formulated in the Progressive Writers Association, and who only later came to literacy activism, spending so much time in villages with learners and rural activists turned their world around. In his memoirs Tamilcelvan reflects on the theory of realism in light of his experience of activism: "Were the books we gave to people in a form that would allow them to grasp reality? If education is meant to reflect reality, is it a real mirror? My head spun when we would discuss these things in literary circles. Is literature a mirror of the times that could reflect social life [*ilakkiyam camūka vāḻvaip pirapalikkum kālattiṉkaṇṇāṭiyā*]?" These are some of the many questions he had been debating with his fellow progressive writers for years before becoming an activist and coming to the conclusion that "it was only in Arivoli that these literary questions could be answered. What is the point of reading and writing reality [*yatārttattai vācippatum eḻutuvatum etaṟkkāka*]? To change it [*atai māṟṟavataṟkāka*]" (2004b, 27). The authors of the Tamil Nadu Progressive Writers Association who took part in activism would have to rethink the political efficacy of realism altogether.

Cultural Dimensions of Literary Activism

While living in Pudukkottai, I took a trip down south to visit Tamilcelvan at his home. He lives in the rural town of Pattamadai, which is known throughout India for its fine, handwoven mats, and located just up the river from the district center of Tirunelveli. I had been reading his serialized memoirs about his Arivoli activism in the literary journal *Tīmtarikiṭā* (Drumroll) for several months. I was also beginning to read his short stories with help from my Tamil teacher, many of which are set in the dry countryside of southern Tamil Nadu. Within the field of Marxist politics, Tamilcelvan is known as someone who has a special sensitivity to questions of culture, history, and literature. In the wider literary world, many people I had talked to recognized his awareness of these issues, but then went on to question why he should be so devoted to the progressive writers group and a form of Left politics that has so consistently turned a deaf ear to questions of culture and even denigrated those who fall prey to the "intoxicating" powers of language. I was therefore eager to interview him and to ask more pointed questions about his views on Tamil literature and the problem of devising an activist literature.

Tamilcelvan lives in the Brahman quarter of Pattamadai, the *akirakāram*, despite not being a Brahman himself, because it is near the school where his wife works as a teacher and because they had found a beautiful old, traditional Tamil house there. Walking up from the bus stop on the main road of this small town, I asked where the author Tamilcelvan lives, and I was guided by a young boy to a recently whitewashed house with a dramatically sloping tile roof sheltering the front veranda and an open courtyard in the middle. Tamilcelvan was sitting at a desk in the shade of his office, a room just off the veranda entrance, writing something on his computer and surrounded by tall piles of books. I noticed that on top of one of these stacks sat open a photocopied version of Clifford Geertz's collected essays, *The Interpretation of Cultures*. As I walked in, Tamilcelvan looked at me and smiled, "You're an anthropologist, right? I just got a copy of this from one of my friends in Madras." He told me that he had been reading widely in cultural theory, and this book had been recommended to him as an essential text by a professor who teaches folklore at a nearby university. I dropped my backpack on the floor, and Tamilcelvan immediately suggested that we go out for a stroll through Pattamadai and have a cup of tea at the local tea shop.

Walking in the late afternoon sun in the schoolyard along green paddy fields by the banks of the Tamiraparani River, he began to explain how his whole orientation to literature, culture, and language transformed dramatically as a result of his work with the Arivoli Iyakkam. The son of a famous playwright and literary figure, Tamilcelvan had worked as an officer in the postal service until taking early retirement to devote himself to literature and politics. There was one incident in particular that was etched in his memory as the moment he understood the political importance of the Arivoli Iyakkam. He was still working at the post office at the time, when a group of Tamil language activists gathered around the building shouting, "Down with Hindi, long live Tamil! [*inti o<u>l</u>i<u>k</u>a tami<u>l</u> vā<u>l</u><u>k</u>a!*]" The post office, a central government of India institution, bore signs written in Tamil, English, and Hindi. One among the group of sixty protesters had brought a ladder and climbed it in an effort to smear tar on the Hindi lettering, while the others encouraged him by shouting their anti-Hindi slogans. Once this young man had climbed the ladder, he looked down and asked his fellow language activists which part of the sign was written in Hindi. It seems that this devotee of the Tamil language could not read, and so could not tell the difference between Hindi and Tamil script. "For the following months, I felt terribly guilty. Here we were singing songs of praise to our language when so many people could not even read it," said Tamilcelvan as we sat down for a cup of tea.

It was just around this time that organizing began for the Arivoli campaigns of the early 1990s. Tamilcelvan was contacted by the leadership of the Tamil Nadu Science Forum in his capacity as a writer to help provide pedagogical literature for the movement. Every district had a literary figure who was called on to help. In Pudukkottai, it was the Tamil teacher and poet Muttu Nilavan, who had risen to national fame because of his song celebrating the women's cycling movement. "In Tirunelveli, they called upon me," Tamilcelvan said. "But I didn't have much experience working with this type of literature. I had already developed a style of writing village stories. My style was realist, but I had never really thought about writing for common people. I wrote about villages and common people quite a lot, but never for common people." His experience of writing *for* villagers would forever change his orientation to literature.

When we returned to Tamilcelvan's house, we sat down in the shade of the front veranda to discuss his Arivoli Iyakkam experience in more detail. "Within a few months of trying to teach the *Aṟivoḷi Tīpam* primers, we soon realized that this was not going to work. We fought hard to begin the lesson with *paṭṭā* and *paṭi*, but as Madasamy, their designer admits, we did not think about the language. There was no spoken language in the early primers." When I asked how that began to change, he told me that it was only when preparing longer texts for those who were already learning to read that the problem became clearer. The first attempts to construct longer texts in Tirunelveli District, where Tamilcelvan was working, were a series of short pamphlets designed to narrate Indian history in four parts, from the onset of colonialism to the story of Indian nationalism in southern India. The final small book focused on "Freedom Fighters of Southern Tamil Nadu," narrating the story of well-known local heroes like the chieftain Vira Pandia Kattabomman, who resisted the British army, later to be immortalized in folktales as well as one of the classics of Tamil cinema. He remarked that "it was an interesting challenge to write history for those who had never gone to school." But Tamilcelvan explained that the more immediate problem in this phase of the Arivoli movement was that posed by government officials. Soon after taking office, the new Tirunelveli District collector called him to his office with a complaint. "The books and pamphlets that you are publishing are all of one 'type' (using the English word). You need to stop teaching these history books and tell villagers about government development plans" (Tamilcelvan 2004b, 56). Shocked that this IAS officer did not understand what they had been trying to accomplish with the Arivoli Iyakkam, Tamilcelvan was not sure how to respond.

Instead of narrating history or simply writing about development plans, Tamilcelvan gathered a group of writers to start a monthly publication consisting of short fictional stories written in simple language for neoliterates. This magazine, named *Cāral* (Driving Rain), like its counterparts in other districts is where the artists of the progressive writers group who had been recruited for the literacy movement first started their experiments in writing prose in the language of village speech. As I asked him about the language commonly used in Tamil literature, Tamilcelvan explained what he saw as a long-standing prejudice against the language that people generally speak. "This is a *power* politics, a *cultural* politics," he argued, switching briefly from Tamil to English for emphasis, "and it was only through my experiences in Arivoli that I came to realize the depth of this disdain and the damage it has done. We have to break this [*oṭikkaṇum*]." He reflected on the fact that he too had been guilty of this in his own attitudes, and then argued that just as the Tamil nationalist movement had revolted against the dominance of Sanskrit, what is needed now is a new linguistic revolution against the hegemony of "high" *centamiḻ* written varieties of Tamil. "We need self-respect for the spoken word [*pēccunaṭaikku cuyamariyātai*]," he told me, invoking the early twentieth-century self-respect movement against caste and gender domination.

But his attempts to mirror reality, mimetically this time in the form of spoken language itself, led to more confrontations with the district administration. After a few issues of *Cāral* had been released and circulated, Tamilcelvan was called back to the collector's office, this time to meet with the officer in charge of maintaining the purity of Tamil language. He was asked why their literature did not conform to the standards established for schools, and he was told that all further publications that were written under the aegis of the Tamil Nadu state government would need to be approved by an officer from the Department for the Development of Tamil before publication.

Creating a People's Literature

By the mid-1990s, the Arivoli Iyakkam was shifting modes, from running as a Total Literacy Campaign focusing on basic letters, words, and signatures, to addressing the issue of continuing education for those who had learned simple reading and writing skills in the first phase of the movement. This shift meant that the Arivoli learners' circles would be fewer in number and smaller in size than the initial lessons. "But," Tamilcelvan explained, "it also meant that this was the time to broaden our focus not just on literacy education, on teaching people to sign their names. . . . This was the time to address problems facing society as a whole." The literature that developed in this phase would eventually be published by the Tamil Nadu Science Forum and the All-India Science Network (BGVS), not the state government or government of India, and it marks some of the most interesting experiments in trying to develop a literature that would be appropriate to a village readership while remaining true to the Left politics that the progressive writers were charged with fostering.

It was in this series of small books, written in large letters, that the writers of the Arivoli Iyakkam began to translate stories from a range of literary traditions into simple, spoken Tamil. The pamphlets prepared for the Makkal Vacippu Iyakkam included adaptations of classics of Tamil fiction, such as Pudumaippithan's "Caṅkut Tēvaṉiṉ Tarmam" (Sangu Devan's Dharma), which had been renamed "Muttācci." Other stories printed in Science Forum pamphlets were adaptations of classics from other languages, like *Les Misérables* and "How Much Land Does a Man Need." All these stories were chosen because they address the questions of poverty and survival in some respect or another, although not all of them were as didactic as Tolstoy or Hugo. O. Henry's "The Last Leaf," for example, tells the story of a young girl who was sick with pneumonia and decided that she would die when the last leaf fell from the tree outside her window. A poor artist living next door decided that he would brave terrible weather the night he was sure the final leaf would fall, to paint a leaf on the tree and thereby give hope to the young girl. The artist himself died in the process, but his masterpiece saved that girl's life. Many of the Science Forum pamphlets were also aimed at questions of religion. Another story published as a pamphlet and read aloud in villages tells of how a stone mile marker by the side of the road came to be worshipped as a deity, illustrating the means by which everyday objects come to be imbued with religious significance by humans.

The search for a new language in which to present these materials involved a great deal of experimentation. Writers of the movement would compose a rough draft of a story they wanted to use in the movement, and then go out in the evenings to a village that was participating in the reading movement and try it out. They would ask the villagers assembled to listen and then ask them which parts of the story were interesting or difficult to understand. Over the course of the following days, adjustments were made to the language in order to make the text more readable in consultation with other authors who were similarly involved in creating this new literature. This process could take several weeks of trials in various villages. It was through these experiments that a certain tension emerged between the desire to produce a literature in the regional dialects that villagers speak and the recognition that reading aloud requires it own special forms of language. Although all the authors involved in these efforts shared in the commitment to avoid standard written Tamil as it is taught in schools, they found that pamphlets written using purely spoken Tamil were more difficult to read aloud, and that the use of this language was even deemed inappropriate in some contexts. The desire to create a realist literature for Tamil villagers led them to focus on using realistic language, in an attempt to mimetically reproduce the sound of village Tamil on the written page. But the villagers who gathered regularly to listen to stories being read aloud in the Makkal Vacippu Iyakkam would often ask why activists used *ḵoṭuntamiḻ* (broken Tamil) or village speech in their reading materials. It seems that even when spoken aloud, the detour through writing demanded a language that was quite different from earlier efforts to render the spoken in written form. The authors of the movement would have to devise a language that was specifically designed for reciting aloud.

In 1996 the authors of the Makkal Vacippu Iyakkam established a main office in the centrally located southern city of Madurai, called the Bharat Gyan Vigyan Samiti (BGVS) Resource Center, where they would meet to discuss these issues and to learn from each other's efforts to devise a new language. The center was so named after the all-India network of science activists that I have described in chapter 1. Writers from all around the state would regularly travel by bus to meet at the BGVS Resource Center office, where they were given guidance by some of the luminaries of the Tamil folklore movement, like Ki. Rajanarayanan, who also participated in these experiments himself by writing an adaptation of *King Lear* set in rural Tamil Nadu. It was only after several experimental runs in different villages and a series of meetings critiquing the work that illustrations were added. Two thousand copies would then be printed up in Madurai and distributed through the Tamil Nadu Science Forum and Tamil Nadu Progressive Writers Association networks across the state. These pamphlets were then sold to local activists in villages for one rupee per pamphlet, about the price of a cup of tea.

The Turn to Folklore

Much early experimentation in the Makkal Vacippu Iyakkam had to do with the language of reading—that is, how to tell the story. As the search to develop a new genre of literature for villagers expanded in scope, however, writers in the movement became increasingly interested in studying the techniques and themes in stories told by Arivoli's village learners themselves. Still sitting next to me on the veranda in front of his house, Tamilcelvan explained, "We wanted to give them world literature and lessons about exploitation. We wanted to lift their consciousness with these stories. But people have their own calculations [*kaṇakku*]. They'll only put up with our talk for so long, then they'll stop coming to Arivoli classes to go prepare for the village festival or go take care of their fields. People have their own calculations about what to do, when, and it took us a long time to understand."

It was under the leadership of Madasamy and Tamilcelvan that the office that had been established in Madurai to discuss literary technique for the Makkal Vacippu Iyakkam eventually turned into a research center. Activists started collecting sayings, proverbs, riddles, tales of gods, and other folklore. They had trained a group of Arivoli volunteers at the resource center to read a story aloud, like the one about how a milestone turned into a god or the adaptation of *King Lear*, and then, after discussing it, they would ask one of the learners to tell a story they knew. These stories would be written down and brought back to the BGVS Resource Center in Madurai, where a substantial collection had developed. As their archive increased in size, many among the Arivoli Iyakkam movement leaders grew enthusiastic about the possibilities of fusing technique and theme by finding narrative material that could be turned into pamphlets to be read aloud among these stories, thus finally dissolving the distinction between author and public.

Tamilcelvan looked out from the veranda into the fields under the dimming sky while telling me how they established this research center for the BGVS working group that had been publishing pamphlets. Night was falling. "People already have a critique of their social situation buried in their folktales and in their proverbs," he explained. He then shared a favorite *colavaṭai* (adage) that he had learned over the course of his work in the villages of Tirunelveli to give me an example.

> tattippōṭṭa roṭṭi
> poṟaṭṭippōṭa nātiyillai.
>
> The roti that is cooking
> has no one to flip it.

These short, staccato lines manage to communicate a whole world of suffering through the metaphor of desiccation: like a burning chapati that has been left on the cooking stone without being turned over, the poor have been created and cast onto this earth without any protection. "Think of the knowledge in that, how sharply it is phrased! There are hundreds like this, and there are new ones coming up all the time," Tamilcelvan continued, switching to English again for emphasis, "where you can see social criticism. It's there in stories about village gods too. There is a history behind these gods. They are not like those at the big Brahmanical temples." But these forms of critical consciousness had not been recognized by those on the Left who thought that it was their job to bring consciousness to the countryside. He included himself in this group, telling me that it was the Arivoli Iyakkam that had helped him understand this.

Tamilcelvan brought me inside from the veranda, turned on a light and went to open the door of the metal cabinet sitting to the side of his office. He took out several boxes full of papers. "This is some of what came out of our project," he told me while taking out these materials. The papers piled up in those boxes contained hundreds, maybe thousands, of stories, proverbs, and songs. Arivoli volunteers who participated in this project had also made maps of where the shrines to gods were located in villages and they had kept notes about which communities propitiate which deities. The writers of the Makkal Vacippu movement had published some reading materials from this archive through the BGVS, including a collection of stories about "Witty Women" (*Putticāli Peṇkaḷ*, 1996) and a collection of adages and riddles, titled "Tongue without Bones" (*Eḻumpillāta Nākku,* 1999). But other stories that they had collected in the literacy movement would be published only later, in a set of pamphlets called "A Guidebook Series for Socio-Cultural Activists." Unlike the Makkal Vacippu Iyakkam pamphlets, these guidebooks were not necessarily to be read aloud. They were intended to sensitize activists of the Left to connections between politics and the sphere of cultural production that are often overlooked.

The guidebook that Tamilcelvan had written based on this archive was specifically about the role of religion in the cultural life of the rural poor. It is called "Village Gods: Our Allied Front" (*Nāṭṭār Teyvaṅkaḷ: Namatu Nēca Aṇi*, 2003). In this book, Tamilcelvan makes the argument that many local gods that inhabit villages represent a form of critical consciousness that exhibits some parallels with secularism. The stories of these gods should be thought of as resistance to the modes of cultural hegemony (*paṇpāṭṭu mēlātikkattai*) reproduced in more institutionalized religious settings, be they Saivite, Vaishnava, Christian, or Muslim. Tamilcelvan writes in this book that these stories provide a vantage point for an immanent critique of caste and gender domination, from within folklore itself. This critique may not be the same as that of science, but it is nevertheless important for activists of the Left, especially those in the Tamil Nadu Science Forum, to respect the forms of reason that inform these narratives, rather than dismiss religion altogether. This book draws both on anthropology and his own experience collecting and reading stories with villagers, through a series of stories about gods who came about because of the violence of humans toward each other, to show the forms of historical consciousness that are manifest in village folklore. Tamilcelvan ends with the argument that "these village gods are not there for us to use as instruments, we must rather understand them as our natural allies in our struggle against oppression" (2003, 30).[10] While I sat reading and taking notes from this handbook and other files he had collected from the BGVS research project, Tamilcelvan moved to the kitchen and started to warm up some dinner. I then joined him at the table. He told me that his latest project was writing a cookbook for rural men, who do not normally cook if they live with women, based on recipes he had been collecting. After eating, we went to sleep, and I took a bus back home to Pudukkottai the following morning.

Tamilcelvan's story, as he told it to me that day in Pattamadai and as he was writing at the time in his memoirs, was that of a seemingly endless search for techniques of storytelling that are adequate to the Marxist theory of class struggle he held as foundational. I have told his story in some detail because I think it is representative of a range of authors who sought to engage with villagers through the medium of literature, and furthermore because he is, in fact, at once a talented storyteller and activism theorist. The desire to find that perfect fit, a mode of narrative production that would revolutionize the villages they had become intimate with and transform activists themselves into a conduit for critical energies that already existed, was a source of consistent unease for middle-class writers like Tamilcelvan. More often than not, his reflections took the form of questioning and self-criticism for failing to live up to what he must surely have understood to be rather utopian goals. But his search never ceased, even when, shortly before I met him, he decided to take his literary activism in a different direction as he withdrew from the literacy movement to devote himself full-time to his work with the Tamil Nadu Progressive Writers Association. Tamilcelvan remains a prolific author as president of the Tamil Nadu Progressive Writers Association, and his more recent pamphlets include an introduction to the history of Left politics and basic Gramscian theory for working-class readers, called "I Like Politics" (*Araciyal Eṉakku Piṭikkum,* 2004a), as well as his cookbook for men.

In their efforts to expand what Koselleck (2004) would call the "horizon of expectation" among Tamil Nadu's villagers through a refiguration of existing "spaces of experience," the authors of the Makkal Vacippu Iyakkam succeeded to a large extent in devising truly innovative genres of literature and new modes of literary production. "Revolution on the government tab" might not have been in the cards, and there will always be severe social and material constraints on literature's capacity to mobilize the rural poor. But similar efforts to forge a people's literature are continuing in Tamil villages today, as a new generation of activists draw on this literary genre. Apart from the literary genre they developed, the authors of the early phases of the Makkal Vacippu Iyakkam also left a trail of theoretical reflections, a set of practical guides for fellow travelers, and perhaps most important, a general model of activism based on a sort of textual reciprocity.

It was precisely this model of activism that defined the search for a method in the Makkal Vacippu Iyakkam that would continue to animate the efforts of people like Karuppiah and Neela in Pudukkottai. These two were among the young volunteers who read texts aloud to large groups in the late 1990s and reported back to the authors about how the readings were received in villages. During the time of my fieldwork, in the early 2000s, they had become authors in their own right, representing a generation of villagers who were forever changed by the model of activism Tamilcelvan had helped devise. Let us now turn to some of their engagements with using literature in the service of activism in an attempt to understand the lasting effects of this model of activism and the complexity of this project in action.

The Practice of Reading in Katrampatti

Back in Pudukkottai, Karuppiah decided to hold small-scale Makkal Vacippu Iyakkam reading events in the village of Katrampatti for the group of Dalit women he had been working with. These learners had gotten about six months into their lessons when they began to set aside one night every week from studying the normal primers to read a story and discuss it. After fifteen minutes of practicing their signatures and writing out the name of their village, the group would be rewarded with a storytelling session. Everyone in the group preferred listening as someone read aloud to struggling with the script. Sometimes Karuppiah would read the stories to the group himself, and on other occasions he would ask one of the three young women who acted as the local Arivoli volunteers to do so. These events were not as large as the reading of *A Doll's House* we had seen before in Mayakkurichi, a reading that must have attracted at least thirty listeners. But the reading sessions that were incorporated into lessons in Katrampatti did seek to include other interlocutors, not only the women who were taking literacy lessons and the Arivoli volunteers. Everyone from the small village was called to come enjoy and discuss the stories. It was mainly the younger children who also participated, while some of the older men of the village would sit off to the sides and listen in.

Karuppiah began these efforts by reading stories from a new series of pamphlets that he had collected at the Arivoli Iyakkam and Tamil Nadu Science Forum offices in Pudukkottai.[11] The stories that he and the volunteers read from these pamphlets were borrowed from a range of literary traditions, as earlier Makkal Vacippu Iyakkam efforts had been. The first set of stories they tried out with the Katrampatti group, for example, included comic tales from North India of the Mughal emperor Akbar and his minister Birbal, bringing folklore from other regions into the mix, along with European and Tamil short stories. Watching Karuppiah's efforts and learning about the earlier Makkal Vacippu Iyakkam trials, I had begun to collect the original pamphlets that had been published by Tamilcelvan and his team. After a series of visits to Science Forum members across Tamil Nadu and Pondicherry, I had managed to collect most of the forty or so publications they had issued over the course of the 1990s, and Karuppiah soon switched from the new pamphlets back to these for storytelling. He found that the original pamphlets were more suited to the aims of raising critical awareness than the newer ones were, and he held a certain fondness for that time in the movement, when anything seemed possible.

On several occasions, after reading these stories aloud to the group, Karuppiah tried to elicit other stories from the women of Katrampatti in response. He hoped to make use of my recording equipment to capture these stories as a contribution to the larger project that had begun earlier under the leadership of the Madurai research group. But the women of Katrampatti always claimed that they were not good storytellers and that he should ask his own aunt, who was known by all to be an expert in this domain. The learners in this group always preferred to reciprocate through song. Sometimes Neela would come to take part in these events and she would trade songs, mainly lullabies and work songs, with the women from Katrampatti. She too had taken a deep interest in village folklore as a result of her activist work and her engagement with fellow writers in the Makkal Vacippu Iyakkam like Tamilcelvan. While they never managed to record stories in the context of Arivoli lessons, several critical discussions about social conditions that would have been of interest to the writers of the Makkal Vacippu Iyakkam did take place as a result of these reading sessions. However, these arose in a fashion that could not have been anticipated by the authors of the texts. Here, I present two examples from Katrampatti.

On Leaving Home

Among the pamphlets I had managed to track down from the original Makkal Vacippu Iyakkam experiments, Karuppiah especially liked one that consisted of a collection of Tamil tales, drawing on a moral folk literature somewhat akin to Aesop's fables. These stories were already known to most listeners, but the pamphlet presented them in such as way as to elicit discussion from the literacy group with a series of questions about the fable after the main text. He decided to try these very short tales out in Katrampatti.

One evening, after nearly half an hour of practicing signatures and writing out the first words in the literacy primers, Karuppiah began the reading lesson, "OK, shall we read a story?" Karuppiah proceeded to read the first short story in the collection aloud to the group of women and children who had come for the lesson that evening. This was a story about a village householder who is determined to leave his family in pursuit of spiritual awakening, becoming an ascetic renouncer and living in the forest. The renouncer decides that he must get a cat because mice are eating away at his loincloth, which is his only possession. But in order to keep a cat, he needs to secure milk to feed the cat, and so he decides to get a cow, which, in turn requires someone to keep it and take it out grazing, eventually leading him to ask a man to come tend to the cow. Finally, the man keeping the cow demands that his family come to live with him, or he will not be able to tend to the cow, which was required for the milk, to keep the cat, which would keep away the mice, landing the renouncer right back where he started in the world of householders and material possessions. Even though the pamphlet Karuppiah was reading from had been written in a language meant to be read aloud, he did nevertheless feel the need to reword some phrases or ideas using the local village language normally used in storytelling. His tone of voice would also change when rewording, slipping into an intimate drawl when directly addressing his listeners. It seems that even when reformulated for reading aloud, stories need to go through a further "intralingual translation" in the act of telling itself. While he was reading the story, several listeners said that they had heard it before.

When the tale was finished, Karuppiah read the final lines from the pamphlet, "You tell [*nīṅkaḷē colluṅkaḷ*]. Is it all right to leave your wife and people to go live as a renouncer?" Then, switching into the voice he used when talking to the group, he asked, "Then? What do you think? [*eṉṉa niṉekkiṟīṅka?*]" Those who had gathered for the reading quickly responded in agreement that it is not. On this point, there was not much debate. Several women did go on to point out, however, that sometimes life in the village could become so unbearable that it was temping for people to leave and go off on their own. But it was not religious renunciation that they had in mind. What had animated their reflections on the need to escape village life was a desire to go to somewhere where caste would have less of a bearing on their identity and where greater opportunities were available. The option to reject the social world and to follow the spiritual path of an ascetic was far more remote for women than it was for men, in any case.

In one of the most explicit critical comments on local caste dominance I had yet heard in Arivoli Iyakkam lessons, one of the learners, Racamani, turned to me and declared, "This place is no good! [*ūr ceriyille!*] There is nothing for us here [*oṉṟumēyille*]. My two sons have already moved to Chennai and I want to go join them. I need to get out of here. As soon as I've given Thangammal to get married, I'm leaving," she said, referring to her twenty-two-year-old daughter, who had already fallen asleep, too tired to attend lessons that evening. Her fellow learners appeared a little surprised that she should be so forthright in front of outsiders. But they understood the sentiment very well. Almost every one of the Dalit families in Katrampatti had sent their boys to find work in Chennai. When I asked Racamani why she wanted to leave, a number of other learners joined into the conversation, agreeing with her that work in the fields was too sporadic and that there was no progress in the village of Katrampatti. They mentioned the fact that they had no cremation ground because the dominant Kallar caste would not let them use their old one. Govindammal also chimed in, "What do we get paid here? My son works with computers and makes good money in Madras. But I'm too old to go anywhere [*eṉakku vayicāyipōccu*]. I'll just stay here. Let the children go [*puḷḷaiṅkayellā pōkaṭṭum*]." This was the time of the village festival and many of the young people who had grown up in Katrampatti had come back home from Chennai for a short holiday, to visit their families and have some fun. It appeared as if many had asked their parents to join them, and thoughts of moving to the city were weighing on many people's minds.[12]

Karuppiah contributed little to this conversation, and many of their comments were addressed to me, not him. But he was clearly saddened by their condemnation of the village, whose improvement he had put all his energies into as an activist. He had not anticipated this reaction to his question about leaving one's family, which was aimed at provoking discussion of the role of religion in making life decisions. For the women of Katrampatti, any thought of leaving the village would be motivated by the desire to join one's family in pursuit of a better life. The pull of city life for the Dalit residents of Katrampatti was something Karuppiah was already very familiar with through his experience, even if it was not something he would normally discuss with the women who came to Arivoli lessons. He was, in fact, friendly with many of the young men who had gone to Chennai in search of a better life, and he would see them there regularly when he visited. Some of the young men that he would relate to as an "aṇṇaṉ" (older brother) worked for a taxi service that had been started by his childhood friend from Kovilpatti, and some were trying to find work in the film industry. Karuppiah would eventually try to enable the literacy group to solve the problem of the cremation ground by getting them to write a petition. But on this occasion, the frank discussion of how bad the village is for those he hoped to come closer to through literacy lessons disturbed him. It was a direct indictment of caste relations, and furthermore, it seemed to contain the underlying claim that there was little scope for the improvement of local conditions of oppression for Dalits. Karuppiah went on to read another story from the pamphlet, remaining much less animated than usual throughout the rest of the Arivoli lesson.

On Defying Tradition

The second event of reading I would like to describe took place in Katrampatti several months later, during the rainy season, and it illustrates how the context of the literacy lesson itself can be more important than the text being recited in the Makkal Vacippu Iyakkam. The rainy season is a time of extra work requiring the women from Katrampatti to put in long days in the fields, and it is also when flu viruses are most troublesome. A number of the women had been complaining to me about their body aches for a few days, and lessons had been canceled for nearly a week because of weather conditions. But the sky cleared one day, and they had promised Karuppiah on their way to the fields in the morning that they would be ready for class at about nine o'clock in the evening, after cooking dinner and putting their children to bed. Although Karuppiah normally led the literacy classes in Katrampatti, he was feeling ill that day, so it was up to Neela to come and conduct the class and to read a story aloud from one of the older pamphlets I had been collecting.

I met Neela at the bus stop near the temple entrance in Kovilpatti on the main road, and we went up the dark dirt road that leads through the rice fields to Katrampatti together by motorbike. On our arrival, all the women who were participating in the literacy classes were already assembled, sitting on the damp ground under a streetlamp next to the small, empty room built to store a public television set that someone had stolen long ago. They had been called to come by the volunteers. In addition to the regular group, two young women visiting from a neighboring village had joined the class that evening. The lesson began as usual, with Sumathi, one of the young local village volunteers, singing some Arivoli songs about the need to send children to school. The women then started practicing their signatures. Some of them had to practice on the wet mud with their finger because they had given the small slates and chalk that Karuppiah had earlier distributed to their children for use at school.

Neela then suggested that they turn to storytelling, and she started to read aloud from "*Kāycca Maram*" (Fruit Tree), the adaptation of *King Lear* that had been prepared for the Makkal Vacippu Iyakkam by the author and folklorist Ki. Rajanarayanan. About one or two minutes into the story, Neela looked up and saw half her audience falling asleep in front of her. It was already getting late and everyone had put in a very hard day of work. Realizing she would not get far with the reading, Neela closed her book and started to ask questions of the two visitors to the literacy circle that night, trying to place them socially by asking which village they belonged to. Through her questioning, she learned that they had come to deliver news of the death of their maternal uncle, who once had connections to Katrampatti. The two young women went on to describe the unusual funeral that followed the old man's demise, where the eldest daughter of the deceased defied tradition by lighting the funeral pyre, instead of a male relative lighting it as it was traditionally done. Sensing an opportunity to liven up the meeting, Neela asked the others who had gathered if it was right for her to do so, taking into account the fact that she had no brothers and she was especially close to her father. If the tragic story of children who abandoned their parents that she had tried to read aloud was not keeping her listeners' attention, Neela thought that this story might be of more interest.

Everyone began to wake up and involve themselves in the heated debate that ensued. Some fought for the daughter's right to light the pyre, while others argued that was simply wrong, no matter what other changes in women's social position had been taking place. The two visitors, who supported a woman's right to play a ritual role usually reserved for men, invoked the principle of equality between the sexes. They told Neela and the others how they had been discussing gender in their Arivoli Iyakkam classes back home and they saw no reason why the tradition cannot change. But this argument made no impact on those who said that such behavior simply goes against the rules of "*cāstiram*" (Sanskrit, *shāstra*). "You can't just go around doing what you want," Govindammal reasoned. Eventually people began asking questions of me about the United States, and whether such a thing would be done there. After clumsily responding with an explanation that in the United States, as in India, women's roles in society had changed dramatically over the past thirty years, I was told that U.S. women were not civilized in any case (*nāḵarīḵam illāma*) because they walked around with their hair loose, they didn't wear bindis on their foreheads, and there was no affection between people as there was in Indian villages.[13] The United States they had seen in films on television was clearly not an attractive model to follow.

Once the debate had lost some steam, Neela decided to draw the meeting to a close. She never managed to finish the story from the pamphlet that she had started reading. Neela took her leave, and I gave her a ride back to the bus stop on the main road. While we were waiting for the bus to come take Neela back to her village, I felt the need to apologize for the fact that the group was unresponsive to the reading. But she was not disappointed at all. "Look at all the important things that we discussed! Gender equality, the power of religious belief, and we are able to learn about America because you are here. To get them to speak about what they think, that's a politics too, right? [*atuvum oru araciyal illaiyā?*]" She then repeated something she had told me over a year before, shortly after I had met her, a phrase that had stuck with me ever since, and that I have already mentioned in the introduction to this book. As the bus was coming to a stop in front of the temple gate, she said, "We get all these books and instructions from big people in Chennai and Madurai. But we need to run this movement according to the mud of this place [*inta maṇ tavunta mātiri inta iyakkam naṭakkaṇum*]." Having summed up her position on activism through the idiom of agriculture and the quality of place once again, Neela got on the bus and went home.[14]

I was already aware of the fact that the Makkal Vacippu Iyakkam had collected folktales and proverbs from learners, and I had seen interesting stories emerge from casual conversation at Arivoli Iyakkam lessons before; but it was only at this point, well into my fieldwork, that I came to fully appreciate how the vigilant activist could turn what appeared to me as a failed lesson into an opportunity. It turns out that Neela had, in fact, taken note of how this reported story spurred critical conversation in Katrampatti. She had been keeping a diary of such conversations, some of which would reappear in her short stories. When I saw her at the main Arivoli office two days later, she told me that she would be using what she had learned that night from the two visiting Arivoli students to initiate similar discussions in some of the other Arivoli circles she visited regularly by telling them about the woman who defied tradition by lighting the funeral pyre. Whether or not the story ever made it into print, it appears that a new pedagogical text had been born that evening.

The Social Lives of Texts

The two episodes I have related from Katrampatti illustrate the degree to which the lives of artistic works escape authorial intention, a well-worn theme in poststructuralist thought. They illuminate, more specifically, the specific *social mediations* conditioning the trajectory of what linguistic anthropologists refer to as "entextualization," the process of uptake and subsequent recontextualization of discourse that allows for the circulation of texts and the formation of publics around texts (Bauman and Briggs 1990; Silverstein and Urban 1996). The story about the renouncer, which Karuppiah read out, had been taken out of the context envisioned by the Madurai research group that had collected it elsewhere and published it. The story had been reinserted by the women of Katrampatti into a critique of local caste relations, and tied to a desire that seems to have conflicted with Karuppiah's. His aim was certainly not to provoke a discussion on leaving the village. In the second case, the story that Neela had intended to read was replaced with another one that grew out of questions she posed to the two visitors that evening, sparking a debate that could not have been anticipated. The text that emerged, the story of an unorthodox ritual, would subsequently be recontextualized in later literacy lessons with the aim of producing similar effects. I do not know how well Neela's strategy worked. But it is not for these reasons that we should deem the massive efforts that went into producing a literature for the Makkal Vacippu Iyakkam irrelevant.

That a certain underdetermination of effective meaning is built into the process of textual production and circulation is something that the authors who worked with the Arivoli Iyakkam had become well aware of, especially those with personal experience teaching classes. Any activist with experience teaching and reading texts in a village soon became very conscious of the fact that learners come to lessons with their own histories and orientations to textuality that will condition uptake in ways that cannot be known ahead of time. The fact that texts gather new meanings as they are reanimated across contexts was, in fact, at the heart of the desire on the part of activists to bring Ibsen's text, for example, to a "recovered" habit of reading aloud that had been built over generations around a rather different textual corpus, purposefully allowing what Neela referred to as the qualities of "this soil" to continuously muddy the clarity of Arivoli's Enlightenment project. A particular form of reflexivity among activists is born of such experiences, when learners reframe such a text by making it relevant to their concerns. Activists and authors would thus repeatedly experience the limits of authorial intentionality in their attempts to provoke a prescribed set of reactions to the stories they read.

What writers were pursuing in the Makkal Vacippu Iyakkam was a methodology that could incorporate this fact of textual underdeterminacy into their creative practice, and so learn from experience in search of a performative genre that would provide room for public argument. They had moved from a theoretical commitment to realist description, as the self-evident stance a politically engaged progressive author must take, to a position of active participation through forms of textual mimesis and reciprocity. The methods they developed over the course of the Makkal Vacippu Iyakkam would, in the end, more closely resemble the dialogical ideal that they claimed to be pursuing in the basic primers than earlier methods had. A context had certainly been created through this movement for activists to learn more from their fellow villagers and for new stories to arise as materials for instruction, thus pushing against, if not dissolving, the deeply entrenched distinction between author and public that Benjamin had long ago hoped would fade away. But that "degree zero" of communication with the subaltern, a true unification of theory and praxis, would always remain elusive for the authors involved, pulling the movement and motivating experimentation. The writers of the Makkal Vacippu Iyakkam could never understand such transparency as a realizable goal, even when it fueled their desire, motivating new attempts at mediation.[15]

Nor was it the case that writers like Tamilcelvan or Madasamy finally found forms of social critique that would be adequate to their own vision of the political in the stories they collected in villages and then reproduced as printed texts, or even in the discussions that ensued in literacy classes as a result of these experiments. Reading aloud and discussing stories like that of the renouncer, or trading adages and riddles, could only act as a performative context to bring people into a dialogue. But all the artists of the Tamil Nadu Progressive Association, including Neela and Karuppiah, remained committed to radical political change and to forms of social knowledge that are, in some important respects, incommensurable with the textual traditions they rediscovered and engaged with through the reading movement. A full entry into the field of politics, as these writers and activists understood it, would require villagers to join the progressive writers, the Tamil Nadu Science Forum, or perhaps even parties like the CPI(M). Like the village gods described in Tamilcelvan's guidebook, then, the stories and modes of reading that emerged in the Makkal Vacippu Iyakkam could not be used as "instruments" in the project of Enlightenment. These texts and techniques of mediation were perhaps better approached as allies, or friends.

Against Resolution

Much energy in the critical theory of language has been spent emphasizing the irreducibility of poetics and social contexts of performativity as integral to any language use. These elements of communication are inherent to the very materiality of language, enabling discourse to circulate, and not mere appendages to a referential "meaning" or *logos* that would precede them. This common line of argument is nicely summarized by Slavoj Žižek: "What the tradition of Enlightenment dismisses as a mere disturbance of 'normal' communication turns out to be its positive condition. The concrete intersubjective space of symbolic communication is always structured by various (unconscious) textual devices that cannot be reduced to secondary rhetoric" (1994, 10). But it is only recently that researchers have begun to explore the question how this division between the material and the ideal, and corollary distinctions between the poetic and the referential, have come to be so salient in the first place.

Some point to Lockean empiricism as the origin of this particular set of semiotic problems, while others argue that a language ideology that divides the world of language into fleshly matter and divine spirit has deep ties in Protestant theology.[16] Webb Keane (2007), for example, suggests that the materiality and poetic qualities of language have posed serious problems for theories of agency in traditions of thought indebted to what he calls a Christian modern "semiotic ideology." More recently, Bate (2010) has examined how nineteenth-century missionaries incorporated Tamil poetics with great difficulty within a distinctly Protestant orientation to textuality in an effort to create a new public sphere in the bazaars of Ceylon and southern India. In this chapter, I have built on these analytical efforts to understand how such problematics arise in efforts to remake the world through an examination of how those working with the political Left's post-Enlightenment ideology of communication have wrestled with the question of language's materiality. I have also sought understand what this might mean for the theory of realism as social critique. Like the missionaries before them, the literary Marxists had to do a lot of "linguistic and cultural work" to find media and techniques adequate to serve a cause that was nevertheless quite different, even if it was similarly invested in the question of human agency.

I have therefore focused on a series of realizations, experiments, and realignments that took place over the course of the Makkal Vacippu Iyakkam in an attempt to understand the role of texts in activists' efforts to provoke political action. We saw how this reading movement started out as an attempt inspired by the ideals of the Tamil Nadu Progressive Writers Association to bring modern Indian history and realist world literature to the soil of Tamil villages. It had since turned into an ethnographic research project of sorts. The emergence of a new reflexivity among activist authors regarding the roles of language and culture was the result of sustained experimentation with the mediating potentials of literary form in the service of activism. However, this was not a turn to the dominant vision of ancient Tamil language and culture that is propagated by the leaders of Dravidian nationalism. Activists drew instead on a certain cosmopolitan ethos, despite the sometimes dogmatic aesthetic and political leanings of the literary association they belonged to, that allowed them to engage with forms of community and culture that escape the nationalist desire to render these forms as identity. But not all activists in the Arivoli Iyakkam were equally enthusiastic about the new modes of literature and narration that resulted from these experiments.

Those leaders in the Arivoli Iyakkam who were critical of the turn to engage with folklore and village storytelling methods in the movement began to question the value of attaching too much importance to questions of "culture." The search for appropriate learning materials within the history of Tamil textuality, the latter group argued, had obscured the larger mission of Enlightenment that the Arivoli movement had been charged with. One of the founders of the Arivoli Iyakkam in Pondicherry, Dr. Sundararaman, for example, argued for a literature that was more directly political and more oriented toward a discussion of practical issues. "I was very concerned with questions of livelihood," he told me when I interviewed him at his home after telling him about my visit to see Tamilcelvan in Pattamadai. He continued, "And very bothered about messages regarding poverty and exploitation, while some in the movement were going on about folklore and collecting stories. You see, there is the spice of the food, but it is not the food. Salt perhaps, but it's not rice, you know? *I was trying to give them rice*. I've always been concerned with livelihood, life and death issues. We can't take this cultural angle too far." The nutritious core of politics and scientific knowledge, he argued, had been obscured by what he understood as the outer decorative garb of "culture."

Whereas Sundararaman had been supportive of the effort to render stories like *Les Misérables* in a form that could be read by villagers, because it addressed issues of poverty quite directly, he questioned the value of incorporating forms of folklore that had no immediate pedagogical value at the level of politics. When I asked him about what this argument meant for the Arivoli Iyakkam, he continued, explaining his own decision to leave the literacy movement to focus on what he saw as the more concrete realm of political activism around health issues among the poor: "In a sense, the movement needed these tensions, and when the tensions died, so did the movement. So at the time when it was resolved in favor of a particular approach, I think the campaigns had lost their steam. And I myself was against the approach and I never came back." Sundararaman's objections to taking culture too far are indicative of an aspect of Marxist materialism that would, perhaps paradoxically, limit engagement with the very materiality of language in the process of political activism, not unlike the problem of language that had been posed by missionaries before. But Tamilcelvan and others who were also working in the Marxist tradition would likely share his focus on the importance of "tensions" within the movement, as sources of intellectual and practical propulsion.

Back in Katrampatti, where a different set of tensions were still emerging between Karuppiah and the women of the Arivoli Iyakkam learners circle, the conversations that emerged around literacy lessons nevertheless raised some important social problems for public discussion. One of these issues, which Karuppiah had decided could be tied back to the project of literacy, was that of the cremation ground. They still had nowhere to cremate their dead. Although not a direct result either of lessons taught through the basic literacy primers or the stories he read aloud to them in the Makkal Vacippu Iyakkam experiments, the discussions surrounding the lack of a cremation ground for the Dalits of Katrampatti inspired Karuppiah to work toward writing a petition to the collector, demanding a remedy. The final months of Karuppiah's efforts as an activist with the women of Katrampatti were therefore devoted to this project. If they spent nearly a year learning to read and write, being exposed to Arivoli's pedagogy, Karuppiah hoped that it would now be their turn to write back to the state, and solve a very pressing social problem. It is back to these efforts, which I described briefly in the introduction of this book, that we now turn.

5

Subject to Citizenship

Petitions and the Performativity of Signature

Petitioning the state became an act of citizenship for Arivoli Iyakkam activists and their followers in a place where such appeals have long been understood in terms of subjection and even servitude. The literacy movement sought to democratize access to this mode of asserting citizenship by encouraging people who would previously have relied on others to write on their behalf to submit their own petitions at the district headquarters. Explaining the changes she had seen since the beginning of the Arivoli Iyakkam, for example, Sundari, a literacy-movement organizer in Pudukkottai, explained, "Before Arivoli, if village people wanted to give a petition, they'd go to someone else: 'Father! [*ayyā*!] Lord! [*cāmi*!] We need to give a petition to the collector somehow. You take it and give it.' After Arivoli, those people will go see the collector directly [*nēraṭiyāḵa*] themselves. They've come to represent themselves [*cuyacārpuḵḵu vantiṭṭāṅḵa*]." Sundari's story echoes the broader enlightenment narrative of people freeing themselves from the degradation of traditional hierarchies and representing themselves as rights-bearing citizens directly before the state. Activists therefore frame these acts of self-representation as acts of self-determination.

Remember that this book began with such an act when the Katrampatti literacy group embarked on a trip to the collector's office, where they filed a petition regarding land for a cremation ground. In this case, it was a group of Dalit women who took on the role of representing themselves and their community's problems through a petition. Because of their low-caste status, they were denied access to the cremation ground they had been previously using. It was in an effort to contest caste dominance through appeal to the state that Karuppiah had persuaded the literacy group to work toward submitting a petition. To submit a written petition, as this literacy group did, is to engage fields of political power that extend well beyond the village of Katrampatti.

Submitting a petition also means yielding directly to the state bureaucracy and, more specifically, to what Foucault (2007) identified as governmentality: those infrastructures of circulation and classification that enable the modern state to produce and manage populations. A number of scholars have interpreted similar development programs through the lens of governmentality to examine the production of new subjects to regulatory rationality in rural India. Ethnographic accounts have focused on ambivalence among differently positioned social actors who sit in "structurally dependent but antagonistic positions" as a result of government strategies to address poverty and gender inequality (Gupta 2001, 66; see also Sharma 2008). That people like the Dalit petitioners from Katrampatti had become a target population in similar development efforts goes some distance toward explaining their participation in the official grievance process. But this fact does not account for why it was writing in particular that was thought by many to mark their entry into the sphere of modern citizenship nor can it explain how writing technology has produced new relationships to structures of governance more broadly. It is for these reasons that scholars such as Veena Das (2004), Akhil Gupta (2012), Matthew Hull (2012), Nayanika Mathur (2012), Aradhana Sharma (forthcoming), and Emma Tarlo (2001) are also turning their attention to the practices of inscription that are entailed in the production of bureaucratic state power in contemporary South Asia. Their work has pushed beyond the paradigm of governmentality to understand how technologies of literacy produce citizen subjects. The study I have undertaken builds on this reformulated theory of postcolonial statecraft by engaging further with the political claims that cohere around literacy in the process of activist mobilization. Whereas many ethnographers focusing on the state are coming to theoretical terms with the importance of writing practices, I have endeavored to understand how literacy worked as an ethical horizon for activism: a struggle to interrogate the world of rights available to citizens, with political claims made by subjects who do not have the means to demand such rights.

We are nevertheless faced with a paradox insofar as a technology enabling the dissolution of a division of representative labor also stands as the very means by which the political fate of local struggles has been tied to a state apparatus of governance. Petitioning the state in writing marks entry into a new hierarchy of power, one that is already defined by the conflicting values of liberal citizenship and a development-based governmentality. Despite the claims of some literacy activists, it makes little analytical sense to speak of a simple transition from servitude to enlightened citizenship. Contemporary petitioning appears to be suspended somewhere between modernizing ideologies of bureaucratic rationality, democratic self-determination, modes of political action expressed as devotional subjection to the will of a sovereign, and senses of justice that cannot be captured by any of these paradigms. The idioms of caste and gender hierarchy have not been fully subsumed under the logic of citizenship or even that of governmentality; rather, competing value orientations to political action continually jostle with one another, producing new forms of friction, new forms of social critique, and new articulations of governmental power.

Instead of sweeping these complexities under the carpet of a prefabricated theoretical framework, I propose to linger for a moment with the paradoxes of addressing the state in writing. Unlike studies that have sought to understand how textual reifications forged under colonialism became grounds for contemporary politics, I examine the event of textual production itself in a decidedly postcolonial context of governance. I do so with aim of understanding how competing logics of power have been imbricated through the petitioning process, and to make some sense of the dramatic increase in petitioning among rural women who have been encouraged by literacy activism. It is in the very act of composing a petition that agents of government employ a pedagogical stance toward citizen subjects, and it is also in this act of text production that critical orientations emerge among those who are being disciplined in this fashion. The textual structure of petitions themselves constitutes a zone where competing models of social power are also rendered evident. I pay special attention to how the Arivoli Iyakkam has sought to change the language of petitioning to fit its model of Enlightenment, focusing in particular on the tension between self-representation and self-determination. Before turning to the ethnography of contemporary text making at the collector's office, however, we must pause for a moment to understand the broader historical outlines of petitioning in southern India.

Reimagining a Colonial Inheritance

Petitioning the state with one's grievances is a practice that dates back well into precolonial times.[1] It has become clear, however, that the establishment of administrative offices, under the East India Company in the late eighteenth and early nineteenth centuries, gave foundational shape to the forms of petitioning now found in South India (Raman 2012; Swarnalatha 2001).[2] A push to standardize the administrative process in response to accusations of illiberal government led to the official establishment of a formal corps known as the Indian Civil Service (ICS) in 1855.[3] The British collector of a district received petitions both at his office on designated days and "in the field" at specific "camps." As indicated by his title, the collector's job was primarily that of a revenue official. But the smooth collection of taxes required the quelling of rural political disturbances, and petitions offered the colonial administration a means of addressing potential sources of trouble. Scholars who have examined the workings of this new form of administration tend to agree that "many of these colossal structures of colonial 'rationalism' had feet of vernacular clay" (Kaviraj 1984, 227). This is because the structures of governance were not only dominated at the top levels by the English-language medium, they were premised on the institutionalization of a transcendent reason that would consistently define itself against the "natives" it was to rule over. In the princely state of Pudukkottai, petitions were sent to the king, whose crown Nicholas Dirks (1993) has described as "hollow" under indirect British rule. In Dirks's account of the bureaucratization of royal authority, he notes how expedient measures to secure political power nevertheless required the maintenance of forms of political legitimation that were deemed "customary." "Colonialism did not usher in modern institutions and ideologies, instead curiously blending its own forms with those of the old regime" (354). We will see shortly how his "curious blend" persists in some respects today at the collector's office, which is housed in what was formerly the royal palace.

Indians started joining the ICS in large numbers after the Government of India Act of 1919. This moment also marks the development of a more pedagogical orientation to rural populations. According to the Montagu-Chelmsford reforms, the newly Indianized ICS would not only provide the "executive machinery of government; it will be their part to assist as only they can do on the training of the rural classes for self-government; their help will be greatly needed to explain the new principles of Government to *many who will find them strange.*" With independence in 1947, the ICS was renamed the Indian Administrative Service (IAS), and while still controlled through a very competitive examination system, many more women and people from the lower castes have joined, enabled in part through India's affirmative action policy. The political relationship the administration is supposed to have with its petitioning subjects has also changed in theory. Erstwhile subjects are now supposed to be citizens, and collectors are to serve them.

The final major reframing of governance and petitioning in Tamil Nadu prior to the Arivoli Iyakkam was a gesture meant to claim the institutions of rural administration for the Tamil people. In 1969, the recently elected Dravida Munnetra Kazhagam (DMK) government of Tamil Nadu declared every Monday at collector's offices across the state as Grievance Day, known in Tamil as *maṉu nīti nāḷ* (Petition Justice Day). In addition, the state began to run the Mass Contact Program, a monthly event in which the collector and other revenue officials travel to interior villages to receive petitions on location.[4] The Petition Justice Plan gives petitions submitted on Grievance Day and in villages selected for the Mass Contact Program a special status such that they must be "disposed of" within a month. Under the new regime of petitioning, those submitting petitions are also given a receipt saying that they may contact the office or submit another petition if they do not hear back from the authorities within a month of the original submission.

The petitioning process has a complex heritage. When asked about the origins of petitioning, many of the workers I spoke to in the collector's and tahsildar's offices told me about a king, not about British colonial rule. They recounted the story of Manu Needhi, known very well throughout Tamil Nadu: one thousand years ago there lived a just and enlightened Chola emperor whose son, the rambunctious prince, one day ran over a calf while speeding through the countryside on his chariot. The mother cow whose calf had been killed by the prince immediately went in sorrow and rang the village bell demanding justice. On hearing the bell and the mother cow's complaint, the emperor was outraged and judged that his own son's life must be sacrificed in the name of justice. A statue of this mother cow ringing the justice bell now stands in front of the Tamil Nadu High Court in Chennai, and I suspect the story has taken on new life with its use by the DMK as a foundational story for their *maṉu nīti tiṭṭam* (Petition Justice Plan). The DMK government's use of this royal history stands as both a gesture to connect with the people and an invocation of indigenous and enlightened Tamil royal tradition. The institution of Grievance Day was formalized as such by the DMK through an electoral process, but it is important to bear in mind that the collector, to whom all these petitions are addressed, is not elected by the people but is rather an administrative delegate of the government of India.

At the collector's office, governance and the implementation of policy are supposed to be separated from party politics. Contemporary collectors, like their colonial predecessors, are members of the nationwide elite IAS who have passed a rigorous examination system.[5] Both of the collectors in charge during my stay in Pudukkottai were from North Indian states and they were considered by most to be poor Tamil speakers, even if they were ultimately responsible for guaranteeing access to development initiatives. The collector of Pudukkottai in 2004 narrated the history of his job in an interview with me. "As the government took a lot of developmental functions," he said, "the area of administration also increased, covering various spheres of life of the people." Most communication between lower-level officers and the collector took place in English. Apart from assuring a certain standardization of district administration across India, the use of

IAS officers from other regions, supposedly detached from local patronage networks, is also meant to cut down on corruption and to promote Indian unity across regions.

In the contemporary Pudukkottai collector's office, every Monday the collector, district revenue officer, and development project officer sit in a large hall to receive between four hundred and five hundred of these written petitions in person. Petitioners may also have the chance to say a brief word explaining their situation in addition to the written and signed request they must hand in. This hall is also full of representatives of various local government offices who may be called on by the collector receiving petitions to explain why the problem has arisen or how best to solve it through administrative action. Grievance Day is a carefully choreographed display of transparent and responsive government, designed to convince those largely peasant and landless laborers who have come with a problem, and perhaps government workers themselves, that the administration is a responsible agency, at their service, and is there to be communicated with.

Speaking and Writing Grievance

If cows of the Chola Empire could simply ring a bell to air their grievances, the citizens of contemporary Pudukkottai are faced with a more demanding procedure. They must present a written petition, which must also be signed, or at least bear the thumbprint of the petitioner. There are several difficulties that arise in this situation. The first problem lies in the simple fact that many petitioners cannot read or write. They need someone else, usually a paid scribe who sits outside the office, to write a petition on their behalf. There are four or five scribes who sit outside the collector's office every day selling their services to petitioners. A second difficulty is that many who have had formal education, and can read a newspaper or perhaps write a personal letter, feel a great deal of anxiety before the written forms of Tamil they assume should be used in a petition addressed to the collector. They also require scribal mediation. As one of the professional petition writers sitting outside the office put it when I asked about the number of literate customers he has, "There's a separate office style, not everyone understands this. . . . It's only a matter of faith that we'll write it well." This writer and others like him were well aware that their livelihood relied on their capacity to maintain a monopoly on this style of written language. Over the course of my fieldwork, volunteers from the Arivoli movement had also begun to sit outside the office to write petitions for free. The scribe or volunteer nevertheless plays a critical mediating role in framing a grievance in writing.

The third difficulty has to do with the question of what counts as a legitimate problem that can be transcribed onto paper in categories recognizable to government readers. As the collector told me when asked about the role of paid scribes,

> We encourage people to write their own petitions. Sometimes what happens is, though people know how to write, they are not able to put out their thoughts in a very cogent manner. That is where the petition writers' services do come in. Normally what happens is a person has many grievances. And in the official mechanism, what happens is you take one grievance at a time. That is where petition writers . . . their functions do come in. They *reduce* it to a *cogent* and *logical* structure.

The application of abstract laws and categories of governance to particular instances of struggle, often marked by concerns deemed less than logical or legitimate by the state, therefore involves a set of framing techniques establishing a standardized and more legible text (Scott 1998). For instance, caste domination will be successfully invoked in a petition with reference to Scheduled Caste status and development benefits that are supposed to derive from this government category.[6] Similarly, widowhood and physical disability are recognized categories of social disadvantage that can be referred to in a petition. In the process, many of the details that the petitioner finds very relevant are either flattened in the text or erased altogether.

It is very common for people to show up at Grievance Day with ten rupees—half a day's pay for daily wage workers—and simple requests, telling the writer, "I'm poor, I live alone, and I need help." Sometimes the requests are more complicated, involving detailed stories of atrocities against Dalits or demands for official rights to land premised on undocumented histories of use. Petitioners will often come equipped with some documents such as a land deed, a family ration card (referred to by villagers as *cīṉikkarṭu*, "sugar card"), or some certificate proving their Scheduled Caste status.[7] Villagers may not always be able to read these documents, but they know them to be important for any interaction with the government.

In any case, the requests initially made by petitioners are usually of a quality that is not easily legible to the state as a solvable problem. It is then up to the petition writer, who, if he is a professional, is usually more interested in the ten rupees he will soon receive than in the fate of the petition he writes, to come up with something more appropriate to write.[8] Professional scribes appear to have little concern for their reputation among petitioners, who come from across the district. Arivoli volunteers acting as scribes will generally be more invested in writing a successful petition, though they are similarly placed as translators of sorts between different registers of discourse. I analyze the texts scribes and Arivoli workers produce in the following sections. Here, I am concerned with describing the oral interactions that feed into the production of a written document.

Muttammal's Grievance

Like many petitioners, Muttammal, a villager in her forties, first presented her personal problems. She described what brought her to the collector's office that Monday morning. In this case, the petition writer was not a professional charging a fee but an Arivoli Iyakkam volunteer named Rani. Rani was a villager in her twenties who wrote petitions free of charge on behalf of others every Monday. Her role as a literacy activist made her more inclined than professional scribes were to use the petition-writing dialogue as a mode of socialization to state linguistic practice. She was also more polite when speaking to the petitioner. However, I have recorded a number of exchanges between professional scribes and their clients that were similar insofar as they had to reframe a grievance to make it fit the expectations of administrators. Muttammal walked up to the petition-writing table outside the office and said,

1. M: I'm a widow. My husband passed away. I've got nothing to live on [*po̱lapputtalappukku vaḻiyille*]. I'm disabled. I've got two girl children. They need to be married off. I've no help at all. I've got no possessions

> or good health [*eṉakku cottum ille cukamum ille*]. I need help because of all this [*itukkuḷḷukku eṉakku utavi vēṇum*]. That's what I need to ask for.

Muttammal is widowed, poor, physically handicapped, alone, and the mother of two girls who must give dowry to get married. This introduction anticipates some relevant governmental categories, but it also presents a case for help that is both very moving and very reasonable to the average listener, invoking common problems. She made listeners around her feel for her situation, in which there is apparently no way out. Muttammal was creating what Arjun Appadurai (1990) calls a "community of sentiment," a frame to establish understanding and to excite pathos among her listeners.[9] She seemed to be talking as much to her fellow petitioners standing around her as she was to Rani, who was sitting at the petitioning table. As in the logic of praise that is the focus of Appadurai's essay in which he outlines the contours of a "community of sentiment," grievance too is a matter of public performance and negotiation. Such a performance of suffering is "not a matter of direct communication . . . but rather involves the public negotiation of certain gestures and responses" (94). That Muttammal had two daughters who will be able to marry only if she supplies a large dowry is very much at the root of her problem. Since her own husband passed away and she was unable to do physical labor because of her disabled hands, there was no way to come up with the sort of money required to find husbands for her daughters.

But dowry is a concern that lacks legitimacy because dowry is illegal. Rani, in the businesslike fashion one needs to adopt if the politics of compassion are to be effectively routinized, promptly failed to take up Muttammal's implicit invitation to play the role of compassionate community member. Instead, she initiated the following sequence, which was meant to define the grievant in more clearly standardized terms. What Muttammal thought to be a simple informational question turns out to have been a pedagogical routine associated with state literacy.

2. R: oṅka aṭrēcu colluṅka.
   Tell me your address.
3. M: mēṟkalappaṭṭi.
   Merkalappatti.

4. R: oṅka pēru colluṅka.
   Tell me your name.
5. M: pēru muttammā.
   Name's Muttamma.
6. R: pēru muttammāḷā? oṅka vīṭṭukkārar pēru?
   Name's Muttammal? Your husband's name?
7. M: kaṇṇaiyā.
   Kannaiya.
8. R: kaṇṇaiyāvā? apporam pēru colṟīya . . . ka tāṉē varum.
   Kannaiya? Then you're telling me the name . . . "Ka." should come then.
9. M: ām.
   Yeah.
10. R: ka tāṉē varum? iṉciyal?!
    "Ka." Should come then? . . . the initial?!
11. M: ām ka tāṉ varum.
    Yeah, then "Ka." should come.
12. R: ka?
    "Ka."?
13. M: ka muttammā.
    Ka. Muttamma.

The communicative trouble requiring explicit reference to written forms expected of state literacy begins in line 6. Rani, who was filling out the top of a blank piece of paper with Muttammal's address, had asked for her name, expecting an oral reply but in the written style. This would consist of a more formal pronunciation and a first initial, which would normally be taken from her husband's name. First, Muttammal replied in spoken form, *muttammā*, without pronouncing the final retroflex liquid (*ḷ*) used in the written variety, prompting Rani to repeat her name in question form. Second, Muttammal had failed to include an initial before her name, prompting Rani to ask her husband's name.[10] Muttammal simply answered with her deceased husband's name, failing to grasp the fact that Rani was actually trying to get an initial to write in the address line on the petition.[11] In line 7, Rani becomes more explicit in her tactic for eliciting a written form of Muttammal's name including the initial. "Then you're telling me the name . . . 'Ka.' should come then." By line 10, Rani has gotten a little frustrated and asks, using the English loan, "*Inciyal?*" It is only by line 13 that Muttammal has performed adequately, stating her name as it should be read by the state as "Ka. Muttamma," and Rani can go on with next sequence of questioning regarding her requests, although Muttamma[l] still did not produce that '*ḷ*' at the end of her name.

14. R: oṅka . . . en̲n̲a kēkkir̲īṅka?
    Your . . . what are you asking for?
15. M: en̲n̲akku ētāvatu oru utavi ceyyaṇum.
    I need, anything, some help.
16. R: ille. ētāvatu en̲n̲ā . . . nīṅka en̲n̲a utavi kēkkir̲īṅka? atu con̲n̲ātān̲ē teriyum!
    No. Anything means . . . What help are you asking for? I can only know if you tell!
17. M: nān̲ nālu puḷḷeṅkaḷe vaccukkiṭṭu tavikkir̲ēn̲. vīṭum ille.
    I'm suffering with four kids. Don't even have a house.
18. R: illeṅka. pactu oṇṇu, en̲akku irukka iṭam ille atan̲āle ilavacamā vīṭu oṇṇu koṭuṅka. appaṭiṇṇu collikkēkkaṇum.
    No (honorific). One, first you need to ask like this: "I have no place to live, so give me a free house."
19. M: vīṭṭukku tan̲iyā eḻutikkoṭukkaṇum.
    I need to write and give a separate [petition] for a house.
20. R: appaṭi illeṇṇu con̲n̲āka nīṅka vantu ētāvatu peṭṭikkaṭe vaikkaṇum. itu mātiri kēkkur̲iṅkaṇṇāka oru lōṇ oṇṇu koṭuṅka appaṭiṇṇu collikkēkkaṇum.
    If not that, then you want to set up some sort of small shop. If you're asking for something like that, you should ask, "Give me a loan."
21. M: lōṇtān̲ kēkkir̲ēn̲ nālu puḷḷakaḷe vaccukkiṭṭu poḻakkaṇum.
    I'm just asking for a loan . . . I've got to survive with four kids.
22. R: ippa kaṭan̲ vacati kēkkir̲īṅka.
    So now you're asking for a loan.

In the third and final section of this transcript, we get at the heart of what I have identified as the third difficulty that arises from the need to submit a written petition: Muttammal's approach to petitioning was premised on a model of general pleading for dispensation to a social superior. Rani, who sees herself as an activist serving her fellow people, needed a specific request that fits into governmental development programs for social well-being. Muttammal, throughout this section of the exchange, was reaching out through a strategy Appadurai (1990, 110) calls "coercive subordination" as a "publicly understood code for the negotiation and expectation of obligations," again trying to get Rani and others to feel with her and to exercise their duty to help. Rani, on the other hand, knows she needs to write a "cogent" and "logical" petition that will make some sense to a government official, if there is to be any hope of getting the state to help Muttammal. These two orientations are at odds, and trouble starts right away in the transcript when Muttammal says she needs "anything, some help."

"No," Rani tells the supplicant, asking for "anything" will not do; one needs to ask for *something*, something that can be formalized as a discrete request to be communicated in a clear and efficient manner to the collector. In line 17, Muttammal fails to take up Rani's demand and continues her talk of troubles, still trying to get Rani and others around her (including me) to understand through the experience of her pain that she is seriously destitute. Again, the sort of understanding Muttammal was looking for would not come from the simple transmission of information, but rather from an effective performative evocation of collective affect.

Rani understood. But she also understood that Muttammal was not getting what for Rani was the larger point of the exercise: a successful "disposal" of the petition. She therefore decided to model what an appropriate request would sound like. "One, first you need to ask like this: 'I have no place to live so give me a free house.'" Here, the socialization routine becomes more explicit. The performance of troubles talk is relegated to the category of irrelevant context in the linguistic genre of petitioning. Muttammal partially enters the bureaucratic frame and counters in line 18 that she will need to have another petition written to demand a house. Then Rani proceeds to model another appropriate request someone in Muttammal's position might make. "If not that, then you want to set up some sort of small shop. If you're asking for something like that, you should ask, 'Give me a loan.'" Muttammal's response to this suggests that money is what she was asking for in the first place, if only by implication, but she still adds what for her is critical context for such a request: "I've got to survive with four kids." By line 22, Rani has reached the point where she can start writing, already anticipating the language of the written document by switching from the more colloquial English loanword for "loan" (*lōṇ*) to a written form in pure Tamil (*kaṭaṉ vacati*). She never gives a response to the repeated complaint about taking care of kids, which was critical for Muttammal.

One could understand why Muttammal would be frustrated. Having come from a distant village, out of desperation to ask for help, she encountered a set of impersonal procedures. Her performance of suffering was not taken up, but rather shoved into an explicit request for money from the state. This sort of lack of uptake is why villagers consistently describe the people who live in towns such as Pudukkottai as lacking in compassion and affection (*pācam*). In villages of Tamil Nadu, widows and poor families who must marry off their daughters can evoke sorrow and plead for help. There are many more appropriate ways to ask for help than just saying, "Give me a loan." Rani's frustration stems from the requirements of state bureaucracy for standardization, expedience, and formalization in written discourse. In the struggle over relevance in discourse at Grievance Day the state wins because it has written the very rules of the game. I would furthermore argue that Rani took on a relatively formal demeanor in part because she was a woman trying to assert her authority in a bureaucratic field where men have more often held positions of power.

In some sense they had talked past each other, but a petition had nevertheless been written so that Muttammal's problems could then be represented to the collector. Some sort of communication happened, even if the likelihood that Muttammal will actually get a loan or a new house out of this agonistic encounter is unclear.[12] Petitions regarding local law-and-order problems or requests for land deeds usually elicit a response in the form of a police inspection or a visit from the local revenue officer. Requests for loans made by people without documentation of a special status for which there is an existing government program tend never to hear back from the administration.

Chinnammal's Grievance

In a second example, we will see how much of a grievance can get erased in the transition from speech to a written petition, causing suspicion about the very practice of writing a grievance. Chinnammal, an elderly woman petitioner, first simply walked up to the professional writer sitting outside the collector's office, sat down on the ground, and stated her problem: "I need an official housing site, in Cantaippettai, they tore down my house." Cantaippettai is a large slum in Pudukkottai Town, right next to the collector's office, inhabited almost exclusively by Dalit castes, mainly leather workers, garbage collectors, and sweepers for the municipality. Although as many as one-third of residents of Cantaippettai work for the state, the slum itself is not provided with schooling, electricity, or even running water.[13]

The writer was a poor man in his fifties of the higher, Chettiyar caste. He was among the professional scribes, who deal differently with their clients than Arivoli volunteers do. The scribe responded to Chinnammal, for example, by asking her name using the disrespectful second-person singular possessive pronoun. He then began to ask for facts relevant to writing the petition as he saw it. When he asked Chinnammal how long she had been living in the Cantaippettai slum, she first said, "*rompa varucamā iruntēṉ*" (Been much [many] years). When the scribe yelled at her to clarify, Chinnammal responded with "*irupatu varucam . . . mūppatu varucam . . . nāppatu varucamāccu, atiliruṇṭu*" (Twenty years . . . thirty years . . . forty years . . . since then). He then asked what kind of work she did, and she replied that she did "*ḳūli vēle*" ("coolie," or daily-wage work). Chinnammal then volunteered that she had been living in a blacksmith's shop since her house had been torn down, and the scribe proceeded to write the petition without further inquiries. Theirs was a fairly typical exchange between a scribe and his client (all the professional scribes are men), although marked by a somewhat extreme assertion of superiority by the writer. Whereas an elderly woman could have expected at least some show of deference because of her age, this petition writer was especially disrespectful to women and to people of lower caste.

As the scribe was writing on her behalf, I asked Chinnammal if she had submitted petitions before. She replied that she had already given three to the collector without any satisfactory effects. Chinnammal was then moved to tell her story in more detail for all those who had gathered around the scribe to have petitions written:

> They gathered the whole town to go beat up my son. To tear up the house he built, and we can't get any justice for this. I told the police, but no justice. There's no one to stand up and fight for us. . . . I said, "We'll go seek help at home, somewhere.". . . I just hit my own head and cried [*talaiyile aṭiccuḳiṭṭuaḻutēṉ*]. Nowhere to be, nowhere to live, nothing's left, I stand here suffering, . . . orphaned [*āṉāti*]. . . . I have to go back to my caste [*jātile aṇṭaṇum*]. . . . There's none of the justice I asked for! How many petitions I gave! [*eṉaḳḳu ḳēṭṭuḳḳoṭaḳḳa niyāyam ḳeṭeḳḳalle*! *ettaṉaiyō maṉu ḳoṭuttēṉ*!] I got nothing. It seems they came to ask one day. I had gone out that very day. To check the card. That lady told them I had just gone out. "Just now, just here she was," it seems she said. It seems they said they'd be back on Friday, . . . they didn't come at all. After that, last Monday I brought and gave a petition. No response. If they came I could show them the spot. Eight stone pillars just stand there. They did wrong and tore it up! [*mōcaṭi paṇṇi pariccuḳḳāṅḳa*!]

I asked Chinnammal how many petitions she had given before because I had seen her giving one the previous week at Grievance Day. Her response stands as a powerful indictment of the whole petitioning process, in addition to acting as the invocation of a moral community of sentiment, a community she has almost already given up on: "*There's none of the justice I asked for*!" Chinnammal's speech stands as a call for the presence of an absent state authority that has done nothing to intervene or help in her situation. She appears to be acutely aware of the fact that she does not have the techniques required to represent herself to the state. For justice to be available to her, her predicament would have to be understood in ways that cannot fit into a "reduced," "cogent," and "logical" written structure as required by the petitioning process. Chinnammal had been "orphaned" (*āṉāti*) not only through lack of housing and social support, in the slum and the state, but also semiotically. Living right next to the collector's office, she could find no justice (*niyāyam*).

That she has given petitions before would make it into her official text, but the writer was writing away and not listening to a word she said after his initial questions. Chinnammal's story of suffering, her crying, could not find its way into ink. The writer had lost interest. He knew such emotions and details could not be made to make official sense in a petition and he simply wrote a basic text, based on a template he has used thousands of times over his fifteen years of writing outside the collector's office. Note that in her narrative Chinnammal mentions that some official did in fact come to see about the situation but that she was out that day. This would have been a useful piece of information to include in the petition, and its omission confirms my impression that the writer does not really care about the fate of this woman or her petition. As the writer finished producing the written text, he gave her the inkpad and commanded, "*rēk̲a vaimā*" (Put your thumbprint, lady). Chinnammal did so and walked away after paying him ten rupees. I met with Chinnammal one month later when the authorities still had yet to respond. She was preparing to write another petition. Karuppiah had volunteered to come with me to meet her and to write a petition on her behalf. When we returned to write another petition, her neighbors said that she had left town to go to her village. We never saw her again.

"None of the Justice I Asked For"

I have reproduced Chinnammal's speech in some detail because it captures a feeling of disappointment, anger, and suspicion about the government's will and ability to respond to a written grievance. It is representative of a widespread ambivalence among villagers and the poor to the petitioning process. Although they keep coming by the hundreds, often repeatedly, to Grievance Day at the collector's office and to the mass contact campaigns that are held across the district every month, many people are not sure there is much use in simply handing over a piece of paper. A frequent refrain I heard from petitioners in interviews echoes the words of the petition writer cited earlier: "It's only a matter of faith" (*oru nampik̲k̲aitān̲*). It is, in fact, the chance to see the collector in person, and to hand him the paper, that excites many people about the petitioning process as it occurs in Pudukkottai. They do not know who, if anyone, will actually be reading their petition.

The district administration is often experienced as an abstract and unpredictable player in rural affairs and among the urban poor. *Kūli* workers, daily-wage laborers who make up the bulk of petitioners and who have had little or no schooling, understand the electoral process quite well, operating as it does through caste and kinship networks. People know how elected politicians are swayed by the forces of party affiliation, money, and caste calculus. However, the person of the collector seems contradictory because collectors are symbolically "higher" than the villagers they come into contact with, while making a pretense of serving the people on egalitarian terms. District administration remains opaque, at best ambiguous, and perhaps uncaring.

The following popular song, titled "Petition Justice" (*maṉu nīti*) after the Chola emperor and the Grievance Day plan bearing his name, also captures this feeling quite effectively. This song was written in a folk style by the poet Navakavi, also associated with the Tamil Nadu Progressive Writers Association.

The collector is coming in a car up the tar road,
See the color, colored paper at the office gate.
There, the village meeting goes on for miles,
See the crowds standing in line with petitions.

"Tip-top," "all-top," collector sir!
Silent Tahsildar with his arms folded,
A well-loan, a car, with an application,
Look, in line is our village's own Marigonar.

The village meeting is grand! Dust is flying!
Selling hot bondas and vadais at the tea shop,
Bewildered Marigonar and piles of petitions,
He went like a pilgrim climbing a mountain.

He gave his petition, happy Marigonar,
Got himself a masala vadai and a cup of tea.
See the paper in his hand, used to wrap the bonda,
The petition just given, handed back to him again!

Paper scarcity here where people came to give petitions,
Petitions all end as wrapping paper in the tea shop.
Give a petition and this government won't budge,
Raise your voice and start a movement, Marigonar!

Marigonar, whose excitement turns from bewilderment to happiness on handing over the petition and eventually to absolute disappointment, found his afternoon snack wrapped in the very petition he had just worked so hard to give to the collector. While highlighting the very materiality of paper as well as the marginality of villagers, this song argues for the insignificance of writing to the administration as a form of communication.[14] They just collect petitions, they don't read them, let alone act on them. The petition-giving occasion is exciting, like a village festival, with crowds, colored paper, savory snacks, and most important the "tip-top, all-top" collector stepping out of his big car. All the mass contact programs I attended in villages around Pudukkottai did in fact have music blaring out of loudspeakers and many of the other accoutrements of village festivals held yearly in celebration of the local deity.

The comparison of Marigonar, the petitioner, to a pilgrim climbing a tall mountain in a religious show of faith is not at all accidental in this regard. Do those important officers really care about the plight of a simple small farmer or daily-wage worker? Or is this all a show of connection, lacking in real substance? (After all, the collector can barely speak Tamil.) These are some questions rural residents of Pudukkottai might be asking themselves when consistently telling me that giving a petition is "just a matter of faith" (*oru nampikkaitāṉ*). When describing official petitioning in this way, villagers are drawing on a language of indeterminacy that they also used for religious occasions. One does what one can to help make certain things happen through religious ritual, for example, but there are no guarantees that a particular ritual will have the intended effects. There is, in fact, a temple fifteen miles north of Pudukkottai Town where people submit written petitions to the goddess Viramma Kaliyamman, in a fashion that mimes petitioning at the collector's office. There are even scribes who work at the temple writing petitions to the goddess, fully replicating this idiom of sovereignty in the sacred realm. The collector's visit to accept petitions is all show, the song argues, and the government "won't budge" unless Marigonar raises his voice and starts to participate in mass politics. There are serious limits to the vision of bureaucratic citizenship offered by the petition process. Without claiming that this artful critique of the state represents the view of the majority of rural residents of Pudukkottai, I would nevertheless argue that this song does voice a widely experienced ambivalence toward the state. The story is both funny and disturbing because it is very plausible.

Scribal Mediation and the Legible Artifact

One can find tension between different orientations to grievance and governance, in a concretized form, in the written documents that are handed over to the collector every Monday. Professional scribes write petitions on a standard A4-size white piece of paper in blue ink with a ballpoint pen. Some petitioners find this practice too informal and they may go to a nearby shop to have their petition, once composed, typed on a typewriter. Most of the professional writers took up this occupation later in life after working as manual laborers in their youth. Several of the petition writers had acquired physical disabilities along the way, leaving them unable to perform more intensive manual labor. None of the professional writers of petitions at the Pudukkottai collector's office have studied beyond the eighth standard. They learned to write by copying models and watching others on the job, unlike official scribes who write out land deeds. The latter scribes have gone through schooling and passed an examination to be certified professionals. Petition writers, on other hand, learned through a less formal apprenticeship under older writers.

Petitions are usually referred to as "*ma<u>n</u>u*" or "*viṇṇappam*," both words deriving from the practice of petitioning the gods through prayer.[15] Models for such official letters of application are taught to Tamil students in the eighth standard. Paid petition writers, however, such as the man who wrote for Chinnammal, will tend to hypercorrect and exceed even the archaized formal written Tamil taught in schools. It is almost as if it were their job to do so; they use what distinctive symbolic capital they have got. Scribes exceed certain limits of what the collector had described to me as "cogent" and "reduced." They tend to employ the most archaic-sounding or esoteric—and therefore authoritative, in the eyes of their clients—word or phrase available. But scribes are not masters of refined Tamil (*centami<u>l</u>*), and the grammatical structure of their sentences and even some lexical items remain somewhat awkward by the standards of written Tamil as taught in school. The language of petitions written by scribes has been called "Cutchery Tamil," a hybrid register that first developed with the

Figure 8. Professional petition writers plying their trade on the street outside the collector's office. Photograph by the author.

establishment of collector's offices under the East India Company (Raman 2009). If we compare contemporary texts with those collected by Reverend Pope in 1863 for his *Tamil Prose Reader*, we can see that this register has shown remarkable stability, even when the political context has changed such that petitioners are theoretically now citizens of India.

There is a recurrent structure to these documents that makes them recognizable as working within the Cutchery Tamil idiom. It is especially important to get a sense of the honorifics involved. For example, the receiver of a petition is always addressed as "*uyar*"—literally, "high"—collector. This is followed by the third-person plural pronoun (*avarkaḷ*), an honorific index that pluralizes the referent and thus avoids sharp pointing as done in many traditions of honorification.[16] In the petition written by the scribe on behalf of Chinnammal, for instance, the addressee is referred to as "*uyar tiru māvaṭṭa āṭcittalaivar avarkaḷ*" (his highest great district collector, they). A standard petition will then proceed to invoke the relevant government development programs that are available to disadvantaged populations, all the while showering praise on the benevolent addressee, such as the phrase "*taṅkaḷ mēlāṉa camūkam*" (yourselves [reflexive third-person plural], high presence/society [with objective case form postfix]), used in Chinnammal's petition. The word "*camūkam*" in this honorific phrase presents particular translation difficulties, and is found in contemporary Tamil as a form of deferential address almost exclusively in petition writing.[17] Though used in common contemporary speech as an equivalent of the English "society" or "community" (see chapter 2), it can be translated, when used in petitions as a form of address, perhaps more accurately as "presence."[18] This is clearly a sociolinguistic register that is equally at home in the discourse of kingship as it is in that of modernist governmentality. These uses of deferential language are precisely why few people, prior to the advent of the Arivoli Iyakkam, would claim that petitioning is the act of representation that marks one as a rights-bearing citizen.

The final sentences of petitions also express a relationship of hierarchical dependence in strongly affective language. Chinnammal's petition, for example, ends with the following plea: "Therefore, I very humbly pray [*paṇintu vēṇṭukiṟēṉ*] that your great presence take pity in your heart to take up this petition [*camūkam maṉamiraṅki immaṉuvai ēṟṟu mēlnaṭatti*] and quickly take actions that a housing site be made available." This is followed in her petition by *taṅkaḷ paṇiyuḷḷa*, "in your service," further lowering the supplicant. Chinnammal's petition was closed by the thumbprint, indexing her participation. These "explicitly performative utterances," (Austin 1962, 83) in the last lines are the most consistently formulaic sentences across all the examples of petitions I have collected in Pudukkottai. The final sentence is generally structured as follows:

ākavē aiyā camuka ekemāṉ avarkaḷ karuṉai kūrntu
Therefore, Sir in the grace of your presence, master [3rd pl.] having had

[fill in the blank with request] *paṇiyutaṉ vēṇṭukkolkiṟēṉ*
dutifully prayed [myself—reflexive verb, 1st per. sing.]

All these linguistic means of lowering the petitioning subject before the exalted addressee can be found in oral praise genres and in poetic forms associated with the social world of divine sovereignty, royal duty (Sanskrit, *rājā dharma*), or patron-like status more broadly conceived. In addition to the invocation of presence and the third-person plural pronoun, the collector is usually referred to, and "dutifully" "prayed" to, also as "*ekemāṉ*."[19] This word, like "*camukam*," also performs hierarchy, servitude, and the social controls and responsibilities that go with it. The collector, then, is explicitly put in the position of the kingly patron, literally the "hegemon," and master over a community or dominion. Although kings may be the paradigmatic addressees of such praise, Appadurai argues that the "pragmatic sense of praise could be extended from kings to all patrons," such that "the patron (yajamana) of any ritualized or aesthetic activity is the situational incarnation of the god-king. Thus the ideological and rhetorical forms associated with the praise of patrons can be seen as paradigmatic of inferiors to their superiors in all domains of life" (1990, 96). There is in fact a great degree of continuity between the language of praise and prayer, on the one hand, and that of petitioning, on the other. Both rely on a discursive strategy of "coercive subordination" in that the giving of deference entitles the very *giver* of deference to kindness and compassion (see also Hull 2012, 100–01). These public signs of affect rely on a logic that dominates in a number of social arenas, requiring that king-like patrons and political superiors in general respond to the pleas of subordinates. A certain power to compel therefore lies in one's capacity for the performance of subordination.

We must bear in mind, however, that it is the writer who introduces the language of hierarchical address into the written petition, thereby imposing a new discursive structure onto what was before an oral demand for justice that had been denied. It is therefore the writer who puts the petitioner in their place through language as a low supplicant to a higher power. While this is certainly the case in Chinnammal's petition, even Muttammal's indirect pleading discussed above displays none of the language of address found in written petitions. But written petitions praising the collector as a dharmic hegemon live an awkward social life because, in this case, the sense of public recognition required of a successful performance of coercive subordination is complicated by the fact that it is a written document destined to be detached from the agent it is meant to represent. There is none of the public hierarchical intimacy that such discursive genres presuppose, in practice, in order to perform effectively. So thoroughly mediated by scribal agency, in addition to the fact of being written as a detachable text, these petitions bear only the largely ineffective traces of oral complaint.

Petitions are usually read back aloud by the scribe to the client, in front of other potential clients, so that they can appreciate the production, which is now suitable for circulation in the collector's office. It is in the honorifics and esoteric grammar, as well as the official-sounding language, apart from the simple fact of writing that I assume clients believe they are getting their money's worth. Petition writers will also sometimes charge petitioners for an official-looking, but completely unnecessary, stamp affixed to the piece of paper, giving it an even grander and official look.

Struggles over Representation

To understand how the Arivoli Iyakkam can claim that petitioning the collector counts as an act of citizenship, and not just an exercise in servitude, we must return to the petitioning event described at the beginning of this book, also mentioned in the beginning of this chapter. Recall that the Katrampatti literacy group that petitioned the collector for a pathway to their own cremation ground ended up taking the bus a little later than hoped for that morning. Their domestic duties in the village had made it difficult to catch an early ride to town. This lack of time and flexibility to travel to town at will is built into the practiced rhythms of life and weighs particularly on women. When they arrived at the collector's office in Pudukkottai Town, Karuppiah and other literacy volunteers at the main Arivoli Iyakkam office somewhat regretfully decided that there would be no time for the group to write their own petition out, and that it would be best for him to write the main text and the petitioners should merely sign their names at the bottom. If they could not show off their still weak skills through the main text of the petition itself, at least some of them would be signing their names officially for the first time, and they assumed they would be able to see the collector and talk to him directly when handing over the petition in person. Many of the Arivoli students were a little anxious about being asked to write out a longer text in any case.

It turned out that another resident of Katrampatti, a village council member who met us that day on our way to the office, had once already submitted a petition, written by a professional scribe, regarding the cremation ground, but without any results. Given the time pressure, Karuppiah proceeded to copy, in his own quick, disciplined, and well-schooled handwriting, from this petition, originally written by a professional scribe on behalf of a Katrampatti villager to the tahsildar, the subdistrict revenue officer. Karuppiah simply changed the addressee line to address the collector and he indicated that the petition was from the Arivoli Iyakkam literacy group. Below is my English translation of the original petition commissioned by the council member and written by a scribe at the taluk (the subdistrict revenue division) office:

Petition Text

Sender:
Receiver: *uyar* [high] Mr. Tahsildar *avarkaḷ* [3rd-per. pl. pronoun]
Alangudi Taluk [revenue division]
Subject: Regarding request for path to cremation ground
Sir,

We have lived at the above-mentioned village since the time of our ancestors. Fifty Hindu Adi-Dravidars ["Original Dravidians," administrative term for Dalits] have inherited twenty-four cents of land in Kilattur Village survey number 140.3 for a cremation ground. This is the only ground where we can dispose of our dead. Caste-Hindus own all the land surrounding our cremation ground. We can reach the cremation ground only by carrying the dead through these fields. Before, these fields were left completely fallow. No one ever stopped us from taking bodies to the cremation grounds. Now, all around our grounds they have started farming. They now stop us, saying we must not take our dead through the crops. Now we are all fearful and do not take our dead. As Adi-Dravidars we have requested a path to our grounds from the officer concerned many times. Having given many petitions requesting a path, no actions have yet been taken. Therefore, in the name of Adi-Dravidars we very humbly ask for your compassion, they, dharmic master so that we may be given a cremation-ground path.

Sincerely,

————-Signature————-

This petition exhibits many of the features I have identified above as characteristic of Cutchery Tamil. After stating that the petitioners had ancestral claims to their village, the following sentence enters directly into the language of governance, explaining that the petitioners claim Scheduled Caste status, or that they are Adi-Dravidars, in the parlance of Tamil administration. This invocation of a caste status for which special government provisions have been made is accompanied by the exact amount and survey number of the land they claim rights to in order to cremate their dead. Following a brief history of their use of this cremation ground, the petition then explains the community's fear before the threats of the dominant castes and explains that petitions have been submitted before without any results. The original petition ends with a fairly standard final performative sentence, again invoking the petitioners' low-caste status.

What I did not notice until looking over my photos later, however, is that Karuppiah, who copied the original scribal petition, had changed the last sentence in the second version to be given to the collector by the literacy group. Both versions of the last sentence are reproduced below:

Original Final Sentence:

ākavē ātitirāviṭar pēril karuṉai kūrntu
Therefore, original Dravidian name (loc.) grace (gen.) having had (adv. participle)

tarma ejamāṉ avarkaḷ eṅkaḷukkum mayāṉa pātai amaittu
dharma master 3rd pl. [to] us (dative) cremation ground path made (adv. participle)

tarumpaṭi mika paṇiyuṭaṉ kēṭṭukkoḷkiṟōm
give + as to very [with] duty (ass.) we [ourselves] ask (reflexive verb)

Therefore, in the name of Adi-Dravidars we very humbly ask for your compassion, they, dharmic master, so that we may be given a cremation-ground path.

Reformed Final Sentence:

ākavē tayavuceytu eṅkaḷukku mayāṉap pātai ēṟpaṭutti
Therefore, please [to] us (dat.) cremation ground (adj.) path prepared (adv. participle)

tarumāru mikavum paṇiyuṭaṉ kēṭṭukkoḷkiṟōm
give + as to very [with] duty (ass.) we [ourselves] ask (reflexive verb)

Therefore, we very humbly ask that we may please be given a cremation-ground path.

In the original petition to the subdistrict officer, the last sentence reads, "Therefore, in the name of Adi-Dravidars we humbly ask for your compassion, they, dharmic master, so that we may be given a path." The word for master here is "*ejamāṉ*" and is once again tied to caste hierarchy, employment, and the social controls and responsibilities that go with it. Such a performance of subjection to kingly dispensation in a relationship requiring the enactment of deference certainly challenges the premise that petitioners are communicating with the state as full rights-bearing citizens demanding services. An interactional model of pleading has been laminated onto bureaucratic-document discourse genres. This interactional model might have been attractive to literate petitioners, such as the Dalit council member who commissioned the writing of the original document, insofar as it performs the kind of "coercive subordination" I have outlined above.

But it is the very idiom of village hierarchy and the rather explicit index of an intercaste pleading register, here filtered through categories of governance, that Karuppiah the Arivoli teacher did away with in his version of the petition. Instead he wrote, "Therefore we humbly ask that we may please be given a path." The original invocation of the district collector as dharmic hegemon, though perhaps sociologically accurate in a sense, conflicts with the ideologies of participatory, egalitarian, and enlightened government. These are, of course, the very values Arivoli Iyakkam is charged with spreading through literacy. The idioms of village hierarchy, though persistent in most forms of petition writing, were simply out of place in the vision of Karuppiah, the Arivoli worker. He had furthermore deleted the phrase asking for a cremation-ground path "in the name of Adi-Dravidars," and had instead made the request in more universalizing terms than those of caste and dharmic duty.

The demand for rationalized written communication with the government entails movement toward a less elaborated indexical regime of inequality between communicators and perhaps more covert forms of exclusion and marginalization. At the very least it would entail, as Weber would have it, a form of modern loyalty to an office, which "does not establish a relationship to a person, like the disciple's faith under feudal or patrimonial authority, but rather is devoted to impersonal and functional purposes" (1978, 959). After writing about this petition in my dissertation, I visited Karuppiah in India and asked him about the switch. He told me that he shouldn't have even used the word "*paṇiyuṭaṉ*," to "humbly" or "dutifully" ask. But the word for "please," "*tayavuceytu*," was very important in establishing the impersonal and, to him, dignified tone of such a demand. "One shouldn't be going around asking for things like a beggar," he said. This was a decision taken by the literacy volunteer about how these women should represent themselves to the collector, as citizen petitioners, not as abject beggars. The petitioners themselves, however, the women of Katrampatti, simply heard the petition read aloud to them and agreed to sign it. Their authorship, to the degree that we would attribute any authorship to them, had been thickly mediated several times over in the entextualization process. They signed the petition written in their names and told me, "It's just a matter of faith" (*oru nampikkaitāṉ*).

Performativity of Signature

The petitioners from Katrampatti were Dalits, and they were women with no close connections to any political party apparatus. They had little hope of solving the cremation-ground problem through local power struggles in the hamlet or in the village panchayat council. It is therefore important to bear in mind that, in rural Pudukkottai as in many places, the district administration may well be among the more effective powers to appeal to even if it is not always clear how things actually work. My aim is not to portray modern claims to citizenship as simply hollow. Instead, we must understand how such an ideology stretches the limits of representation by recontextualizing the marginality of petitioners, thereby overdetermining their place in an encompassing structure of power premised on the logic of developmental governmentality. We can see that the theory of citizenship conflating self-representation with self-determination and the promises of future development premised on full literacy are two sides of the same coin.

In the final petition, copied and altered by Karuppiah, the still less-than-concrete, somewhat unsteady signatures of the Katrampatti group are allowed entry into a stratified semiotic system in which the template is already written by another hand in the register of a different social stratum. This initial and partial entry into a field of bureaucratic practice is marked in the very form of the signatures, which look different from the schooled hand that wrote the petition. Here we can see an intratextual contrast, replicating other signs of social positioning. In the very form of the petition, then, one can see wider social processes at work.

J.L. Austin (1962) has suggested that signatures are performative, tethering names to intentions, subjects, and agency, and doing things with words. The "I" of the signatures, the subject, is supposed to be the same "I," the agent, who humbly asks of the collector. We have already seen how this logical assumption is a socially complicated one. The signers from Katrampatti had delegated the responsibility of representing their complaint in writing to Karuppiah. Their signatures would attest to something he had rewritten, based on yet another petition, producing a dense intertextuality. Derrida (1986, 1988) extended and challenged the Austinian insight, turning it into a logical paradox, in that signatures appear to create retroactively the very subjects they are also assumed to represent. Signatures clearly stand as signs representing subjects, but it may also just as easily be said, with Derrida, that "the signature invents the signer" (1986, 10). This engagement with the inherent tension between representation (constative structure) and creation (performative structure) is helpful in bringing the problem of signature back to that of the contradictions underpinning the postcolonial state that I outlined throughout this book. Just as the state's will to development often seems to trump democratic recognition in the present, the performative aspect of signature seems to undermine its capacity to represent an already-constituted subject. But what exactly is being performed in this case and through what forms of institutionalized agency?

It is not at all clear whether the signers from Katrampatti are, in fact, already full citizens exercising their agency by representing themselves to an absent addressee through the medium of writing. They are just as much becoming citizens only by virtue of having attended literacy classes and then signing a petition in the first place. In this fashion, the signature creates the modern citizen. The state in fact attempts to create

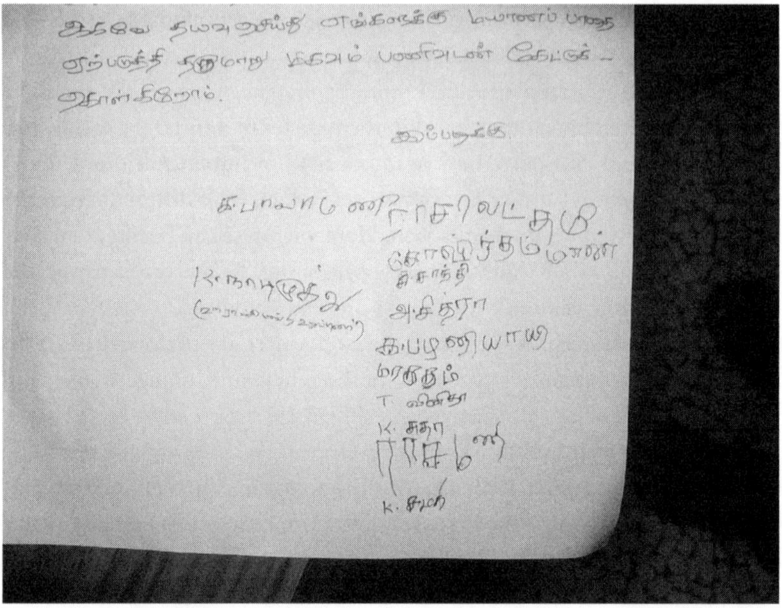

Figure 9. Signatures at the bottom of the Katrampatti petition. Photograph by the author.

proper citizens through pedagogical disciplines in an attempt to align frameworks of representation and performance. Such a perfect alignment, allowing for an already fully constituted citizen to perform her citizenship in a transparent manner, appears as always deferred in the narrative of developmental governmentality. I would thus also like to propose a more multimodal semiotic and social analysis to point out how exactly the narrative of postcolonial development brings a peculiar temporal logic to work on this relationship between representation and performance. This requires attention to at least two other related ways in which the classic paradigm of performance fails to capture completely the distinctive uses of signature in this context, even as it helps bring out points of distinction.

First, the Katrampatti signatures do not refer back to an always-stable individualized subject. They are not the paradigmatic "iterable" signatures used to assure stability of identity in the course of using up a checkbook, for example. They are tied in a semiosis of unsteadiness, of something that can be corrected, to their particular context of production. The event of identity production here is the very partial, uneven product of a massive pedagogical work, and signers have been infantilized in the process. The unsteadiness that marks these signatures as those of neo-signers is subject to change and rectification over time. The force of the Katrampatti signatures is perhaps their very irreproducibility. They index a concrete connection to people coming into the fold as newly legitimate petitioners of the state. Because of the way they were used by Karuppiah, to signal to the collector that the petitioners were neoliterates, the signatures refer back to a type of underdeveloped person coming into the fold of modern citizenship, as much as they do to individual people.

Remember, this is why Karuppiah had hoped to have a neoliterate write the whole petition out: to send a message to the petitioners that they can represent themselves through writing, but also, and just as important, to send a message to the collector that they are "developing," trying for full literacy and representational capacity but not yet there. Some of the rhetorical burden of scribal praise language from the original petition, instantiating an affectively potent relationship of dependence, would have been shifted onto the qualities of the handwriting itself, as bureaucratic rationality is supposed to be replacing kingship or patron status as the dominant modality of power in Pudukkottai. Subjects are now subordinate to the project of development in place of royal sovereignty. The hierarchy of social status is projected onto an ideology of social sameness in delayed time.

A second point of distinction in these signatures, as seen through the lens of performativity, follows as a sociological elaboration of the first point of semiotic distinction. This concerns frames of interpretation and brings us to the question of shared common sense in state practices. The classic felicitous performance assumes a great degree of homogeneity of interpretation among participants, a shared sense of authorized representation. In this case such an assumption cannot be presupposed. Disjunctive frames of interpretation, grounded in different regimes of legitimation remain the rule. The signature would have appeared felicitous for some (Karuppiah, and probably the collector) because it fulfilled the requirements of development-as-pedagogy, by acting as a sign of enlightenment through writing.

But for the women who had come to the office that day from Katrampatti, my sense is that they would have been satisfied that they had performed the act of petitioning at Grievance Day only if they had been able to see the collector and plead with him orally using generic conventions compelling superiors to act on behalf of the weak, not unlike those found in the praise language that had been erased from their petition. Their ambivalence is a product of having been denied the chance to make an affective claim through eye contact, ensuring that the collector would sympathize with their suffering. Karuppiah and I had tried to make it up to the petitioners by taking them all out to lunch after submitting the petition, but the bus ride home was certainly marked by disappointment and uncertainty about what had just taken place at the collector's office. They all knew it would be very difficult to collectively take yet another day off from work and come back to town.

Any governmental claims to rationalized and disenchanted Weberian bureaucracy remain particularly vexed in this context, because the collector does sit in the erstwhile king's seat, in his palace. In fact, he collects

Figure 10. The collector's office remains a royal palace in the eyes of many. Photograph by the author.

petitions in the old *darbār* hall where the king of Pudukkottai would have met with the court and those who had come to plead before royalty.[20] Such an environment does not lend itself easily to a bureaucratic ideology of directness or "reduced," "logical" communication in the eyes of petitioners or even petition writers. The collector does appear to act like a king. It took so much pedagogical work just to get the group from Katrampatti to come to the collector's office, and the journey seemed somehow incomplete, in part because after such effort they simply turned in the sheet of paper at a small office without being able to see and talk to the collector at Grievance Day. The petitioners' idea of seeing the collector directly (*nēraṭiyāḳa*), of having a face-to-face encounter with a powerful patron, conflicts with the ideals of directness as the simple transmission of a communication in written form in which a petitioner has no face. Beyond this sense of disappointment at not connecting visually or verbally with their addressee, these petitioners have repeatedly been deceived or disappointed by the state, as by other higher powers. They know they are dealing with a realm of power that is in some sense beyond their control. This was, after all, an act of faith (*oru nampiḳḳaitāṉ*) as much as it was an exercise in citizenship.

Some Concluding Thoughts

Postcolonial citizenship is structured by a logic of developmental governmentality and its articulation with principles of subordination to sovereignty in ways that require attention to the quality of political address, as well as to the social distribution of representational form. If we return to Sundari's claims about rural Tamils, for example, that "they've come to represent themselves" rather than ask others to engage the administration on their behalf, we must begin by acknowledging the sociological import of this observation insofar as it describes certain empirical changes. More and more Arivoli Iyakkam groups are handing in petitions and making demands in an arena where they would not have before. The number of petitions that the collector receives now is far greater than the numbers received prior to Arivoli activism.[21] More of these petitions are written by the petitioners themselves than ever before. It matters that people can write their own petitions and sign their own names, even if this shift cannot be contained within a story of progressive emancipation toward pure citizenship. The literacy movement has led to an intensified imbrication of political logics, perhaps a degree of minimal commensuration at a certain level of representation.

But the question of what it means to represent oneself through such texts is vexed, at best, and self-representation does not necessarily correlate with self-determination in any simple fashion. The capacity of the Arivoli Iyakkam to mobilize rural women exerts a force that has spread more rapidly and deeply than the practices of full literacy in this context. Claims to representation do not match embodied technique. There is a gap that has been produced between the two, making evident the distance between formal membership and substantive incorporation. In the pedagogical process, however, the "incompleteness" of the spread of representative means and the manifest differences in perspectives on effective action have both been recruited for use in the narrative of development. The integration of communicative logics and techniques, a prerequisite for transparency and directness from a statist perspective that is often shared by literacy activists, also appears as a horizon to be worked toward. It is the narrative of development-as-pedagogy that holds out the promise of arrival, a future integration allowing for the transparent self-representation of an already-constituted citizen. In the process, the marginality of people like the petitioners from Katrampatti is increasingly recontextualized as something *within* the state (Das and Poole 2004), and literacy as a means of self-representation is presented as the solution to this problem of marginality. What is at stake here is not a simple technical transformation.

There is a cultural politics that has been condensed in the signatures I have described and in the wider process of petitioning in twenty-first-century rural India; this is a politics of representation that has been multiply determined by legacies of colonial administration, widespread logics of deference and subordination, postcolonial developmentalism, the neoliberal turn toward development-as-pedagogy, claims for social justice, and the fact of an unequal distribution of representative means. These determining forces have worked at different scales only to come together in an act that many people would take for granted as how one represents one's "self" across space and time. If there is a tension between constative representation and performative creation that inheres to the dual structure of any signature (Derrida 1986, 1988), the signatures of the Katrampatti petitioners must also serve to remind us that there is nothing natural about an interpretive framework that would presume an isomorphism between written subject and social agent. The duality of performative structure in signature in this case, to the extent that a tension between two poles of significance is rendered evident, provides an entry point into the investigation of how and why the multiple contexts of performance matter a great deal in lending plausibility to a historicist temporal logic of interpretation. The magical conflation of subject and agent that is supposed to inhere in the act of signing is thrown into question even further if we take into account the signers' own interpretation of events—interpretations that were shaped by logics of deference and visuality that escape dominant ideologies of the written sign, as well as by a series of past disappointments. It is the very weight of these intersecting histories on the present, and on imagined futures, that must be taken into an account of the performativity of the signed petition. Claims to full citizenship through such media thus appear quite contradictory.

Epilogue

Reflections on a Time of Charismatic Enlightenment

In subsequent visits to meet with the Katrampatti Arivoli Iyakkam literacy group, I learned that the Adi-Dravidar Welfare Office had sent someone to their village to inquire about a path to the cremation ground for Dalits. This was one concrete result of having submitted a petition. The official who was sent appears to have noted the survey number of some land that could potentially be used for the purpose of a path and even talked to some of the men in Katrampatti. The women who actually presented the petition at the collector's office never talked to him. It was only when I visited Katrampatti in 2009, however, a number of years after the literacy group had submitted their petition, that I discovered how the district administration eventually determined that it would be best for the residents of Katrampatti to use the government-owned, dry riverbed as a path to their cremation ground. Dalits would still not be passing through the fields claimed by the Kallars, nor would they be given land of their own. Caste dominance was therefore legitimated by state action taken as a result of the Katrampatti petition. Theirs was a petition and a set of signatures that may well have marked partial entry into a new field of citizenship for the women of Katrampatti, but it cannot be said to have done much to reduce the injustices they continued to face. The promise of emancipation had instead faded into a new form of caste domination, now sanctioned by bureaucratic authority.

In that same year, the National Literacy Mission of India decided to stop funding for the Arivoli Iyakkam continuing-education program in Tamil Nadu. The main office in Pudukkottai was closed. The central government would fund more limited adult-literacy projects only in those districts with especially low rates of literacy among women. Pudukkottai had failed to qualify for these funds. Some of those who had occupied leadership positions in the Arivoli Iyakkam had already gone off to work for one of the many private development agencies that were hiring people with field experience in the literacy movement. A number of private organizations, such as the M. S. Swaminathan Research Foundation, had started "village knowledge centers" designed to advance the project of participatory development that had once been the domain of the state. Some who had worked as volunteers in the Arivoli Iyakkam simply went back to farming or working in any number of small business in the villages and small towns of Pudukkottai. Most of the women from Katrampatti who had participated in literacy lessons are still finding daily-wage work in the fields around their village, while a few have moved to Chennai in hopes of building a better life for their children.

A great number of activists who had been working for the Arivoli Iyakkam, however, have continued about their business of trying to teach their fellow villagers about the world around them in the name of a certain humanist emancipation. They do so now mainly through the Tamil Nadu Science Forum and the Progressive Writers and Artists Association, both of which maintain a strong presence in Pudukkottai and other districts across the state. These activists did not receive even the minimal honorarium that the government had promised them for some years in any case. They had been working out of their own convictions, not because it offered them any special job opportunities in the government or in private firms. Neela and Karuppiah, for example, had started teaching literacy classes for prisoners in the Pudukkottai Town Jail in the last days of the Arivoli Iyakkam. They had already put much effort into this project and had built a degree of goodwill among the inmates and the wardens, so they decided to continue with their lessons, even when the literacy program officially ended. Neela eventually wrote a series of essays reflecting on her experiences teaching in the jail, and about the new methods of imparting literacy that they had experimented with in this context. UNESCO decided to sponsor an English translation of her book to bring this work to an international audience, once again rewarding the actions of Arivoli Iyakkam's volunteer activists after the state had given up on the project. But the broader field of political possibilities for people like Neela in Pudukkottai has changed dramatically since the heady days of mass mobilization.

The time of the Arivoli Iyakkam was one of incredible, sometimes hyperbolic promise, when it seemed perfectly possible to people from a wide range of political positions that rapid changes in technology and structures of governance would lead to a complete remaking of the agrarian world. The then-president of India, Abdul Kalam, could confidently claim that the country would be "fully developed" by the year 2020. The advent of e-governance would ensure that there was a computer in every village where farmers could download their land deeds from the Internet and print them out.[1] For those on the Left who entered into the once-proscribed field of NGO activism, the task would be to steer the changes that were coming to India's villages in a more socially equitable direction. Literacy activism was a means toward this end of building a more unified nation-state. Through mass literacy, India's peasants would finally be able to "represent themselves," in the words of Sundari, the activist I have quoted earlier. A sort of postcolonial Enlightenment in the Tamil countryside appeared imminent in light of the new social energies that had been unleashed.

From a more sober, macrosociological perspective, we can see that the Arivoli Iyakkam and similar efforts of the 1990s and early 2000s were the products of a particular political conjuncture. The demise of a state structure that had long sought to monopolize claims to material development, and even to modernity itself, coincided with the rise of vast social movements making demands on behalf of people who felt they had never been adequately cared for by the paternalist Nehruvian state.[2] The rise of these social movements was indeed concurrent with the growing influence of neoliberalism in India, and a turn toward Hindu nationalism at the national level, prompting a political struggle over the future course of development. Although a number of large-scale movements emerged from the turn to NGO activism during this time—some like the literacy movement working in conjunction with the state, but many working against it—a general sense of disillusionment has since grown among those who took part in these movements, as the ideology of market fundamentalism coupled with corporatist political party apparatuses appear to drown out socialist visions of emancipation.

At a more global level, there is a profound sense in which the imaginary of a common future to be planned for underpinning earlier articulations of modernity has been hollowed out in a number of contexts. Marc Abélès (2010), for example, argues that as a result of the evaporation of the common future under neoliberalism, the North Atlantic world has shifted from a political imaginary organized around the problem of "making a society" together, toward a "politics of survival." Elizabeth Povinelli (2011) tracks a parallel shift in what she terms "late liberalism," focusing on the afterlives of settler colonialism in Australia and the United States, where "the futures of some, or the hopes they have for the future, can never be a *future*. . . . And for others, no matter what harms they do, the truth of these harms is deferred into the future" (27–28). But if much of the global North has entered the post-9/11 era of security without a positive shared sense of futurity, India's love affair with the horizon of what is yet to come has propelled it in somewhat different directions. A shift away from state-led planning in India certainly corresponded to a downturn in the political fortunes of the mainstream Communist parties, coupled with the rise of Maoist violence and repressive paramilitary assaults on *Adivasi* indigenous communities in the name of security. The question of the common future in India nevertheless continues to animate political struggle, now defined primarily by the rise of lower-caste claims on democracy (Jaffrelot 2003; Omvedt 1994; Rao 2009); ultra-Left challenges to the state's monopoly on violence (Shah 2010, 2011; Sundar 2006, 2010); a groundswell of queer critique and activism (Dave 2012; Narrain and Bhan 2005); and the always-present specter of organized religious violence (Chaturvedi 2011; Das 2006; Hansen 2001; Valiani 2011), and it is accompanied by consumerist aspirations animating a range of middle-class populisms (Fernandes 2006; Lukose 2009). The problem of "catching up" to an imagined West does not carry the same weight it once did, survival remains an essentially collective issue, and liberal visions of the political cannot be taken as hegemonic. Efforts to "make a society" together, such as those undertaken by the Arivoli literacy movement, have for the most part taken a backseat to other formulations of what the common future might be.

Such a macrosociology of changes in the neoliberal development state is certainly necessary to interpret the rise and fall of movements like the Arivoli Iyakkam. But this lens also strikes me as inadequate to the task of understanding the forms of social life that the movement enabled, nor can such a perspective provide compelling accounts of why and how activists and learners chose participate in the Arivoli Iyakkam in the first place. It is for this reason that I have felt the need to narrate the story of Arivoli Iyakkam activism in at least two registers. One has focused on questions of social positioning and on the morphology of social action, whereas another has been more attuned to the "spirit" that can be said to have animated the work of activism, immanent to that social field, and to the intellectual problems that were raised through this work. Even when focusing on the perhaps less tangible spirit or ethos of activism, it has been necessary at various points to draw a distinction between the explicit goals and ideology of the Arivoli Iyakkam and the often tacit modes of social relation through which this movement reached hundreds of thousands of villagers. This distinction between ideology and practice is even made by activists in moments of reflection—for example, when Dr. Sundararaman told me that the "concept of empowerment never happened," but that "empowerment did happen in a major way, because of who we were." The enlightenment that literacy activists claimed to spread through literacy and science lessons was belied by the very modes of reciprocal agency calling fellow villagers to action in the movement. It is this less obvious spirit of responsiveness and responsibility animating the peculiar dynamic of give-and-take at the core of activism that I have found to be of most interest in telling the story of the Arivoli Iyakkam.

The Arivoli Iyakkam was a *charismatic* Enlightenment movement. This may sound like a paradoxical formulation to the degree that the forms of secular rationality, scientific objectification, and self-mastery that activists sought to foster among villagers would seem to mitigate against the sense of time-bound mysticism or devotion that inheres in the concept of charisma. But I think that what Weber (1978, 245) would term the "anti-economic force" of charisma captures nicely that particular sense of responsiveness to a call that drove Arivoli Iyakkam activism. This is a charisma that adhered to the movement itself and not necessarily to a particular individual, as this concept is sometimes thought of in the Weberian tradition, even if it may well be said that the Arivoli Iyakkam was populated by a number of extraordinary people who compelled social action through their personalities. It is indeed worth recalling, in this context, the notions of gifting and grace that attach themselves to the Greek roots of this concept. In calling the Arivoli Iyakkam a charismatic Enlightenment project, I am simply claiming the movement was able to articulate the aspirations of a wide set of social actors, less through its ideology of enlightenment, than in its mode of operation through reciprocity.

It is true that the Arivoli Iyakkam promised forms of enlightenment and emancipation that could never be delivered through the propagation of literacy alone, as the story of the Katrampatti petition makes devastatingly clear. The promises it did make, however, appear to have had a performative effect of drawing people to the movement that far outweighs their positive content. That the Arivoli movement should fade out and become routinized even as it produced new generations of activists was a fate that was perhaps built into its charismatic mode of mobilization. But if the movement worked only to the degree that it moved according to the quality of Pudukkottai's soil, as Neela would put it, we can also surmise that the quality of this soil was itself forever changed as a result.

Notes

Introduction

1. "Arivoli Iyakkam" would be translated literally as "the Light of Knowledge movement," although the word "Arivoli" is now commonly used to refer to Enlightenment rationality in Tamil cultural studies.

2. Historical accounts of Soviet and Chinese mass-literacy movements can be found in Clark (2000) and Peterson (1997), respectively.

3. It was as a result of a Total Literacy Campaign that took place in 1991–92, and of repeated efforts to organize literacy classes in villages since that time, that Pudukkottai's female literacy rate rose from 44.2% to 60.9% according to the 2001 Census of India. The 2011 census suggests a 73.8% female literacy rate across the state of Tamil Nadu, with 80.3% overall. The current rural female literacy is estimated at 65.5%. Since its inception over twenty years ago, over thirty thousand volunteers have worked for the movement in the rural district of Pudukkottai alone. During the period of my research, in 2002–4, some five thousand recently trained activists were conducting literacy lessons for women while running four hundred village libraries and reading rooms across the district.

4. India had already begun to liberalize its economy from an import-substitution-based, centrally planned mixed economy by opening markets and reducing protective tariffs under Rajiv Gandhi's leadership in the mid-1980s. It was only after a balance-of-payments crisis in 1991, however, that the rural credit system was completely overhauled as part of a larger structural adjustment plan. Financial sector reforms have been introduced since then in an attempt

to transform credit institutions, leading to an emphasis on microfinance (Kalpana 2005; Lalitha and Nagarajan 2000). See also Deepak Nayyar (1996) for a macroeconomic overview of shifts in development policy under liberalization.

5. Partha Chatterjee (1993) and Sudipta Kaviraj (2010) have argued that the Nehruvian state asserted its legitimacy as the bearer of modernity through development projects that often were at odds with the very principals of democracy.

6. The early 1990s also marks the universalization of Panchayati Raj (decentralized democracy). The findings of Heller (2005) and Tanabe (2007) have given reason for hope that the general devolution of state power has in fact opened new spaces for what Tanabe calls "vernacular democracy." Corbridge et al. (2005) remain more equivocal in their studies of local governance in northern and eastern India.

7. As James Ferguson and Akhil Gupta (2002) have argued, it is not always easy to distinguish between state projects and social mobilization in the sphere of "civil society" in an era when some of the most important development work is being done by GONGOs—government organized nongovernmental organizations.

8. See Arturo Escobar (1995) and Akhil Gupta (1998) for classic accounts of how the discourse of development has portrayed a good part of the globe as "behind" and needing to "catch up" with the industrialized North; Ashis Nandy (2003) on how development requires a sacrifice of the present for the sake of the future; and Tania Li (2007) on continuities in development ideology from the colonial to the postcolonial.

9. I borrow the language of "infrastructure" from Craig Calhoun's (1991, 1992) essays on modernity and from Brian Larkin's (2008) ethnography of media technologies in northern Nigeria.

10. Benedict Anderson (1991), Elizabeth Povinelli (2006), Charles Taylor (2004), and Michael Warner (2002) are among the social theorists who have sought to theorize the sort of "stranger sociality" first enabled by writing that sits at the core of modern understandings of national citizenship.

11. Maurice Bloch argues that it is within the paradigm of Enlightenment that "systems of communication are therefore to be judged in terms of their transparency," that is, in terms of writing's capacity to circumvent forms of social mediation (1998, 166). Both Goody (1977, 1986) and Lévi-Strauss (1973) are writing within this paradigm of Enlightenment insofar as they are both concerned with the question of the relation between writing and transparency. Jacques Derrida's (1976) classic critique of Lévi-Strauss elaborates this argument concerning the role of transparency in the anthropologist's fear of the written word. See Akhil Gutpa (2012, 192–95) for an overview of this debate and its significance for the study of literacy and democracy in India.

12. Voter turnouts in recent elections are, in fact, consistently higher in constituencies with lower average rates of literacy in India (Yadav 2000).

13. Places where the Arivoli Iyakkam was a strong movement with widespread involvement at the grass roots include Virudunagar, Sivagangai, Tirunelveli, and Pudukkottai districts, and the Union Territory of Pondicherry. The neighboring state of Kerala was also a strong center for this type of literacy and science activism.

14. These people are what Steven Feierman (1990) calls "peasant intellectuals" whose livelihood often still depends on agriculture, or what Gramsci (1971, 14) would call "rural-type intellectuals."

15. In the words of Pierre Bourdieu and Loïc Wacquant, we stand in a "differential distance to the necessity immanent to the universe under examination" (1992, 41).

16. Venkatesh B. Athreya and Sheela Rani Chunkath (1996) and L. S. Saraswathi (2004) have provided the most comprehensive accounts of Arivoli Iyakkam activism in Pudukkottai District.

Krishna Kumar's (1993b) critique of the mass-literacy programs used the Pudukkottai Arivoli Iyakkam as a case to argue that these movements extended the penetration of the market economy. The journalist P. Sainath's (1996) best-selling *Everybody Loves a Good Drought: Stories from India's Poorest Districts* made Pudukkottai famous across India through its descriptions of the Arivoli Iyakkam. A number of other reports and critical essays have appeared on similar National Literacy Mission efforts across India (e.g., Agnihotri 1994; Kumar and Sankaran 2002; Mukherjee 2003; Rao 1993; Saxena 1992, 1993).

1. On Being a "Thumbprint"

1. The thumbprint as a means of identifying criminals and policing populations was first developed in colonial Calcutta (Sengoopta 2003). In the southern Tamil-speaking region, males from certain castes deemed "criminal" under the Madras Presidency Criminal Tribes Act of 1911, such as the Piramalai Kallars, were systematically fingerprinted and even restricted to their villages (Pandian 2009). It is in part because of these histories of colonial policing and population control that using one's thumbprint to document even attestation to a statement such as a petition carries with it an air of lowliness and criminality.

2. As when Rajnikanth's character in the hit film *Annamalai* (1992) is referred to by the villains as a "*ḳaināṭṭu*" [thumbprint] while signing away his family's land. A similar usage can be found in Hindi, as when Jonathan Parry discusses how the son of an uneducated steel worker derisively called his father "stupid and ignorant, how he had done nothing for his children, how he was 'nothing but a thumb-impression man!' (*angutha-chhap admi*)" (2004, 292).

3. I have placed the term "*cēri*," the Dalit hamlet that sits outside the main upper-caste settlement, in quotation marks because of its derogatory connotations in contemporary Tamil. In Kovilpatti, where my fieldwork was conducted, elders from the upper castes would still refer to the local Paraiyar settlement as the "*cēri*," whereas younger residents of the main settlement would refer to it as the "colony." Dalits themselves would simply call it their "*ūr*" or refer to it by name as Katrampatti Colony. No one called it by its official government name of Indira Gandhi Nagar. See Diane Mines's (2005) ethnography for a detailed account of contests over naming in Tirunelveli district.

4. There is plenty of evidence that such views may not be shared by Dalit agricultural laborers themselves. See Kapadia (1995) for a critique of Moffat's (1979) emphasis on consensus.

5. Part of the all-India Public Distribution System (PDS).

6. This is an office established as a government order under M. G. Ramachandran's chief ministership in 1980, consolidating the three older hereditary offices of accountant, security guard, and tax collector into one post, though popularly still referred to by the older term of "*ḳaṇaḳḳuppiḷḷai*."

7. Below poverty line (BPL) status was granted to any household making less than 24,200 rupees per year at the time of my research in 2002–4. Most households in Kovilpatti qualified at the time.

8. This claim is quite suspect given all the evidence pointing toward widespread support for Hindu nationalist politics among the highly educated middle classes (Hansen 1999).

9. Charles E. Clark's *Uprooting Otherness: The Literacy Campaign in NEP-Era Russia* (2000) provides a detailed account of the campaigns of 1923–27, and a useful point of comparison.

10. According to a communiqué issued by the CPI(M) in Kerala, Parameswaran was expelled for his "open rejection of Marxism-Leninism and the fundamental tenets of the party" (*Hindu*, Feb. 16, 2004).

11. Note the execution of a very Nehruvian ideal of developmental pedagogy in the name of modernization: "Simple science experiments, peeps into the microscope, and an explanation of

the ordinary phenomenon of nature bring excitement in their train, and understanding of some of life's processes, and a desire to experiment and find out instead of relying on set phrases and old formulae. Self-confidence and the co-operative spirit grow, and frustration, arising out of the miasma of the past, lessens" (Nehru, quoted in K. Kumar [2005, 188]).

12. Krishnamurthy's vision of Arivoli's function resembles Habermas's (1989) normative ideal of a public sphere, although Krishnamurthy is probably drawing directly on his reading of Freire (1970) here, in theorizing Arivoli as a collective dialogue.

13. This is according to the TNSF leadership I have interviewed in Chennai.

14. See Anandi (1991), Geetha and Rajadurai (1998), and Hodges (2005) for more detailed analyses of gender politics in the self-respect movement.

15. Tiruvalluvar, translated by P. S. Sundaram (1990).

16. In Karunanidhi's text there is a footnote inserted here, attributing the line to Yeats's "Easter 1916," which ends, "Wherever green is worn, / Are changed, changed utterly: / A terrible beauty is born."

17. Note that the translation is not the author's own but is from *Cemmalar* (Red Blossom), the Communist Party of India (Marxist) literary magazine.

18. He was speaking about "national unity" here in the context of Hindu-Muslim communal violence in North India.

19. A *vēṣṭi* is a white, cloth wrap tied around the waist and worn by Tamil men, here taking significance as a sign of tradition and rural working-class status in opposition to "Westernized" and "middle-class" pants. Like pants, powdering one's face with antiperspirant talcum here stands as the sign of a middle-class office worker as distinct from someone who works in the fields.

2. Feminizing Enlightenment

1. "Nearly 89 per cent of the non-literate women (in the targeted age group of 9–45 years) enrolled themselves in *arivoli* centres as against only 73 per cent for men" (Athreya and Chunkath 1996, 177).

2. These two successful experiments are recounted in detail in a book that became standard reading in syllabi on adult education around the world, cowritten by Chunkath and her colleague in the literacy movement, Venkatesh B. Athreya. The book was funded in part by UNESCO and it is titled *Literacy and Empowerment* (1996). The fame of Pudukkottai's women collectors, activists, cyclists, workers, and learners was also spread by high-profile articles written in national newspapers, such as the *Hindu*, and in the best-selling nonfiction book about India's poorest districts by the renowned journalist P. Sainath, *Everybody Loves a Good Drought* (1996).

3. It was in this period that the welfare-based women in development (WID) paradigm that had been formulated in response to the UN's Decade for Women (1975–85) was starting to give way to new strategies among development professionals. What eventually came to be known as the gender and development (GAD) paradigm was framed as a critique of the earlier model, insofar as WID merely sought to extend existing development programs to women. GAD, by contrast, was meant to provide a gendered critique of top-down development planning itself, instead offering a model of participatory development as local "empowerment." The new paradigm of giving NGOs access to state resources is what allowed literacy movements to become strong forces in the "*ruralization* of the women's movement" (Mayaram 2002, 23).

4. What has been called the "NGOization" of development coincided with a corresponding "NGOization" of the political Left in India, away from political parties toward social movement politics (Kamat 2002).

5. The shift toward an emphasis on women's empowerment and citizenship through literacy classes I am describing is not limited to India. Lila Abu-Lughod (2005, 63–69) describes a similar shift in Egypt, where women's literacy classes were used to teach liberal models of citizenship. Laura Ahearn's (2001, 162–71) work on textbooks used in adult literacy classes for women in Nepal of the mid-1990s reveals a similar emphasis on "self-sufficiency" in the service of national development. See Anna Robinson-Pant's (2004) edited volume for critical accounts of similar programs in Africa, Asia, and the Americas.

6. Mary John notes that this new focus on the "importance" of women masks a "crucial shift in signification, such that these findings [on the centrality of women to economic reproduction] are no longer arguments about *exploitation* so much as proofs of *efficiency*" (1996, 3074).

7. Keith Baker (2001) draws specifically on French thought from the Enlightenment to track the history of the concept of society's relation to that of "nature." See also Mary Poovey's (1998) analysis of how the concept of society was paired with the emergent abstraction and objectification of "human nature" in eighteenth-century English moral philosophy.

8. For instance, Susan Gal (2003) has shown how critiques of pornography imported from U.S. feminism into Hungarian academic circles can be interdiscursively aligned with Communist-era censorship, so as to render such critiques suspect by association.

9. Upon their first menstruation, young women are ritually secluded for seventeen days because they are filled with *shakti*, while also being polluted (*tīṭṭu*), potentially causing harm to anyone who comes near. See Kapadia (1995, 92–123) for a full description of puberty rituals similar to those one would find in contemporary Pudukkottai. By marking a woman's entry into the state of fertility, this major life-cycle ritual also tends to mark a change in her relationship to boys and men. From that time onward, when menstruating, women must keep distance (*tūram*) from all other people because they are in a polluted state.

10. *Camūkam* can also be used to refer to a religious community, such as Hindus, Christians, or Muslims, a category that *jāti* or *iṉam* is less likely to be used for.

11. I point readers to Bhaskar Mukhopadhyay's (2005, 44–47) discussion of how "*samāj*" was reformulated as "society" in Bengal. Mukhopadhyay comes to this point through an ethnography of miscommunication between himself and contemporary Bengali villagers, turning on different visions of the semantic field and pragmatics of "*samāj*." See also Gyan Prakash (2002) for a "Colonial Genealogy of Society," in which he analyzes the contrast between "society" and "community" in the making of a specifically colonial governmentality that would render South Asian social institutions as "archaic failures."

12. This song was written by Pralayan, a dramatist and poet affiliated with the Communist Party of India (Marxist).

13. I am indebted to Blake Wentworth for help in finding English approximations for these classical ideals that appear in aphoristic forms in a number of literary contexts.

14. Women's empowerment in this idiom rests on a purification of nature from culture, premised on a nevertheless cultural distinction, leading theorists like Judith Butler (1990) to question the very sex/gender distinction.

15. Valentine Daniel's (1984) semiotic approach to substance and personhood went a long way in reorienting the ethnosociological paradigm away from earlier obsessions with caste hierarchy, and toward a more open-ended theory of culture.

16. *Muṉṉēṟṟam* refers to progress in the sense of forward and upward motion, or "social uplift." It is used this way, for example, in the name of the political party, the *Tirāviṭa Muṉṉēṟṟak Kaḻakam,* or the Dravidian Progress Association (DMK).

17. Lakshmibai, the Rani (queen) of Jhansi in central India, played a leadership role in the Indian uprising of 1857 and was killed in the battle for Gwalior. According to legend, Jhansi Rani

jumped off a cliff in order to escape British capture. She has since become a symbol of women's role in the struggle for independence.

18. I only later found out that these women also belonged to the Velar caste whose traditional occupation was that of making pottery and votive clay horses to be sold as offerings given to the god Ayyanar at his temples.

19. During my fieldwork period the government of Tamil Nadu was offering subsidies and technical assistance for self-help groups to run wireless Internet centers in villages. Most of those who tried to start computer businesses through this scheme failed.

20. The educationalist L. S. Saraswathi (1995), who has written extensively about Pudukkottai's Arivoli Iyakkam, has suggested that women's *ḵōlam*-drawing skills, among other forms of "folk-math," are based on cognitive skills that could be used in the service of planning literacy programs that are more responsive to what she terms "indigenous learning cultures." Saraswathi, however, is equally interested in forms of folk math among men. Also recall how Murugan discussed *ḵōlams* along with women's cooking skills in order to argue for women's special sense of symmetry and their capacities to measure.

21. Neela, whose intellectual formation owes much to Bharathi's poetry and to the leftist tradition that has since appropriated these poems, has recently been rethinking her relationship to Bharathi in light of her participation in feminist writers' circles.

22. Published by the district literacy office as the *Maḵaḷir Aṟivoḷi Iyaḵḵam Kaiyēṭu* (2004).

23. Early twenty-first-century political economic research projects on microcredit and self-help groups in India have found that the "associational" effects of collective savings in this movement have far outweighed any large-scale economic change made through loans. Access to credit through the self-help group's collective account, not necessarily bank loans, is what made the biggest impact on the lives of women who formed such groups (Lalitha and Nagarajan 2000; Kumar and Varghese 2005). Most of the groups in the village where I did fieldwork never made it to the point of actually receiving a loan, but members did borrow from the collective savings fund.

24. The primary authors of the primer are development professionals with higher degrees in education who live in the city of Chennai. They wrote these learning materials in consultation with government development officers and NGO leaders from across the state of Tamil Nadu and from Pondicherry. These are the people who have been charged by the state with the task of translating government development plans into a specific pedagogical form.

25. I do not want to downplay economic incentives, but I want emphasize that such incentives are commonly interpreted through values that are not reducible to economic interest alone.

26. Mines is here using the concept of mutuality as first elaborated by Raheja (1988, 203–48) in her study of prestations and social dominance in a North Indian village.

27. Examples of *tāṉam* in Tamil villages and elsewhere also include gifts made to Brahman priests on completion of rituals associated with death. Brahman priests have a larger capacity to "eat" the inauspiciousness of such gifts than other people (Mines 2005, 69–71; see also Parry 1994).

28. The now very widespread use of signatures might then be seen in terms of a primarily *phatic* literacy. This use of signature is primarily phatic in Jakobson's sense of a linguistic event focused primarily on signaling the openness of a "contact" or channel (writing in this case) rather than on referring to an object or to other linguistic functions. Signatures in this context "communicate without sending or receiving information . . . to confirm the continued attention of an interlocutor" (1985 [1960], 152–53). It is the very *fact of signing* that is significant and communicative as a token of mutuality and the acknowledgment of a bind. I am indebted to Laura Brown for first pointing me toward this perspective on literacy.

3. Labors of Objectification

1. Sumathi Ramaswamy's (2003) work on the cartographic imagination demonstrates how such pedagogical uses of the globe in India date back to the colonial state's efforts to propagate a properly "modern" scientific rationality among "natives" and have precedents in the even earlier efforts of German missionaries in southern India.

2. In his most widely read book in southern India, *Pedagogy of the Oppressed* (1970), Freire quotes from the section on self-consciousness regarding lordship and bondage in Hegel's *Phenomenology of Spirit*, and then more extensively from Sartre's writings on intentionality.

3. This detachable aspect of writing is what introduces an element of uncertainty into documentary practices, as has been argued by Veena Das (2004), for example, insofar as what she terms the "signature of the state" lends itself to forgery, unauthorized circulation, and effects that escape intention while extending networks of state power.

4. Linguistic anthropology has provided a compelling theory of "entextualization" to account for the ways in which large units of language appear to maintain textual integrity across contexts of usage through both oral and written channels (Bauman and Briggs 1990; Silverstein and Urban 1996).

5. See essays in Lankshear and McLaren's (1993) edited volume, *Critical Literacy: Politics, Praxis and the Postmodern*, for a good introduction to applications of Freire's model of education in a range of postcolonial and feminist literacy initiatives. Very similar educational experiments, motivated by comparable postcolonial nationalist concerns, have taken place, for example, in Brazil and lusophone Africa (Freire and Macedo 1987); in Nicaragua under the Sandinistas (Arnove 1988; Weber 1981); in Castro's Cuba (Kozol 1978); and more recently in the REFLECT programs in Uganda, Zambia, and Lesotho (Attwood, Castle, and Smythe 2004; Friedrich 2004).

6. Most of the Arivoli Iyakkam workers I knew who had read Freire had done so in translation, from photocopies that circulate through leftist activist networks. A new version of Freire's *Pedagogy of the Oppressed*, translated by Ira. Nataracan, was published as *Oṭuḵḵappattavarḵaḷiṉ Viṭutalaiḵḵāṉa Kalvimuṟai* in 2008. This version has since become the standard in Tamil.

7. Daniel has noted similar forms of linguistic domination in the tea estates of Sri Lanka, where teachers from Jaffna teach Tamil through more classical varieties: "This dialect of Tamil, which is alien to the student, is called *centamiḻ* (elegant or pure Tamil) by the teacher while he or she simultaneously brands the Tamil spoken by Estate Tamil students *ḵoṭuntamiḻ* (coarse or corrupt Tamil)" (1996, 29). Such a "hegemonic culture of the standard" (Silverstein 1997) is, of course, very widespread and not limited to Tamil Nadu or India (see also Bourdieu 1991; Milroy and Milroy 1991). The dominance and superiority of a separate written standard, though, is perhaps more explicitly elaborated in Tamil pedagogies used in school than some other places.

8. In the National Literacy Mission literature this method is called the "Improved Pace and Content of Learning" method. The broad outlines of the method, which was designed to teach nonliterates how to read and write over the course of ten months, were developed through government collaboration with the BGVS, the state-recognized agency representing the all-India science movement. Primers were all designed locally by activists in the science movement, though there has been a good deal of standardization among the Arivoli Iyakkam literacy programs operating in different Tamil-speaking districts.

9. The document for registering land, which the man is holding, has been written on a piece of stamp paper worth five thousand rupees, more money than learners who labor as daily-wage workers might earn in an entire year.

10. It is not an accident that Ricoeur's language of liberation through textual mediation should resemble that of Freire's, given their common Left-Christian-phenomenological philosophical

world. The text (note its singularity) is not only a "model for culture," as Ricoeur has famously argued, but also a *tool for the cultivation of subjects*, in a concept of culture that draws on tropes of civilization.

11. The word is the very medium that would most effectively separate subjects from objects in a fashion of modernization characterized by Bruno Latour (1993) as "purification." See Webb Keane's (2007) account of the Protestant roots of this particularly modern orientation to language and subjectivity in Indonesia.

12. Outside the context of literacy lessons, both men and women from Katrampatti would couch their claims to land in terms of hoping to use the land and irrigation resources of particular landowners by performing services for them. Such desires resonate with those articulated in the rural Tamil Dalit autobiography of Viramma, collected, edited, and translated by Josiane Racine and Jean-Luc Racine as *Une vie paria* (1995).

13. Compare to Mines's (2005, 188–202) description of a Dalit religious procession through the middle of the main caste-Hindu settlement as a mode of protest.

14. Trawick argues that, in contrast to sociological understandings of the "great tradition" of Sanskritic Hinduism that would emphasize the Brahmanic origin of dominant cultural patterns in village India, Dalit "crying songs" allow for an alternative understanding of how cultural patterns are "communicated upward in the status hierarchy rather than downward, as seems usually to be the case" (1991, 297).

15. In his memoirs, the activist Tamilcelvan reports being asked the very same question when he tried to teach the first lessons from the primer (2004b, 23).

16. The letter *A* also marks the beginning of the great Tamil philosophical text, the *Tirukkuṟaḷ*, with the couplet, *ak̲ara mutala eḻuttellām āti pak̲avaṉ mutaṟṟē ulak̲u* (*A* begins the alphabet, / And God, the primordial, the world).

17. The *aricuvaṭi* is a teaching text that was traditionally used in Tamil village schools as a mnemonic device. Through recitation of this text, which appears as a religious devotional poem, students learned the alphasyllabary in an order that corresponded to the first syllables of every line in the poem. Older men in the villages of Kovilpatti and Katrampatti had learned to read by means of this text when they were children.

18. The *Naṉṉūl* (literally, "The Good Book") is a Tamil grammar attributed to the sage Pavanandi and written in the eleventh century. It is the most frequently cited grammar text in modern Tamil schooling.

19. This order of emphasis is exactly what Krishna Kumar finds troubling about traditional Indian education in general. "In brief, this approach is characterized by the treatment of script as a complex package of information to be learned for its own sake. Children must learn the names of different letters and they must develop the ability to recognize them separately and as part of a word. . . . Reading is treated as an end product which the child must wait for, suspending the desire to find meaning in written material, especially to find meaning with which he or she can relate" (1993a, 105–6).

20. In an attempt to rescue an understanding of the mnemonic learning system meant to cultivate the powers of recollection and calculation from its transformation into "rote learning" in the colonial era, historical research suggests that both Christian missionaries and the early East India Company administration began a fundamental reordering of South Indian orientations to writing (Raman 2012).

21. Learners may well have seen attempts to teach normal spoken forms from people who had already mastered literary varieties as condescending. It is partly for this reason, I suspect, that it has been very difficult to produce educational texts more closely resembling everyday forms of language use among the poor in Tamil Nadu.

22. See Collins and Blot (2003) for a useful overview of the debates around technological determinism, the "new literacy studies," and ideological approaches to literacy studies.

23. Roger Chartier's (1994) work on early modern reading practices in Europe shows that this type of silent individual reading is a new phenomenon, and A. R. Venkatachalapathy's (1994, 2012) work on the birth of silent reading in Tamil Nadu connects this practice to the rise of a middle class in the mid-twentieth century.

24. Michael Jackson's critique of "the intellectualist tendency to regard body praxis as secondary to verbal praxis" (1983, 328) once again assumes that verbal praxis is not already embodied. See Dominic Boyer's (2005a) argument about the place of professionalization in obscuring the role of the body in intellectual production.

4. Search for a Method

1. Stuart Blackburn's (2003) research on the origins of Tamil print culture in the eighteenth and nineteenth centuries is worth noting in this context because folktales appear to be among the first texts to enter print. These were used in missionary activities and later in teaching the British Tamil at the College of Fort St. George in Madras.

2. It is clear from Constantine G. Beschi's (1822 [1782], 1831 [1730]) early grammars that what is known as *centamiḻ* (refined or cultivated Tamil) has long been distinguished as a privileged register from *koccaittamiḻ* (vulgar Tamil) or *koṭuntamiḻ* (broken Tamil). However, the exact form of the variety known as *centamiḻ* has changed over time. See Bate (2009) for a more detailed theoretical discussion of diglossia and heteroglossia in Tamil.

3. Roman Jakobson (2000) distinguishes among three types of translation, each of which would play a role in devising this literature: "(1) Intralingual translation or *rewording* is an interpretation of verbal signs by means of other signs of the same language. (2) Interlingual translation or *translation proper* is an interpretation of verbal signs by means of some other language. (3) Intersemiotic translation or *transmutation* is an interpretation of verbal signs by means of signs of nonverbal sign systems."

4. See Annamalai (2007) for a good overview of the struggle to render distinct language varieties in written literature in Tamil, and Kailasapathy (1979) on early critiques of the Tamil nationalist purification efforts in the struggle to bring spoken language into writing.

5. A. R. Venkatachalapathy (1994, 2012) emphasizes the fact that *vācippu*, the word now often used to refer to reading, used to refer to the act of reciting aloud, and he shows how this shift from reading aloud to reading silently developed with the rise of modern literature.

6. Fuller accounts of the history of the Tamil Nadu Progressive Writers Association can be found in books published on the occasion of their statewide meetings, such as *Paṇpāṭṭut Taḷattil Māṟṟuppātai Tēṭi*. The group officially changed its name to the Tamil Nadu Progressive Writers and Artists Association in 2008, in an effort to incorporate performing and visual artists.

7. This passage is quoted almost verbatim in *Paṇpāṭṭut Taḷattil Māṟṟuppātai Tēṭi* (2006, 6), published by the Tamil Nadu Progressive Writers Association on the occasion of their tenth general meeting in Tiruvannamalai.

8. The writers of the All-India Progressive Writers Association who worked primarily in Urdu and Hindi also took inspiration from similar literary movements forming in Europe at the same time. Their manifesto demanding that creative literature be relentlessly critical of both traditional society and modern fascism was published in English by Sajjad Zaheer and Mulk Raj Anand in the *Left Review* in London, as well as in Hindi by Premchand in the journal *Hans*, printed in Varanasi (see Ahmed 2009; Gopal 2005).

9. The Communist Party of India split in 1964, leading to a division among artists associated with offshoot parties. Karthigesu Sivathamby (1978) provides a more ecumenical account of the role of realism in the Tamil progressive writers' movement than that told by the Tamil Nadu Progressive Writers Association, emphasizing earlier Left literary movements in Tamil, in addition to European precedents.

10. See the ethnographic monographs written by Stuart Blackburn (1988) and Diane Mines (2005) for accounts of gods who came about as a result of violence in Tamil village narratives, or what Blackburn (1986) elsewhere calls "Violation-Death-Deification-Revenge" story-types.

11. These pamphlets were prepared in 2002 by the education activist and scholar L. S. Saraswathi, who was among the first to study the Arivoli Iyakkam in Pudukkottai (see Saraswathi 2004).

12. See Margaret Trawick's (1991) discussion of the trope of "placelessness" in Dalit song and narrative.

13. The ideal of *nākarīkam* refers to a certain civility, which the women of Katrampatti found surprisingly lacking in U.S. culture considering the relative freedom women there appeared to enjoy. See Karin Kapadia's (1995, 66–67) ethnography for a discussion of this sense of civility in the context of marriage alliances, and Anand Pandian's (2009) more extended account and interpretation of the virtues of "agrarian civility."

14. Neela's formulation of the problem facing activism fits well with Valentine Daniel's (1984) account of how villagers speak of compatibility between people and their village (*ūr*) in terms of the quality of its mud.

15. In certain respects, this dynamic of what has been called "remediation" in search of a certain effect of transparency is similar to what we are learning from research on the ideological vicissitudes of computer technology in rural India (Mazzarella 2006, 2010). In rural Tamil Nadu, some of the very same people were involved in both literacy activism and the development of a rural computer infrastructure for low-cost wireless Internet.

16. Richard Bauman has been an important voice in this line of research, first focusing on Quaker language ideologies (Bauman 1983), and then shifting to work with Charles Briggs on language philosophy from Lock and Herder to later folklore movements (Bauman and Briggs 2003).

5. Subject to Citizenship

1. See Majid Siddiqi (2005) for an overview of this historiography.

2. We can tell from the Tamil scholar Rev. G. U. Pope's training manuals for British officers stationed in the Tamil country from the 1850s and 1860s that, by the mid-nineteenth century, a distinct variety of written prose language had already been well established for petitions and other official correspondence. See chapters 5 and 6 of Pope's (1982 [1905]) *Handbook of the Tamil Language: A Tamil Prose Reader*, "Magisterial Business: 'Cutchery Tamil,'" and "Petitions and Official Correspondence" respectively, for examples of petitions collected in 1863.

3. Membership was determined through standardized examination (Chakrabarty and Bhattacharya 2003; Maheshwari 1994).

4. The DMK had just won control of the state legislature from Congress on the promises of a Dravidian nationalist populist platform. M. Karunanidhi, who had just taken over the position of chief minister of Tamil Nadu after the death of the party founder C. N. Annadurai in 1968, gave a government order formalizing and opening the petitioning process as the *maṉu nīti tiṭṭam* (Petition Justice Plan).

5. I use the word "elite" here, noting that contemporary IAS officers are an educational elite, and that collectors may well come from relatively socially disadvantaged backgrounds.

6. Scheduled Caste is a census category used for the castes I refer to as "Dalit." A number of special development programs are designed for this community in particular, and they are also given preferential treatment in government hiring through India's affirmative action program.

7. It is also common to see people coming in with newspaper clippings if, for instance, their house had burned down or if they were struck by some other misfortune that made it into the local column. One man I saw talking to the petition writers insisted, against their advice, that the

petition be written on the very piece paper on which he had photocopied a news item relating to his problems.

8. I use the male gender for the professional scribes because they were all men. Arivoli volunteers, on the other hand, are men and women.

9. Laura Bear (2007) has noted how such performances of suffering entered into the very texts of petitions among railway workers in early twentieth-century Calcutta. See also Trawick's description of Paraiyar "crying songs," through which singers hope to "convince the listener of the singer's intrinsic worth, and the fact that she has been wronged, perhaps by the listener himself" (1986, 302).

10. Women would generally be reluctant to say their husband's names. Some women hesitate in responding to this question, but Muttammal did not.

11. See Parry's discussion of how, when he sent his informant a registered letter in the name of "'Somvaru Ram,' he had to go sign for it at the main post office, where he was put through the mill by the babus because, though his grandchildren had taught him 'Somvaru,' he could not manage the 'Ram'" (2004, 291). See also James Scott's (1998, 64–71) discussion of the development of surnames as a means of making populations "legible" to the state.

12. Again, this encounter might have been a little different in the details if the writer were a young man, but the same problems of making demands legible to the state would persist.

13. This information is based on an unpublished census and survey taken in June of 2003 by the Arivoli Continuing Education Programme. I participated in taking the census and, after analyzing the data, submitted a formal report to the collector in August of 2003.

14. Petitions can be written on any plain piece of paper. Some petitioners, however, will insist on having their petition written on official government stamp paper, which must be bought for an additional twenty rupees.

15. The *Tamil Lexicon* (1931) entries for *maṇu* and *viṇṇappam* both assert the religious origins of petitioning vocabulary.

16. See Irvine (1998) on how "the expression of deference is grammaticalized" across a number of languages and cases, and Levinson (1982) for the most systematic study of deferential pronoun usage in Tamil.

17. This form was also in common use in the petitions collected by Reverend Pope from 1863 and published in his prose reader in 1905.

18. The Cre-A contemporary Tamil dictionary (1992, 405) defines *camukam*, as it is more commonly spelled in petitions, as an archaic, increasingly rare form, meaning "presence (of a king, etc.)."

19. The Cre-A Tamil dictionary (1992, 170) has a rather lengthy definition of "*ecemāṉ*": "in villages, one who provides employment in his house or land, master." It derives from the Sanskrit *yajamāṉa*, meaning "master of the sacrifice" (Monier-Williams 1920). This word is variously written in Tamil as "*eḵemāṉ*," in many petitions written by unschooled writers; "*ejemāṉ*," using a more Sanskritic phonology; or "*ecemāṉ*," as in the standard Dravidianization of Sanskrit phonology expected of schooled literacy, though not commonly found in petitions. This lexical item is probably also related to the Greek *hegemon*, meaning "leader," the root of the modern English word "hegemony."

20. The *darbār* hall is a special room in a royal palace for public viewing of royalty. It is derived in part from Persianate courtly traditions requiring that the king make himself visible and available to his court and subjects. The idea of a *darbār* was also significantly altered and reconstructed under a contradictory form of colonialism that Bernard Cohn (1987) and Nicholas Dirks (1993) convincingly argue sought to maintain India as a "feudal" order even while claiming to dismantle patrimonial authority in the name of modern governance. The effects of this contradictory project can be felt even now insofar as the collector occupies a dual relation to his citizen/subjects, as both royal patron and government servant.

21. The collector of Pudukkottai told me that he received between four hundred and five hundred petitions every week at Grievance Day, and that these numbers are much higher than those before the beginnings of literacy activism in the 1990s.

Epilogue

1. See William Mazzarella's (2006, 2010) attention to the hyperbole surrounding information technology during this time. A number of Tamil literacy activists were similarly involved in establishing rural computer centers.

2. See the volume edited by Ray and Katzenstein (2005) for a compelling overview of these political changes and the rise of new social movements in India. Amita Baviskar's (1995) ethnography of the social movement to halt the building of the Sardar Sarovar Dam also provides insight into the contradictions that emerged within the field of activism at this time.

Works Cited

Literacy Primers and Pamphlets

Anandamurthy, V., and V. Harikumar. 2001. *Cakti*. Chennai: State Resource Centre.

BGVS Working Group. 1999. *Eḻumpillāta Nākku* [Tongue without bones: Adages told by Arivoli learners]. Madurai: BGVS Resource Center Tamil Nadu.

——. 1996. *Putticāli Peṇkaḷ* [Intelligent women: Folktale collection]. Madurai: BGVS Resource Center Tamil Nadu.

——. 1992. *Nīṅkaḷē Colluṅkaḷ* [Tell me yourself: Story collection]. Madurai: BGVS Resource Center Tamil Nadu.

Kadiresan, M. 1996. *Victor Hugo's Ēḻai Paṭum Pāṭu* [Victor Hugo's les misérables]. Madurai: BGVS Resource Center Tamil Nadu.

Pudukkottai Arivoli Continuing Education Programme. 2004. *Makaḷir Aṟivoḷi Iyakkam Kaiyēṭu* [Women's enlightenment movement handbook]. Pudukkottai: Arivoli Iyakkam.

Pudukkottai Mavatta Arivoli Iyakkam. 1993. *Aṟivoḷi Veṟṟiviḻā Malar* [Enlightenment celebration booklet]. Pudukkottai: District Literacy Society.

Rajanarayanan, K. 1995. *Kāycca Maram* [Fruit tree, based on King Lear]. Madurai: BGVS Resource Center Tamil Nadu.

Ravichandran, S. 1995. *O. Henry's Kaṭaici Ilai* [The last leaf]. Madurai: BGVS Resource Center Tamil Nadu.

State Resource Centre and Arivoli Continuing Education Officers. 2004. *Aṟivoḷi Tīpam Pakuti—1* [Lamp of enlightenment, part one]. Pudukkottai: District Development Office and Pudukkottai Continuing Education Programme.

Tamilcelvan, S. 1997. *Muttācci* [Based on Pudumaipittan's *Caṅkut Tēvaṉiṉ Tarmam* (Deva's duty)]. Madurai: BGVS Resource Center Tamil Nadu

Secondary Literature

Abélès, Marc. 2010. *The Politics of Survival*. Translated by Julie Kleinman. Durham, NC: Duke University Press.

Abu-Lughod, Lila. 2005. *Dramas of Nationhood: The Politics of Television in Egypt.* Chicago: University of Chicago Press.

Agnihotri, R. K. 1994. "Campaign-Based Literacy Programs: The Case of the Ambedkar Nagar Experiment in Delhi." *Language and Education* 8 (1–2):47–56.

Ahearn, Laura. 2001. *Invitations to Love: Literacy, Love Letters, and Social Change in Nepal*. Ann Arbor: University of Michigan Press.

Ahmed, Talat. 2009. *Literature and Politics in the Age of Nationalism: The Progressive Episode in South Asia, 1932–56*. New Delhi: Routledge.

Althusser, Louis. 1994. "Ideology and Ideological State Apparatuses (Notes towards an Investigation)." In *Mapping Ideology*, edited by Slavoj Žižek, 100–140. London: Verso.

Amin, Shahid. 1995. *Event, Metaphor, Memory: Chauri Chaura 1922–1992*. New Delhi: Oxford University Press.

Anandi, S. 1991. "The Women's Question in the Dravidian Movement, c. 1925–1948." *Social Scientist* 19 (5–6): 24–41.

Anderson, Benedict. 1991. *Imagined Communities: Reflections on the Origin and Spread of Nationalism*. London: Verso.

Annamalai, E. 2007. "The Challenge of Spoken Language to Creative Writers in Modern Tamil." In *History and Imagination: Tamil Culture in the Global Context,* edited by R. Cheran, Darshan Ambalavanar, and Chelva Kanaganayakam, 63–75. Toronto: TSAR Publications.

Appadurai, Arjun. 1990. "Topographies of the Self: Praise and Emotion in Hindu India." In *Language and the Politics of Emotion,* edited by Catherine Lutz and Lila Abu-Lughod, 92–112. Cambridge: Cambridge University Press.

Arnove, Robert. 1988. "The Nicaraguan National Literacy Crusade of 1980." In *Perspectives on Literacy*, edited by Eugene Kintgen, Barry Froll, and Mike Rose, 410–20. Carbondale: Southern Illinois University Press.

Arokianathan, S. 1988. *Language Use in Mass Media.* New Delhi: Creative Publishers.

Aruna, R. 1999. "'Learn Thoroughly': Primary Schooling in Tamil Nadu." *Economic and Political Weekly* 34:1011–14.

Athreya, Venkatesh B., and Sheela Rani Chunkath. 1996. *Literacy and Empowerment*. New Delhi: Sage and UNESCO.

Attwood, Gillian, Jane Castle, and Suzanne Smythe. 2004. "'Women Are Lions in Dresses': Negotiating Gender Relations in REFLECT Learning Circles in Lesotho." In *Women, Literacy and Development: Alternative Perspectives*, edited by Anna Robinson-Pant, 139–58. London: Routledge.

Austin, J. L. 1962. *How to Do Things with Words*. Cambridge, MA: Harvard University Press.

Babu, Senthil. 2004. "Popularising Science for Social Change: R. Singaravelar." *Economic and Political Weekly* 39 (3): 234–37.

Baker, Keith. 2001. "Enlightenment and the Institution of Society: Notes for a Conceptual History." In *Civil Society: History and Possibilities*, edited by Sudipta Kaviraj and Sunil Kilnani, 84–104. Cambridge: Cambridge University Press.

Bakhtin, M. M. 1981. *The Dialogic Imagination*. Edited by Michael Holquist. Translated by Caryl Emerson and Michael Holquist. Austin: University of Texas Press.

Bartlett, Lesley. 2005. "Dialogue, Knowledge, and Teacher-Student Relations: Freirean Pedagogy in Theory and Practice." *Comparative Education Review* 49 (3): 344–64.

Bate, Bernard. 2010. "The Ethics of Textuality: The Protestant Sermon and the Tamil Public Sphere." In *Ethical Life in South Asia*, edited by Anand Pandian and Daud Ali, 101–15. Bloomington: Indiana University Press.

———. 2009. *Tamil Oratory and the Dravidian Aesthetic: Democratic Practice in South India*. New York: Columbia University Press.

Bauman, Richard. 1983. *Let Your Words Be Few: Symbolism of Speaking and Silence among Seventeenth-Century Quakers*. Cambridge: Cambridge University Press.

Bauman, Richard, and Charles Briggs. 2003. *Voices of Modernity: Language Ideologies and the Politics of Inequality*. Cambridge: Cambridge University Press.

———. 1990. "Poetics and Performance as Critical Perspectives on Language and Social Life." *Annual Review of Anthropology* 19:59–88.

Baviskar, Amita. 1995. *In the Belly of the River: Tribal Conflicts over Development in the Narmada Valley*. New Delhi: Oxford University Press.

Bear, Laura. 2007. *Lines of the Nation: Indian Railway Workers, Bureaucracy, and the Intimate Historical Self*. New York: Columbia University Press.

Benjamin, Walter. 1999. "Experience and Poverty." In *Selected Writings,* edited by Michael Jennings, 2:731–38. Cambridge, MA: Harvard University Press.

———. 1978. "The Author as Producer." In *Reflections*, edited by Peter Demetz, 220–38. New York: Schocken Books.

———. 1968. "The Work of Art in the Age of Mechanical Reproduction." In *Illuminations*, edited by Hannah Arendt, 217–52. New York: Harcourt, Brace, and World.

Bernal, J. D. 1961. *The Social Function of Science*. Cambridge, MA: MIT Press.

Berry, Kim. 2003. "Developing Women: The Traffic in Ideas about Women and Their Needs in Kangra, India." In *Regional Modernities: The Cultural Politics of Development in India*, edited by K. Sivaramakrishnan and Arun Agrawal, 75–98. New Delhi: Oxford University Press.

Beschi, Constantine G. 1831. *A Grammar of the Common Dialect of the Tamulian Language, Called Koduntamij*. Translated by Christopher Henry Horst. Madras: Vepery Mission Press.

——. 1822. *A Grammar of the High Dialect of the Tamil Language, Termed Shen-Tamil: To which is added, an Introduction to Tamil Poetry*. Translated by Benjamin Guy Babington. Madras: College Press.

Besnier, Niko. 1995. *Literacy, Emotion, and Authority: Reading and Writing on a Polynesian Atoll*. Cambridge: Cambridge University Press.

Blackburn, Stuart. 2003. *Print, Folklore, and Nationalism in Colonial South India*. Delhi: Permanent Black.

——. 1988. *Singing of Birth and Death: Performance as Paradigm*. Philadelphia: University of Pennsylvania Press.

——. 1986. "Performance Markers in an India Story-Type." In *Another Harmony: New Essays on the Folklore of India*, edited by Stuart Blackburn and A. K. Ramanujam, 167–94. Berkeley: University of California Press.

Bloch, Maurice. 1998. *How We Think They Think: Anthropological Approaches to Cognition, Memory, and Literacy*. Boulder: Westview Press.

Bourdieu, Pierre. 1999. "Rethinking the State: Genesis and Structure of the Bureaucratic Field." In *State/Culture: State-Formation after the Cultural Turn*, edited by George Steinmetz, 53–75. Ithaca, NY: Cornell University Press.

——. 1991. *Language and Symbolic Power*. Translated by Gino Raymond and Matthew Adamson. Cambridge, MA: Harvard University Press.

——. 1977. *Outline of a Theory of Practice*. Translated by Richard Nice. Cambridge: Cambridge University Press.

Bourdieu, Pierre, and Loïc Wacquant. 1992. *An Invitation to Reflexive Sociology*. Chicago: University of Chicago Press.

Boyer, Dominic. 2007. "Of Dialectical Germans and Dialectical Ethnographers: Notes from an Engagement with Philosophy." In *Ways of Knowing: New Approaches in the Anthropology of Knowledge and Learning*, edited by Mark Harris, 27–41. London: Berghahn Books.

——. 2005a. "The Corporeality of Expertise." *Ethnos* 70 (2): 243–66.

——. 2005b. *Spirit and System: Media, Intellectuals and the Dialectic in Modern German Culture*. Chicago: University of Chicago Press.

Brenneis, Donald. 1994. "Discourse and Discipline at the National Research Council: A Bureaucratic *Bildungsroman*." *Cultural Anthropology* 9 (1): 23–36.

Britto, Francis. 1986. *Diglossia: A Study of the Theory with Application to Tamil*. Washington, DC: Georgetown University Press.

Butler, Judith. 1990. *Gender Trouble: Feminism and the Subversion of Identity*. New York: Routledge.

Calhoun, Craig. 1992. "The Infrastructure of Modernity: Indirect Relationships, Information Technology, and Social Integration." In *Social Change and Modernity*, edited by Hans Haferkamp and Neil J. Smelser, 205–36. Berkeley: University of California.

——. 1991. "Indirect Relationships and Imagined Communities: Large Scale Social Integration and the Transformation of Everyday Life." In *Social Theory for a Changing Society*, edited by Pierre Bourdieu and James S. Coleman, 95–120. Boulder: Westview Press.

Chakrabarty, Bidyut, and Mohit Bhattacharya, eds. 2003. *Public Administration: A Reader*. New Delhi: Oxford University Press.

Chakrabarty, Dipesh. 2000. *Provincializing Europe: Postcolonial Thought and Historical Difference*. Princeton: Princeton University Press.

Chari, Sharad, and Henrike Donner. 2010. "Ethnographies of Activism: A Critical Introduction." *Cultural Dynamics* 22 (2): 75–85.

Chartier, Roger. 1994. *The Order of Books*. Stanford: Stanford University Press.

Chatterjee, Partha. 2004. *The Politics of the Governed: Reflections on Popular Politics in Most of the World*. New York: Columbia University Press.

——. 1993. *The Nation and Its Fragments: Colonial and Postcolonial Histories*. Princeton: Princeton University Press.

——. 1989. "Colonialism, Nationalism, and Colonized Women: The Contest in India." *American Ethnologist* 16:622–33.

Chaturvedi, Ruchi. 2011. "'SOMEHOW IT HAPPENED': Violence, Culpability, and the Hindu Nationalist Community." *Cultural Anthropology* 26 (3): 340–62.

Cheah, Pheng. 2003. *Spectral Nationality: Passages of Freedom from Kant to Postcolonial Literatures of Liberation*. New York: Columbia University Press.

Clark, Charles. 2000. *Uprooting Otherness: The Literacy Campaign in NEP-Era Russia*. London: Associated University Presses.

Cody, Francis. 2011. "Arivoli's Humanism: Literacy Activism and the Senses of Enlightenment." In *World without Walls: Being Human, Being Tamil*, edited by R. Cheran, Dalbir Singh, Chelva Kanaganayakam, and Sudharshan Duraiyappah, 1–14. Toronto: TSAR Press.

——. 2009. "Inscribing Subjects to Citizenship: Petitions, Literacy Activism, and the Performativity of Signature in Rural Tamil India." *Cultural Anthropology* 24 (3): 347–80.

Cohn, Bernard. 1987. "Representing Authority in Victorian India." In *An Anthropologist among the Historians, and Other Essays,* edited by Bernard Cohn, 632–82. New Delhi: Oxford University Press.

Collins, John, and Richard Blot. 2003. *Literacy and Literacies: Texts, Power, and Identity*. Cambridge: Cambridge University Press.

Corbridge, Stuart, Glyn Williams, Manoj Srivastava, and René Véron. 2005. *Seeing the State: Governance and Governmentality in India*. Cambridge: Cambridge University Press.

Cre-A. 1992. *Kriyāviṉ Taṟkālat Tamiḻ Akarāti: Tamiḻ-Tamiḻ-Āṅkilam*. Chennai: Cre-A.

Daniel, E. Valentine. 1996. *Charred Lullabies: Chapters in an Anthropography of Violence*. Princeton: Princeton University Press.

——. 1984. *Fluid Signs: Being a Person the Tamil Way*. Berkeley: University of California Press.

Das, Veena. 2006. *Life and Words: Violence and the Descent into the Ordinary*. Berkeley: University of California Press.

——. 2004. "The Signature of the State: The Paradox of Illegibility." In *Anthropology in the Margins of the State,* edited by Veena Das and Deborah Poole, 225–52. New Delhi: Oxford University Press.

Das, Veena, and Deborah Poole, eds. 2004. *Anthropology in the Margins of the State*. New Delhi: Oxford University Press.

Dave, Naisargi. 2012. *Queer Activism in India: A Story in the Anthropology of Ethics*. Durham, NC: Duke University Press.

De Beauvoir, Simone. 2011. *The Second Sex.* Translated by Constance Borde and Sheila Malovany-Chevallier. 1949. Reprint, New York: Vintage.

de Certeau. Michel. 1984. *The Practice of Everyday Life*. Berkeley: University of California Press.

Derrida, Jacques. 1988. "Signature Event Context." In *Limited Inc*., edited by Gerald Graff, 1–23. Evanston, IL: Northwestern University Press.

——. 1986. "Declarations of Independence." *New Political Science* 15 (1): 7–15.

——. 1976. *Of Grammatology*. Translated by Gayatri Chakravorty Spivak. Baltimore: Johns Hopkins University Press.

Diehl, Anita. 1977. *E.V. Ramaswamy Naiker-Periyar: A Study of the Influence of a Personality in Contemporary South India*. Lund, Sweden: Esselte Studium.

Dirks, Nicholas. 2001. *Castes of Mind: Colonialism and the Making of Modern India*. Princeton: Princeton University Press.

——. 1993. *The Hollow Crown: Ethnohistory of a Small Indian Kingdom.* Ann Arbor: University of Michigan Press.

Drèze, Jean. 2004. "Patterns of Literacy and Their Social Context." In *Oxford Handbook of Indian Sociology*, edited by Veena Das, 345–64. New Delhi: Oxford University Press.

Dube, Leela. 1986. "Seed and Earth: The Symbolism of Biological Reproduction and Sexual Relations of Production." In *Visibility and Power*, edited by Leela Dube, Eleanor Leacock, and Shirley Ardener, 22–53. New Delhi: Oxford University Press.

Escobar, Arturo. 1995. *Encountering Development: The Making and Unmaking of the Third World*. Princeton: Princeton University Press.

Fabian, Johannes. 1983. *Time and the Other: How Anthropology Makes Its Object*. New York: Columbia University Press.

Feierman, Steven. 1990. *Peasant Intellectuals: Anthropology and History in Tanzania*. Madison: University of Wisconsin Press.

Ferguson, Charles. 1959. Diglossia. *Word* 15:325–40.

Ferguson, James. 1994. *The Anti-Politics Machine: "Development," Depoliticization and Bureaucratic Power in Lesotho*. Minneapolis: University of Minnesota Press.

Ferguson, James, and Akhil Gupta. 2002. "Spatializing States: Toward an Ethnography of Neoliberal Governmentality." *American Ethnologist* 29 (4): 981–1002.

Fernandes, Leela. 2006. *India's New Middle Class: Democratic Politics in an Era of Economic Reform*. Minneapolis: University of Minnesota Press.

Foucault, Michel. 2007. *Security, Territory, Population: Lectures at the Collège de France, 1977–1978*. Edited by Michael Senallart. New York: Picador.
———. 1987. "What Is Enlightenment?" In *Interpretive Social Science: A Second Look*, edited by Paul Rabinow and William M. Sullivan, 157–76. Berkeley: University of California Press.
Freire, Paulo. 2008. *Oṭukkappattavarkaḷiṉ Viṭutalaikkāṉa Kalvimuṟai* [Pedagogy of the oppressed]. Translated by Ira. Nataracan. Chennai: Books for Children.
———. 1970. *Pedagogy of the Oppressed*. Translated by Myra Bergman Ramos. New York: Continuum Press.
Freire, Paulo, and Donaldo Macedo. 1987. *Literacy: Reading the Word and the World*. London: Routledge.
Friedrich, Marc. 2004. "Functional Participation? Questioning Participatory Attempts at Reshaping African Gender Identities: The Case of REFLECT in Uganda." In *Women, Literacy and Development: Alternative Perspectives*, edited by Anna Robinson-Pant, 219–32. London: Routledge.
Fuller, C. J., and Veronique Bénéï, eds. 2001. *The Everyday State and Society in Modern India*. London: Herst.
Gal, Susan. 2003 "Movements of Feminism: The Circulation of Discourses about Women." In *Recognition Struggles and Social Movements: Contested Identities, Power and Agency,* edited by Barbara Hobson, 93–120. Cambridge: Cambridge University Press.
Gee, James Paul. 1996. *Social Linguistics and Literacies: Ideology in Discourses*. 2nd ed. London: Falmer Press.
Geertz, Clifford. 1973. *The Interpretation of Cultures: Selected Essays.* New York: Basic Books.
Geetha, V., and S. V. Rajadurai. 1998. *Toward a Non-Brahmin Millennium: From Iyothee Thass to Periyar*. Chennai: Bhatkal and Sen.
Goodwin, Jeff, James M. Jasper, and Francesca Polletta, eds. 2001. *Passionate Politics: Emotions and Social Movements.* Chicago: University of Chicago Press.
Goody, Jack. 1986. *The Logic of Writing and the Organization of Society*. Cambridge: Cambridge University Press.
———. 1977. *The Domestication of the Savage Mind*. New York: Cambridge University Press.
———, ed. 1968. *Literacy in Traditional Societies*. Cambridge: Cambridge University Press.
Gopal, Priya. 2005. *Literary Radicalism in India: Gender, Nation, and the Transition to Independence*. London: Routledge.
Goswami, Manu. 2004. *Producing India: From Colonial Economy to National Space*. Chicago: University of Chicago Press.
Gottlieb, Esther E., and Thomas J. La Belle. 1990. "Ethnographic Contextualization of Freire's Discourse: Consciousness-Raising Theory and Practice." *Anthropology and Education Quarterly* 21 (1): 3–18.
Graeber, David. 2009. *Direct Action: An Ethnography*. Oakland: AK Press.
Gramsci, Antonio. 1971. *Selections from the Prison Notebooks*. Translated and edited by Quintin Hoare and Geoffrey Nowell. New York: International Publishers.

Guha, Ranajit. 1983. *Elementary Aspects of Peasant Insurgency in Colonial India*. New Delhi: Oxford University Press.

Gupta, Akhil. 2012. *Red Tape: Bureaucracy, Structural Violence, and Poverty in India.* Durham, NC: Duke University Press.

——. 2001. "Governing Population: The Integrated Child Development Services Program in India." In *States of Imagination: Ethnographic Explorations of the Postcolonial State*, edited by Thomas Blom Hansen and Finn Stepputat, 65–96. Durham, NC: Duke University Press.

——. 1998. *Postcolonial Developments: Agriculture in the Making of Modern India*. Durham, NC: Duke University Press.

Gupta, Akhil, and K. Sivaramakrishnan, eds. 2010. *The State in India after Liberalization: Interdisciplinary Perspectives*. London: Routledge.

Habermas, Jürgen. 1989. *Structural Transformation of the Public Sphere: An Inquiry into a Category of Bourgeois Society*. Translated by Thomas Burger. Cambridge, MA: MIT Press.

——. 1987. *The Philosophical Discourse of Modernity*. Translated by Fredrick Lawrence. Cambridge, MA: MIT Press.

Hale, Charles, ed. 2008. *Engaging Contradictions: Theory, Politics, and Methods of Activist Scholarship*. Berkeley: University of California Press.

——. 2006. "Activist Research v. Cultural Critique: Indigenous Land Rights and the Contradictions of Politically Engaged Anthropology." *Cultural Anthropology* 21 (1): 96–120.

Hansen, Thomas Blom. 2001. *Wages of Violence: Naming and Identity in Postcolonial Bombay*. Princeton: Princeton University Press.

——. 1999. *The Saffron Wave: Democracy and Hindu Nationalism in Modern India*. Princeton: Princeton University Press.

Harvey, David. 2005. *A Brief History of Neoliberalism*. Oxford: Oxford University Press.

Heath, Shirley Brice. 1983. *Ways with Words: Language, Life, and Work in Communities and Classrooms*. Cambridge: Cambridge University Press.

Heller, Patrick. 2005. "Reinventing Public Power in the Age of Globalization: Decentralization and the Transformation of Movement Politics in Kerala." In *Social Movements in India: Poverty, Power and Politics*, edited by Raka Ray and Mary Katzenstein, 79–106. New Delhi: Oxford University Press.

——. 2000. "Degrees of Democracy: Comparative Lessons from India." *World Politics* 52:484–519.

Heller, Patrick, K.N. Harilal, and Shubham Chaudhury. 2007. "Building Local Democracy: Evaluating the Impact of Decentralization in Kerala, India." *World Development* 35 (4): 626-48.

Hodges, Sarah. 2005. "Revolutionary Family Life and the Self-Respect Movement in Tamil South India, 1926–49." *Contributions to Indian Sociology* 39 (2): 251–77.

Holmes, Douglas, and George Marcus. 2008. "Collaboration Today and the Re-Imagination of the Classic Scene of Fieldwork Encounter." *Collaborative Anthropologies* 1:81–101.

——. 2005. "Cultures of Expertise and the Management of Globalization: Toward the Re-Functioning of Ethnography." In *Global Assemblages: Technology, Politics, and Ethics as Anthropological Problems*, edited by Aihwa Ong and Stephen Collier, 235–52. London: Blackwell.

Hull, Matthew. 2012. *Government of Paper: The Materiality of Bureaucracy in Urban Pakistan*. Berkeley: University of California Press.

Irvine, Judith. 1998. "Ideologies of Honorific Language." In *Language Ideologies: Practice and Theory*, edited by Bambi Schieffelin, Kathryn Woolard, and Paul Kroskrity, 51–67. New York: Oxford University Press.

Isaac, T.M. Thomas, and Richard Franke. 2002. *Local Democracy and Development: The Kerala People's Campaign for Decentralized Planning*. London: Rowman and Littlefield.

Jackson, Michael. 1983. "Knowledge of the Body." *Man* (n.s.) 18:327–45.

Jaffrelot, Christophe. 2003. *India's Silent Revolution: The Rise of the Lower Castes in North India*. New York: Columbia University Press.

Jakobson, Roman. 2000. "On Linguistic Aspects of Translation." In *The Translation Studies Reader,* edited by Lawrence Venuti, 113–18. London: Routledge.

———. 1985. "Closing Statement: Linguistics and Poetics." In *Semiotics: An Introductory Anthology,* edited by Robert Innis, 145–75. Bloomfield: University of Indiana Press.

Jay, Martin. 1973. *The Dialectical Imagination: A History of the Frankfurt School and the Institute of Social Research, 1923–1950*. Toronto: Little, Brown.

Jeffrey, Robin. 1992. *Politics, Women and Well-Being: How Kerala Became "a Model."* New Delhi: Oxford University Press.

John, Mary. 1996. "Gender and Development in India, 1970s–1990s: Some Reflections on the Constitutive Role of Contexts." *Economic and Political Weekly* 31 (47): 3071–77.

Kailasapathy, K. 1979. "The Tamil Purist Movement: A Re-Evaluation." *Social Scientist* 7 (10): 23–51.

Kalpana, K. 2005. "Shifting Trajectories in Microcredit Discourse." *Economic and Political Weekly* 40 (51): 17–25.

Kamat, Sangeetha. 2002. *Development Hegemony: NGOs and the State in India*. New Delhi: Oxford University Press.

Kapadia, Karin, ed. 2002. *The Violence of Development: The Politics of Identity, Gender and Social Inequalities in India*. New Delhi: Kali for Women.

———. 1995. *Siva and Her Sisters: Gender, Caste and Class in Rural South India*. Boulder: Westview Press.

Karunanidhi, N. 2003. *Pēraḻaku Piṟantatu*. Chennai: Bharathi Puttakalayam.

Kaviraj, Sudipta. 2010. *The Imaginary Institution of India: Politics and Ideas*. New York: Columbia University Press.

———. 1997. "Filth and the Public Sphere: Concepts and Practices about Space in Calcutta." *Public Culture* 10 (1): 83–113.

———. 1984. "On the Crisis of Political Institutions in India." *Contributions to Indian Sociology* 18:223–43.

Kayalvili Devi, J. 1999. *Kuṭi Aracu Itaḻk Kavitaikaḷ*. Chennai: Manimekalai Piracuram.

Keane, Webb. 2007. *Christian Moderns: Fetishism and Freedom in the Missionary Encounter*. Berkeley: University of California Press.

——. 2003. "Semiotics and the Social Analysis of Material Things." *Language and Communication* 23:409–25.

Koselleck, Reinhart. 2004. *Futures Past: On the Semantics of Historical Time*. New York: Columbia University Press.

Kozol, Jonathan. 1978. "A New Look at the Literacy Campaign in Cuba." *Harvard Educational Review* 48:341–77.

Kumar, Hajira, and Jaimon Varghese. 2005. *Women's Empowerment: Issues, Challenges, and Strategies; A Sourcebook*. New Delhi: Regency Publications.

Kumar, K. K. Krishna, and S. R. Sankaran. 2002. "The BGVS Experience in Mass Literacy." In *Practice and Research in Literacy*, edited by Aditi Mukherjee and Duggirala Vasanta, 238–52. New Delhi: Sage Publications.

Kumar, Krishna. 2005. *The Political Agenda of Education: A Study of Colonialist and Nationalist Ideas*. New Delhi: Sage Publications.

——. 1993a. "Literacy and Primary Education in India." In *Knowledge, Culture and Power: International Perspectives on Literacy as Policy and Practice,* edited by Peter Freebody and Anthrony Welch, 104–15. Washington, DC: Falmer Press.

——. 1993b. "Market Economy and Mass Literacy: Revisiting Innis's Economics of Communication." *Economic and Political Weekly* 28 (50): 2727–33.

——. 1986. "Textbooks and Educational Culture." *Economic and Political Weekly* 21 (30): 1309–11.

Lalitha, N., and B.S. Nagarajan. 2000. *Self Help Groups in Rural Development*. New Delhi: Dominant.

Lankshear, Colin, and Peter McLaren, eds. 1993. *Critical Literacy: Politics, Praxis, and the Postmodern.* Albany: State University of New York Press.

Larkin, Brian. 2008. *Signal and Noise: Media, Infrastructure, and Urban Culture in Northern Nigeria*. Durham, NC: Duke University Press.

Latour, Bruno. 1993. *We Have Never Been Modern*. Cambridge, MA: Harvard University Press.

Leve, Lauren. 2007. "'Failed Development' and Rural Revolution in Nepal: Rethinking Subaltern Consciousness and Women's Empowerment." *Anthropological Quarterly* 80 (1): 127–72.

Levinson, Steven. 1982. "Caste Rank and Verbal Interaction in Western Tamilnadu." In *Caste Ideology and Interaction*, edited by Dennis McGilvray, 98–203. Cambridge: Cambridge University Press.

Lévi-Strauss, Claude. 1973. *Tristes tropiques*, translated by John Weightman and Doreen Weightman. New York: Penguin.

Li, Tania Murray. 2007. *The Will to Improve: Governmentality, Development, and the Practice of Politics*. Durham, NC: Duke University Press.

Ludden, David. 1992. "India's Development Regime." In *Culture and Colonialism*, edited by Nicholas Dirks, 247–88. Ann Arbor: University of Michigan Press.

Lukács, Georg. 2001. "Realism in the Balance." In *The Norton Anthology of Theory and Criticism*, edited by Vincent B. Leitch, 1938 Reprint, 1033–58. New York: Norton.

Lukose, Ritty. 2009. *Liberalization's Children: Gender, Youth, and Consumer Citizenship in Globalizing India*. Durham, NC: Duke University Press.

Maheshwari, S. R. 1994. *Public Administration in India: The Higher Civil Service.* New Delhi: Oxford University Press.
Mahmood, Saba. 2005. *Politics of Piety: The Islamic Revival and the Feminist Subject.* Princeton: Princeton University Press.
Marriott, McKim, ed. 1990. *India through Hindu Categories.* New Delhi: Sage Publications.
Marx, Karl. 1963. *The Eighteenth Brumaire of Louis Bonaparte.* Translated by Daniel De Leon, 1852. Reprint, New York: International Publishers.
Mathur, Nayanika. 2012. "Transparent-making Documents and the Crisis of Implementation: A Rural Employment Law and Development Bureaucracy in India." *Political and Legal Anthropology Review* 35 (2): 167–85.
Maurer, Bill. 2005. *Mutual Life, Ltd: Islamic Banking, Alternative Currencies, Lateral Reason.* Princeton: Princeton University Press, 2005.
——. 2002. "Anthropological and Accounting Knowledge in Islamic Banking and Finance: Rethinking Critical Accounts." *Journal of the Royal Anthropological Institute* (n.s.) 8 (4): 645–67.
Mayaram, Shail. 2002. "New Modes of Violence: The Backlash against Women in the Panchayat System." In *The Violence of Development,* edited by Karin Kapadia, 393–424. Delhi: Kali for Women.
Mazzarella, William. 2010. "Beautiful Balloon: The Digital Divide and the Charisma of New Media in India." *American Ethnologist* 37 (4): 783–804.
——. 2006. "Internet X-Ray: E-Governance, Transparency, and the Politics of Immediation in India." *Public Culture* 18 (3): 473–505.
Menon, Nivedita, and Adithya Nigam. 2007. *Power and Contestation: India since 1989.* London: Zed Books.
Merry, Sally Engle. 2006. *Human Rights and Gender Violence: Translating International Law into Local Justice.* Chicago: University of Chicago Press.
——. 2005. "Anthropology and Activism: Researching Human Rights across Porous Boundaries." *Political and Legal Anthropology Review* 28 (2): 240–57.
Messick, Brinkley. 1993. *The Calligraphic State: Textual Domination and History in a Muslim Society.* Berkeley: University of California Press.
Milroy, James, and Leslie Milroy. 1991. *Authority in Language: Investigating Language Prescription and Standardization.* New York: Routledge.
Mines, Diane. 2005. *Fierce Gods: Inequality, Ritual and the Politics of Dignity in a South Indian Village.* Bloomington: Indiana University Press.
Moffat, Michael. 1979. *An Untouchable Community in South India: Structure and Consensus.* Princeton: Princeton University Press.
Mohanty, Chandra Talpade. 1991. "Under Western Eyes: Feminist Scholarship and Colonial Discourses." In *Third World Women and the Politics of Feminism*, edited by Chandra Talpade Mohanty, Ann Russo, and Lourdes Torres, 51–80. Bloomington: Indiana University Press.
Monier-Williams, Monier. 1920. *A Sanskrit-English Dictionary.* New York: Oxford University Press.
Mukherjee, Aditi. 2003. *Literacy in India: The Present Context.* Shimla: Indian Institute of Advanced Study.

Mukhopadhyay, Bhaskar. 2005. "The Rumor of Globalization: Globalism, Counterworks and the Location of Commodity." *Dialectical Anthropology* 29:35–60.

Nambi Arooran, K. 1980. *Tamil Renaissance and Dravidian Nationalism*. Madurai: Koodal.

Nandy, Ashis. 2003. *The Romance of the State: And the State of Dissent in the Tropics*. New Delhi: Oxford University Press.

Narrain, Arvind, and Gautham Bhan, eds. 2005. *Because I Have a Voice: Queer Politics in India*. New Delhi: Yoda Press.

Nayyar, Deepak. 1996. *Economic Liberalization in India: Analytics, Experience and Lessons*. Hyderabad: Orient Longman.

Neela, R. 2004. *Vīṇaiyalla Nāṉ Uṉakku*. Alangudi: Vidiyal Patippakam.

———. 2002. *Pāmara Taricanam*. Alangudi: Vidiyal Kalaikkulu.

Omvedt, Gail. 1994. *Dalits and the Democratic Revolution: Dr. Ambedkar and the Dalit Movement in Colonial India*. Delhi: Sage Publications.

Pandian, Anand. 2009. *Crooked Stalks: Cultivating Virtue in South India*. Durham, NC: Duke University Press.

Pandian, M. S. S. 2007. *Brahmin and Non-Brahmin: Genealogies of the Tamil Political Present*. Delhi: Permanent Black.

Parameswaran, M.P. 1992. "The BGVS: What It Is and What It Is Not." In *The Turning Point.* Delhi: Government of India, Directorate of Ault Education.

Parry, Jonathan. 2004. "The Marital History of a 'Thumb-Impression Man,'" In *Telling Lives in India*, edited by David Arnold and Stuart Blackburn, 281–318. Bloomington: Indiana University Press.

———. 1994. *Death in Banaras*. Cambridge: Cambridge University Press.

———. 1989. "The Brahminical Tradition and the Technology of the Intellect." In *Literacy and Society,* edited by Karen Schousboe and Mogens T. Larsen, 39–71. Copenhagen: Akademisk Forlag.

Peterson, Glen. 1997. *The Power of Words: Literacy and Revolution in South China, 1949–95.* Vancouver: University of British Columbia Press.

Poovey, Mary. 1998. *A History of the Modern Fact: Problems of Knowledge in the Sciences of Wealth and Society*. Chicago: University of Chicago Press.

Pope, G. U. 1982. *Handbook of the Tamil Language: A Tamil Prose Reader*. 1905. Reprint, New Delhi: Marwah.

Povinelli, Elizabeth. 2011. *Economies of Abandonment: Social Belonging and Endurance in Late Liberalism.* Durham, NC: Duke University Press.

———. 2006. *The Empire of Love: Toward a Theory of Intimacy, Genealogy, and Carnality*. Durham, NC: Duke University Press.

———. 2005. "A Flight from Freedom." In *Postcolonial Studies and Beyond*, edited by Ania Loomba, Suvir Kaul, and Matti Bunzl, 145–65. Durham, NC: Duke University Press.

Prakash, Gyan. 2002. "The Colonial Genealogy of Society: Community and Political Modernity in India." In *The Social in Question*, edited by Patrick Joyce, 81–96. New York: Routledge.

Pudumaippithan. 2004. *Putumaipittaṉ Moḻipeyarppukaḷ.* Edited by A. R. Venkatachalapathy. Nagercoil: Kalachuvadu Pathippagam.

——. 2002. *Putumaipittaṉ Katturaikaḷ*. Edited by A. R. Venkatachalapathy. Nagercoil: Kalachuvadu Pathippagam.

——. 2000. *Putumaipittaṉ Kataikaḷ*. Edited by A. R. Venkatachalapathy. Nagercoil: Kalachuvadu Pathippagam.

Raheja, Gloria Goodwin. 1988. *The Poison in the Gift: Ritual, Prestation, and the Dominant Caste in a North Indian Village*. Chicago: University of Chicago Press.

Rahman, Aminur. 1999. "Micro-Initiatives for Equitable and Sustainable Development: Who Pays?" *World Development* 27 (1): 67–82.

Raman, Bhavani. 2012. *Document Raj: Scribes and Writing in Early Colonial South India*. Chicago: University of Chicago Press.

——. 2010. "Disciplining the Senses, Schooling the Mind: Inhabiting Virtue in the Tamil *Tiṇṇai* School." In *Ethical Life in South Asia*, edited by Anand Pandian and Daud Ali, 43–60. Bloomington: Indiana University Press.

——. 2009. "Tamil *Munshis* and *Kacceri* Tamil under the Company's Document Raj in Early-Colonial Madras." In *The Madras School of Orientalism*, edited by Thomas Trautmann, 209–32. New Delhi: Oxford University Press.

Ramaswamy, Sumathi. 2003. "Visualizing India's Geo-Body: Globes, Maps, Bodyscapes." In *Beyond Appearances? Visual Practices and Ideologies in Modern India*, edited by Sumathi Ramaswamy, 157–95. New Delhi: Sage Publications.

——. 2001. "Maps and Mother Goddesses in Modern India." *Imago Mundi* 53:97–114

——. 1997. *Passions of the Tongue: Language Devotion in Tamil India, 1891–1970*. Berkeley: University of California Press.

Rao, Anupama. 2009. *The Caste Question: Dalits and the Politics of Modern India*. Berkeley: University of California Press.

Rao, Nitya. 1993. "Total Literacy Campaigns: A Field Report." *Economic and Political Weekly* 28 (19): 914–18.

Ray, Raka, and Mary Katzenstein, eds. 1995. *Social Movements in India: Poverty, Power and Politics*. New Delhi: Oxford University Press.

Ricoeur, Paul. 1991. "The Hermeneutical Function of Distanciation." In *From Text to Social Action: Essays in Hermeneutics*, 2:75–88. Translated by Kathleen Blamey and John B. Thompson. Evanston, IL: Northwestern University Press.

Riles, Annelise. 2000. *The Network Inside Out*. Ann Arbor: University of Michigan Press.

Robinson-Pant, Anna, ed. 2004. *Women, Literacy, and Development: Alternative Perspectives*. London: Routledge.

Sainath, P. 1996. *Everybody Loves a Good Drought: Stories from India's Poorest Districts*. New Delhi: Penguin Books.

Sanford, Victoria, and Asali Angel-Ajani, eds. 2006. *Engaged Observer: Anthropology, Advocacy, and Activism*. New Brunswick, NJ: Rutgers University Press.

Saraswathi, L. S. 2004. "Total Literacy Campaign: Pudukkottai, Tamil Nadu." In *Paradigms of Learning: The Total Literacy Campaign in India*, edited by Malavika Karlekar, 132–176. New Delhi: Sage.

——. 1995. "Indigenous Learning Cultures Basic to Sustainable Literacy." *ABD* 26 (1): 4–7.

Sarkar, Tanika. 2008. *Rebels, Wives, Saints: Designing Selves and Nations in Colonial Times*. Delhi: Permanent Black.

Saxena, Sadhna. 1993. "Limits and Consequences of Literacy Programmes." *Economic and Political Weekly* 28 (8–9): 321–22.

——. 1992. "The Myth of Total Literacy in Narsingpur." *Economic and Political Weekly* 27 (45): 2408–10.

Scheper-Hughes, Nancy. 1995. "The Primacy of the Ethical: Propositions for a Militant Anthropology." *Current Anthropology* 36 (3): 409–40.

Schieffelin, Bambi. 2000. "Introducing Kaluli Literacy: A Chronology of Influences." In *Regimes of Language: Ideologies, Polities, and Identities,* edited by Paul V. Kroskrity, 293–327. Santa Fe: School of American Research Press.

——. 1996. "Creating Evidence: Making Sense of the Written Word in Bosavi." In *Interaction and Grammar*, edited by Elinor Ochs, Emanuel Schegloff, and Sandra Thompson, 45–60. Cambridge: Cambridge University Press.

Scott, David. 1999. *Refashioning Futures: Criticism after Postcoloniality*. Princeton: Princeton University Press.

Scott, James. 1998. *Seeing Like a State: How Certain Schemes to Improve the Human Condition Have Failed*. New Haven, CT: Yale University Press.

Sen, Amartya. 1999. *Development as Freedom*. Oxford: Oxford University Press.

——. 1993. "The Threats to Secular India." *Social Scientist* 21 (3–4): 5–23.

Sengoopta, Chandak. 2003. *Imprint of the Raj: How Fingerprinting Was Born in Colonial India*. London: Macmillan.

Shah, Alpa. 2011. "India Burning: The Maoist Revolution." In *A Companion to the Anthropology of India*, edited by Isabelle Clark-Decès, 332–51. Oxford: Wiley-Blackwell.

——. 2010. *In the Shadows of the State: Indigenous Politics, Environmentalism, and Insurgency in Jharkhand, India.* Durham, NC: Duke University Press.

Sharma, Aradhana. Forthcoming. "State Transparency after the Neoliberal Turn: The Politics, Limits, and Paradoxes of India's Right to Information Law." *Political and Legal Anthropology Review.*

——. 2008. *Logics of Empowerment: Development Gender and Governance in Neoliberal India.* Minneapolis: University of Minnesota Press.

Siddhartha. 2005. "From Conscientization to Interbeing: A Personal Journey." In *Rethinking Freire: Globalization and the Environmental Crisis*, edited by C. A. Bowers and Frederique Apffel-Marglin, 83–100. Mahwah, NJ: Lawrence Erlbaum Associates.

Siddiqi, Majid. 2005. "The British Historical Context and Colonial Petitioning in India." *XXII Dr. M. A. Ansari Memorial Lecture.* New Delhi: Jamia Islamia University.

Silverstein, Michael. 1997. "Monoglot 'Standard' in America: Standardization and Metaphors of Linguistic Hegemony." In *The Matrix of Language: Contemporary Linguistic Anthropology*, edited by Donald Brenneis and Ronald K. S. Macaulay, 284–306. Boulder: Westview Press.

Silverstein, Michael, and Greg Urban, eds. 1996. *Natural Histories of Discourse*. Chicago: University of Chicago Press.

Sivaramakrishnan, K., and Arun Agrawal, eds. 2004. *Regional Modernities: The Cultural Politics of Development in India*. Delhi: Oxford University Press.

Sivathamby, Karthigesu. 1978. *Ilakkiyattil Muṟpōkkuvātam*. Chennai: Pattalikal Veliyeedu.

Spivak, Gayatri Chakravorty. 2010. "Can the Subaltern Speak?" In *Can the Subaltern Speak? Reflections on the History of an Idea,* edited by Rosalind Morris, 21–80. New York: Columbia University Press.

Staiger, Janet, Ann Cvetkovich, and Ann Reynolds, eds. 2010. *Political Emotions: New Agendas in Communication*. London: Routledge.

Street, Brian, ed. 1993. *Cross-Cultural Approaches to Literacy*. Cambridge: Cambridge University Press.

——. 1984. *Literacy in Theory and Practice*. Cambridge: Cambridge University Press.

Sundar, Nandini. 2010. "Vigilantism, Culpability, and Moral Dilemmas." *Critique of Anthropology* 30 (1): 113–21.

——. 2006. "Bastar, Maoism, and Salwa Judum." *Economic and Political Weekly* 41 (29): 3187–92.

Swarnalatha, Potukutchi. 2001. "Revolt, Testimony, Petition: Artisanal Protests in Colonial Andhra." *International Review of Social History* 46:107–29.

Tamilcelvan, S. 2004a. *Araciyal Eṉakku Piṭikkum.* Chennai: CITU and Bharati Puttakalayam Press.

——. 2004b. *Iruḷum Oḷiyum: Aṟivoḷi Iyakka Aṉupavaṅkaḷ.* Chennai: Bharati Puttakalayam Press.

——. 2003. *Nāṭṭār Teyvaṅkaḷ: Namatu Nēca Aṇi*, vol. 4. Edited by Sentil Babu. Chennai: South Vision.

Tamiḻnāṭu Muṟpōkku Eḻuttāḷar Caṅkam (Tamil Nadu Progressive Writers Association). 2006. *Paṇpāṭṭut Taḷattil Māṟṟuppātai Tēṭi* Madurai: Ta.Mu.E.Ca.

——. 2002. *Amaippu Aṟikkai.* Madurai: Ta.Mu.E.Ca.

——. 1993. *Kālattiṉ Kuralāy.* Madurai: Ta.Mu.E.Ca.

Tanabe, Akio. 2007. "Toward Vernacular Democracy: Moral Society and Post-Colonial Transformation in Rural Orissa, India." *American Ethnologist* 34 (3): 558–74.

Tarlo, Emma. 2001. "Paper Truths: The Emergency and Slum Clearance through Forgotten Files." In *The Everyday State and Society in Modern India*, edited by C. J. Fuller and Véronique Bénéï, 68–90. New Delhi: Social Science Press.

Taylor, Charles. 2004. *Modern Social Imaginaries*. Durham, NC: Duke University Press.

Tiruvalluvar. 1990. *The Kural*. Translated by P. S. Sundaram. New Delhi: Penguin Books.

Trawick (Egnor), Margaret. 1991. "Wandering Lost: A Landless Laborer's Sense of Place and Self." In *Gender, Genre, and Power in South Asian Expressive Tradition,* edited by Arjun Appadurai, Frank J. Korom, and Margaret Mills, 224–66. Philadelphia: University of Pennsylvania Press.

——. 1990. "Untouchability and the Fear of Death in a Tamil Song." In *Language and the Politics of Emotion,* edited by Catherine Lutz and Lila Abu-Lughod, 186–206. Cambridge: Cambridge University Press.

——. 1986. "Internal Iconicity in Paraiyar 'Crying Songs.'" In *Another Harmony: New Essays on the Folklore of India*, edited by A.K. Ramanujam and Stuart Blackburn, 294–344. Berkeley: University of California Press.

Tsing, Anna Lowenhaupt. 2004. *Friction: An Ethnography of Global Connection*. Princeton: Princeton University Press.

Turner, Victor. 1967. *The Forest of Symbols: Aspects of Ndembu Ritual*. Ithaca, NY: Cornell University Press.

Valiani, Arafaat. 2011. *Militant Publics in India: Physical Culture and Violence in the Making of a Modern Polity*. London: Palgrave Macmillan.

Vanamamalai, N. 1966. *Tamilar Varalārum Panpātum*. Chennai: New Century Book House.

Venkatachalapathy, A. R. 2012. *The Province of the Book: Scholars, Scribes, and Scribblers in Colonial Tamilnadu*. Delhi: Permanent Black.

——. 1994. "Reading Practices and Modes of Reading in Colonial Tamil Nadu." *Studies in History* 10 (2): 273–90.

Venkateshwaran, T. V. 2000. "Paṇpāṭṭil Āyvukaḷ Cila Aṟimuka Kuṟippukaḷ." *Pudu Vicai*, March, 76–78.

Viramma. 1995. *Une vie paria: Le rire des asservis*. Translated by Josiane Racine and Jean-Luc Racine. Paris: Plon/UNESCO.

Warner, Michael. 2002. *Publics and Counterpublics*. New York: Zone Books.

——. 1990. *The Letters of the Republic: Publication and the Public Sphere in Eighteenth Century America*. Cambridge, MA: Harvard University Press.

Warren, Kay. 1998. *Indigenous Movements and Their Critics: Pan-Mayan Activism in Guatemala*. Princeton: Princeton University Press.

Weber, Henri. 1981. *Nicaragua: The Sandinista Revolution*. Translated by Patrick Camiller. London: Verso.

Weber, Max. 1978. *Economy and Society*. Edited by Guenther Roth and Claus Wittich. Berkeley: University of California Press.

Yadav, Yogendra. 2000. "Understanding the Second Democratic Upsurge." In *Transforming India: Social and Political Dynamics of Democracy*, edited by Francine Frankel, R. Z. Hasan, and Rajiv Bhargava, 120–45. Oxford: Oxford University Press.

Zachariah, Mathai, and R. Sooryamoorthy. 1994. *Science for Social Revolution: Achievements and Dilemmas of a Development Movement; The Kerala Sastra Sahitya Parishad*. London: Zed.

Žižek, Slavoj. 1994. "The Spectre of Ideology." In *Mapping Ideology*, edited by Slavoj Žižek, 1–33. London: Verso.

Zvelebil, Kamil. 1990. "The Dimension of Orality in Tamil Literature." In *Language versus Dialect: Linguistic and Literary Essays on Hindi, Tamil and Sarnami*, edited by Mariola Offredi, 127–69. New Delhi: Manohar.

Index